Gender, Generation and Identity in Contemporary Russia

This book explores the lives and expectations of young women in the new Russia, looking at the enormous changes that the new social and economic environment has brought.

The contributors, all of whom either live and work in Russia or spend a significant amount of their time there, focus on the emergence of the 'beauty myth', the growth of the sex industry and the rise in sexual violence, on women's views of marriage and child rearing, on youth culture and the role of girls within it, on education, and on career expectations and difficulties. The book discusses both the actual experience of young women in Russia and the context of that experience in contrast to that of the West, looking at how the media, academia and state institutions in Russia and in the West have viewed the interaction of gender and youth.

Gender Generation and Identity will appeal to students and scholars of contemporary Russia and to sociologists interested in the interaction of gender and youth, who will find the book presents a fascinating comparison to the growing literature on gender and generation in the West.

Hilary Pilkington is Lecturer in Russian Politics and Society at the Centre for Russian and East European Studies, The University of Birmingham.

Gender, Generation and Identity in Contemporary Russia

Edited by Hilary Pilkington

London and New York

First published 1996
by Routledge
11 New Fetter Lane, London EC4P 4EE

Simultaneously published in the USA and Canada
by Routledge
27 West 35th Street, New York, NY 10001

Routledge is an International Thomson Publishing company

Phototypeset in Times by
Intype London Ltd
Printed and bound in Great Britain by
Mackays of Chatham PLC, Chatham, Kent

British Library Cataloguing in Publication data
A catalogue record for this book is available from the British Library

Library of Congress Cataloging in Publication Data
Gender, generation and identity in contemporary Russia / edited by
  Hilary Pilkington.
      p. cm.
   Includes bibliographical references and index.
   1. Young women—Russia (Federation)—Social conditions. 2. Women–
–Russia (Federation)—Social conditions. 3. Gender identity—Russia
(Federation) 4. Russia (Federation)—Social conditions—1991–
I. Pilkington, Hilary, 1964–
HQ1665.15.G46   1996
305.4′0947—dc20   96–11343
                                   CIP

ISBN 0–415–13543–5 (hbk)
ISBN 0–415–13544–3 (pbk)

For
Mavis, Malcolm,
Rachel and Louise

Contents

List of figures and tables   ix
List of contributors   x
Acknowledgements   xiii

1 Introduction   1
   Hilary Pilkington

Part I Surviving the new social environment: strategies at home, work and school

2 Gender and generation in the new Russian labour   21
   market
   Sue Bridger and Rebecca Kay

3 Employment strategies and the formation of new   39
   identities in the service sector in Moscow
   Marta Bruno

4 Women's career patterns in industry: a generational   57
   comparison
   Irina Tartakovskaia

5 Orientations, re-orientations or disorientations?   75
   Expectations of the future among Russian school-
   leavers
   Elena Dmitrieva

Part II The new Russian woman: femininity, sexuality and power

6 Young people, sex and sexual identity   95
   Lynne Attwood

 7 Love, sex and marriage – the female mirror: value   121
    orientations of young women in Russia
    Mariia Kotovskaia and Natal'ia Shalygina

 8 Young people's attitudes towards sex roles and sexuality   132
    Lynne Attwood

 9 Beliefs about reproductive health: young Russian   152
    women talking
    Anne Murcott and Annie Feltham

10 Sexual violence towards women   169
    Tat'iana Zabelina

Part III Gender, identity and cultural practice

11 'Youth culture' in contemporary Russia: gender,   189
    consumption and identity
    Hilary Pilkington

12 Young women in provincial gang culture: a case study
    of Ul'ianovsk
    Elena Omel'chenko

13 Farewell to the *tusovka*: masculinities and femininities   237
    on the Moscow youth scene
    Hilary Pilkington

14 The body encoded: notes on the folklore of pregnancy   264
    Tat'iana Shchepanskaia

    Bibliography   282
    Index   296

Figures and tables

FIGURES

12.1 Changes in the basis of association among gangs   223
12.2 Relationship between youth gangs and the mafia   225
12.3 A typology of girls in youth gangs   228
A13.1 Taxonomy of Moscow *neformaly* in 1991   259

TABLES

8.1 Information about respondents   150
12.1 Change in gang membership, 1991–3   220
13.1 Biker groups in Moscow: organizational differences   246

Contributors

Lynne Attwood is Lecturer in Russian Studies at the University of Manchester. She has published widely on the construction of gender identity in the Soviet Union and post-Soviet Russia as well as on representations of gender in the media. She is author of *The New Soviet Man and Woman: Sex Socialization in the USSR*, Indiana University Press, 1990 and editor of *Red Women on the Silver Screen*, Pandora Press, 1993. Her current research interest is in the changing representations of women and gender relations in the press and in films.

Sue Bridger is Senior Lecturer in Russian Studies at the University of Bradford. She is author of *Women in the Soviet Countryside*, Cambridge University Press, 1987 and numerous articles on Russian women. Most recently she has jointly authored *No More Heroines? Russia, Women and the Market*, Routledge, 1995 with Rebecca Kay and Kathryn Pinnick.

Marta Bruno is completing her doctoral thesis on gender differences, employment and social change at the Department of Geography, University of Cambridge. She is a Research Fellow at the Russian and East European Research Centre at the University of Wolverhampton, where she is working on Russian women in financial services, and gender and the economic aspects of nationalism and ethnic conflicts.

Elena Dmitrieva is a doctoral student in sociology at Moscow State University and Lecturer at the Moscow Medical Academy. In addition to her study of youth attitudes to education and family she has a keen research interest in women's reproductive health and qualitative research methodologies, particularly focus group methods.

Annie Feltham is a Senior Teaching Fellow at the University of Essex. She has been researching into Soviet and post-Soviet social issues for twenty years and is particularly interested in women's issues, the family, health and addictive behaviours. With the new opportunities to conduct primary research which began to emerge in the mid-1980s, she has been keen to develop our understanding of Russian society at the local level.

Rebecca Kay is a doctoral student at the University of Bradford studying the position of women in the new Russia and the role of women's organizations in fighting for their equality. She has worked as research assistant to Dr Sue Bridger on a Leverhulme Trust funded project on 'Women and marketisation in Russia' and in this capacity co-authored the book *No More Heroines? Russian, Women and the Market*, Routledge, 1995.

Mariia Kotovskaia and **Natal'ia Shalygina** are researchers at the Centre of Ethnic and Gender Research at the Institute of Ethnology and Anthropology (RAN), Moscow. Their contribution to this volume is part of a broader research project on inter-generational value orientations and behavioural models of women in contemporary Russia, which will provide a gender analysis of Russia in the transition to democracy.

Anne Murcott holds a research post as Professor of the Sociology of Health at South Bank University, London. She has a long-standing interest in cultural conceptions of health, gender and the body, as well as of food, eating and diet. She is past editor of the international journal, *Sociology of Health and Illness* and is currently Director of the ESRC Research Programme 'The Nation's Diet'.

Elena Omel'chenko, is Director of the interdisciplinary research centre, 'Region', Moscow State University (Ul'ianovsk branch) where she has undertaken wide-ranging research on aspects of contemporary Russian society, politics and culture. She has a long-standing interest in the sociology of Russian youth and her current research interests include 'deviant behaviour' among young people, and advertising and its impact on youth attitudes and orientations. She is editor of *Advertising in Russia: Problems and Prospects*, MGU-Ul'ianovsk Press, 1993 (in Russian) and author of *Interviewing Methods and Training of Interviewers*, MGU Press, Moscow, 1995 (in Russian).

Hilary Pilkington, is Lecturer in Russian Politics and Society at the

Centre for Russian and East European Studies at The University of Birmingham. She is author of *Russia's Youth and its Culture: A Nation's Constructors and Constructed*, Routledge, 1994 as well as numerous articles on gender relations in contemporary Russia. She is currently engaged in research on Russian forced migrants and the implications of their resettlement for ethnic and national identity.

Tat'iana Shchepanskaia is an academic anthropologist working at the Museum of Anthropology and Ethnography (Russian Academy of Sciences) in St Petersburg. She has published widely on youth culture and gender identity.

Irina Tartakovskaia lives in the Russian city of Samara and works at the Institute for Comparative Research on Labour Relations. She is currently working in the field of gender relations and is a participant on a joint Russian–British research project on the restructuring of management and industrial relations in Russia.

Tat'iana Zabelina is Director of the Centre for Women, Family and Gender Studies at the Moscow Institute of Youth, where she also works as a lecturer. She is the author of numerous publications (both in Russia and abroad) on women's issues and is co-author and editor of the first Russian handbook on how to start and manage a women's crisis centre. Dr Zabelina is a founding member and volunteer at the Moscow Assault Recovery Centre, 'Sisters'.

Acknowledgements

Thanks must go primarily to all those women and men, young and old, in Russia without whose co-operation our research, and this book, would have been impossible. Our thanks are also expressed to our colleagues, families, friends and partners with, and against, whom we have ourselves shaped our own identities.

1 Introduction

Hilary Pilkington

WHY GENDER? WHY IDENTITY?

There is a growing literature on gender and generation in the West that has arisen as a result of the recognition that the experience of youth is classed, raced and gendered and the experience of gender is mediated by class, race, ethnicity, sexuality and age. The commitment to exploring 'difference and diversity' is very real and in the area of youth studies these themes have replaced the notion of 'resistance' amongst those researchers seeking to challenge the discourses of deviance, disaffection, consumption and dependence which have dominated the mainstream debate (Griffin 1993: 199–200). Both radical and mainstream discourses have traditionally been rooted in perceived truisms about the alienating experience of modern societies. But simple resolutions of this modern condition (via class, ethnic or national consciousness) appear increasingly problematic. This is why the notion of 'identity' is important, since it is at the level of individual identity formation and reformation that the negotiation between different socio-cultural identities takes place. There is, in the times we live in, no collective social identity birthright; rather, identities of gender, generation, sexuality, class, race, ethnicity and religion are constructed in time and space.

WHY GENERATION?

Age has never been accepted as a macro social category of the significance of class, race and gender. Nevertheless, renegotiations of identity through the life-cycle are significant. For many this may conjure up a single image: of the transition from childhood to adulthood, the infamous 'adolescent' frustrated by inadequacies and intermediary positions. There are, however, many other moments in the life-cycle at which one's identity may be renegotiated, such as: entrance to college or higher education, military service, the death or disappearance of family members, entrance into a long-term sexual relationship or marriage, the birth of children, significant change in career direction or promotion, the birth of grandchildren, retirement from (or move out of) paid employment, the loss of a partner. All these experiences are, among other things, gendered.

Identity formation also takes place in space and whilst to some extent, in the current period, experience has been 'globalized', Stuart Hall aptly notes that, 'The new times seem to have gone "global" and "local" at the same moment' (Hall 1989: 133). Despite this, English language publications on youth rarely consider either the experience of European youth in general or, still less often, youth of the new Europe. Gender issues in Eastern Europe, however, have been increasingly taken up by the disciplines of women's studies whilst Russian studies has provided a blossoming literature on gender in Russia past and present. However, the distinct agendas of this literature (particularly a concern to intervene in the process of the discursive re-formation of gender relations) means that it rarely fully recognizes the great diversity in the experience of women and 'women's issues' tend to be falsely universalized. In Russia there is also a growing gender literature which is sustained by a small community of highly committed researchers and activists. However, publishing outlets for these are extremely limited, due to the political unacceptability of gender analysis compounded by the general economic crisis in Russian publishing. Thus, there is currently an anomalous situation whereby much Russian feminist work has been published in English rather than Russian.

Work (primarily survey work) also continues on youth issues. The Russian literature on youth tends to feed directly into policy debates, especially concerning education, social problems and morality. Even at the height of glasnost and democratization in 1988, one researcher surveying the debate on youth in the press found that the most common themes in such publications were: bureaucratism and administration (raised in over one-third of articles); the low professional and moral qualities of youth 'instructors' (raised in 14 per cent of articles) and their conservatism (also 14 per cent); the gap between ideology and reality (raised in 22 per cent of articles); the moral and aesthetic education of youth (15 per cent of articles) and the construction of new, more democratic relations with youth (15 per cent) (Semenov 1992). Whilst the obvious conclusion from this might be thought to be the need to let young people define the youth debate for themselves (since these motifs are clearly about state, not youth, concerns – social control, socialization and education), in fact, the author concludes that 'we cannot just give young people independence, but [must] help them understand it, teach them how to use this great right', which, he argues, requires a return to good old-fashioned 'moral education' (*vospitanie*) (ibid., 26).

My own study of the press on youth in the perestroika period (employing a textual rather than content analysis approach) reveals a major paradigm change in the discussion of youth (Pilkington 1994a: 89–193). If in the Soviet period young people were heralded as the 'constructors of communism' (on a material and symbolic level), then by the beginning of the 1990s, they had become seen as a 'lost generation'. Images of patriotic, work-loving, ideologically committed and morally upright youth were replaced by those of economically deprived, socially marginalized and morally disorientated young people. Social surveys ceased to be paraded as evidence of the educational level, professional expertise and ideological conviction of young people and now are used instead to indicate: poor housing conditions (the majority of young people continue to live at home or accept hostel rooms on a long-term basis because there is no other choice); lack of patriotism (10 per cent of youth are reported to want to leave Russia for the West permanently); the rise in juvenile crime (in the post-Soviet period the proportion of youth among convicted criminals has risen from 46 per cent to 59 per cent); low levels of political interest and trust (only 5 per cent of youth positively evaluate the activity of parliament, 12 per cent the government, and 27 per cent the president, while belief in various political parties or movements is negligible); and a reciprocal lack of trust in youth (only 2.8 per cent of professional managerial posts are occupied by young people) (all figures cited in Alekseenkov, Baranov and Nevar 1993). This change in discourse is closely connected to the institutional crisis of the late perestroika period; faced with imminent implosion, due to the abolition of Article 6 of the Constitution which had given the Communist Party a monopoly of the political arena, the *Komsomol* (official communist youth organization) redefined its role as the protector of youth and the defender of its social interests in the state sphere (Pilkington 1994a: 162–93). This, in turn, required an objectification of youth as a social policy issue; youth became repositioned as a marginalized and dependent group in need of social protection.

Where gender is brought into the youth debate at all at this abstract level, it is in order to give an added moral dimension to the symbolic role youth plays for society in general. If, in the Soviet period, youth symbolized the bright future which young people themselves would build and live in, then in post-Soviet Russia youth symbolizes the depths to which the country has fallen. The moral state of young women (defined only in terms of their reproductive role) symbolizes the degradation of the country as a whole:

> Surely if the family is the basis of society, then the woman, the mother is the basis of the family. If the mother is moral, the family is moral and society is moral. Like many other simple and eternal truths, we have spurned this. Now we have an abundance of [female] continuers of the species who swear and indulge in alcohol and tobacco. But the worst is still to come ... The situation is such that today we really need to struggle for women, the protector of the hearth, the continuer of the species, the basis of our spiritual and moral self-preservation, to protect them from false morality and false freedom, from the pernicious influence of cynicism and shamelessness.
>
> (Semenov 1992: 27)

WHY RUSSIA?

The temporal and spatial dimensions covered in this book – contemporary Russia – are considered to be important not only because Russia is a significant absence in the wider discussion on gender and generation but because she is currently experiencing massive social and cultural dislocation. Although economic and political events in Russia are well-documented in academic writings, social and cultural transformations are much more difficult to chart and are largely posited as a kind of 'fall-out' of economic breakdown. In considering these transformations, the authors hope to avoid the temptation of placing gender and generation in any 'hierarchy' of oppression. The aim is rather to consider patterns and strategies adopted by women of different generations and by young people of both sexes in order to negotiate the ongoing crises. This is not to minimize the real poverty, social tension, dislocation and trauma experienced by many people in the current period, but also not to decontextualize these experiences and externalize their solutions (via macro economic polices or Western aid, both of which will be slow in resolving the problems, if they materialize in any kind of effective form at all). All the while people are acting and changing their environments and reshaping their identities to re-place themselves in a new and still changing world. The research presented in the book does not seek to evidence the 'state of things' in contemporary Russia, therefore, but to chart the social processes and relations shaping people's experiences and strategies.

In order to realize these aims the book brings together contributors who either live and work in Russia or who, over a number of years, have spent a significant amount of their time there. Many of the contributors have worked together in the past and have been in dialogue on these research issues for some time. In addition to their experiential expertise, however, the contributors share a common approach to their research subjects. All the research presented in this volume has been conducted employing qualitative research methods, drawing on a number of social science disciplines (social anthropology, sociology, geography, cultural studies). The methods are varied (including textual analysis, structured and semi-structured interviewing, participant observation and open-question questionnaires) but the principle behind them is shared; a commitment to the integrity of the subject and the incorporation of the subjective factor into the research process. Whilst many Western researchers still find themselves marginalized because of their use of qualitative methods, for Russian scholars, qualitative sociology still borders on the completely unacceptable. Traditionally, Soviet sociology has been heavily quantitative reflecting the desire to show uniformity, conformity and objective 'progress' rather than difference, diversity and the individual experience. Although ideological double-speak may no longer constitute a problem for Russian academics, today the fierce competition for external grants necessary for survival means that many researchers still have little choice about their direction; qualitative work takes time, commitment and sacrifice. The authors brought together in this volume share this commitment and its consequences.

Of course, academic traditions vary significantly between Russia and the UK in both institutional and cultural terms and it would be wrong to ignore the problems of engaging in collaborative writing projects. Such problems have not been eradicated from the current volume, but, it is hoped, they have been minimized. All Russian contributors were invited to submit articles in their native language and these were translated and edited by the editor. This process was a dialogue inhibited by the problem of communication with Russia but which, nevertheless, was a useful one during which many issues of difference as well as similarity in approach became apparent. These differences in many ways reflect the subject matter of the book and the chapters remain free-standing; no author is bound to the conclusions of any other. In order to facilitate cross-cultural understanding, however, each section begins with a chapter of slightly broader brush than the subsequent empirical case studies designed to contextualize issues in the areas of: employment, education and family; sex, sexuality and relations between the sexes; and cultural and 'subcultural' activity.

Difference is by its nature inexhaustible and the current volume can only scratch the surface. The book draws on as wide a regional experience as was possible: case studies include data from St Petersburg, Samara, Ul'ianovsk and Piatigorsk, as well as Moscow, while analyses of media discourse attempt to include a wide range of regional as well as national newspapers and journals. However, significant gaps remain. In particular, the experience of women of non-Russian ethnicities, rural women and disabled women is not represented. Insufficient attention is given to older women, especially in relation to family, sex and sexuality (their experience in the field of work does receive attention in the first part of the volume). Issues of masculinity are also inadequately raised. These absences are deeply regretted but it is hoped that at least the primary objective has been achieved: to provide space for young women's experience to be written about in a way other than as a sideline or peripheral element of larger research projects. The book aims simply to begin the kind of dialogue which might encourage others to write and talk about generational differences among women and the gendered experience of age; it does not by any means seek to define what this experience is, or should be, and thereby to exclude other experiences.

SURVIVING IN POST-SOVIET RUSSIA: ONE AIM, DIVERSE STRATEGIES

The themes of structural blocks but also choice and strategy permeate the first part of the book, as authors balance their analysis of the structures and constraints within which women move in the new market environment with the opportunities and the survival mechanisms they develop. Sue Bridger and Rebecca Kay outline the reasons why women are more prone to redundancy and why they find it harder to re-enter paid employment than their male counterparts. However, their chapter focuses on the generational aspects of the structuring of the labour market in post-Soviet Russia and they emphasize the reluctance amongst employers to take on women of 'pre-pensionable age' and those who have young children (since social protectionism on the part of the state effectively prices women out of the labour market). Younger women, they argue, suffer more from a process of de-skilling, as women are employed as 'representatives' of firms, to look good and please clients (and managers) rather than for their professional skills. Although, as Irina Tartakovskaia shows in her chapter, the question of the linking of careers for women with 'sexual favours for the bosses' is not new, marketization and the open growth of the sex industry 'normalizes' the marketing of women's bodies, including at the workplace. This is still more problematic in Russia given the weak definition of what constitutes sexual harassment and the lack of prosecution culture in this area. According to one legal expert, on average only about five men a year are charged with using their official position to compel female subordinates to perform more than their professional duties (Yakov 1993).

On the structural level, Marta Bruno pays attention to the significance of the Soviet past (both state ideology and popular *mentalité*) in shaping the new market environment and women's place in it. On the basis of a case study of women working in foreign firms and joint ventures in Moscow, however, she also explores women's ability to devise strategies and resist their positioning in the new, gendered labour market and the way in which generational differences shape these survival strategies. While Bruno suggests that older women, who have more experience of 'surviving the system', may prove to be more flexible than younger women in defining a space for themselves in the new environment, Irina Tartakovskaia's study of women managers in the heavy industrial environment of Samara suggests that it is younger women who are better able to act in market conditions. It is the latter, Tartakovskaia argues, who are more able to leap the psychological barrier of perceiving themselves as 'career women' and to act to achieve their aims. All three chapters thus conclude that generation is a significant factor shaping women's experience of the market, but that there is no natural connection between age and ability to survive; the difference among women of the post-Soviet generation may be greater than that between women of different generations.

All the authors also concur on the fact that although successful careers can be made by women, the resurgence of masculinity in the post-Soviet era limits the space for the reworking of feminine identities in the new environment. This is evident from Elena Dmitrieva's study of gender differences in school-leavers' professional and educational aspirations. Dmitrieva shows that young women still find it difficult to combine images of 'woman' and 'career' and that this is primarily a result of the interference, when thinking about future, of the 'family factor'. By this she means the expectation among young women that family commitments will limit the scope for realization of professional and educational potential. Although Dmitrieva argues that the connection between education and future work is relatively weak among both male and female respondents – a finding supported, incidentally, by sociological surveys which suggest that only 10 per cent of young people connect the possibility of a professional career with their level of education (Alekseenkov, Baranov and Nevar 1993) – the gender factor is nevertheless significant. The relative roles played by family and work or education in young women's ideal images of themselves and their partners is taken up at greater length by Natal'ia Shalygina and Mariia Kotovskaia in the second part of the book.

An unfortunate absence from the discussion is the experience of rural women. Over the last two decades there has been an increasingly high outflow of young women from the countryside, with women often being the first to leave (Bridger 1989: 92). This has been due to the shortage of skilled, mechanized work for women on the farms as well as extremely poor infrastructural development in rural areas. In crop-growing about 90 per cent of the work is still performed manually and one-third of women aged 46–55 have illnesses caused by the arduous or hazardous nature of their work (Terkhov 1993). As in urban areas, women are the first to be made unemployed; in the first quarter of 1993, 72 per cent of unemployed people living in rural areas were women, mainly young women (under the age of 30). It is not expected that market relations or privatization will improve life for Russian rural women; land is likely to fall under the control of men, considered to be the heads of the family, while single-parent families and elderly women, especially widows, will be left 'landless' (ibid.).

Much attention has been paid recently to the negative consequences of current social, economic and cultural changes in Eastern Europe and the former Soviet Union for women (see Einhorn 1993; Funk and Mueller 1993; Watson 1993a). This is quite justified, but it would be wrong to assume that women in general, and young women in particular, are happily buying the ideology of 'returning women to the home'. They are, more accurately, seeking ways to survive in the new market environment. For older women this may involve a painful process of abandoning past professions or even waged employment for more risky survival economics based on petty trading or commerce. Younger women, on the other hand, often extremely critical of their mothers' experience, but still forming their own, seek real choice (as opposed to the mythical choice of contemporary Western societies) which will allow them to balance rather than juggle family and work. This first section of the book seeks to explore such different strategies via the articulated experiences of women of different generations.

THE NEW RUSSIAN WOMAN: FEMININITY, SEXUALITY AND POWER

Part II of the book focuses on a theme currently at the heart of much feminist debate and intervention into general social theory; the question of 'equality' and 'difference'. Lynne Attwood sets the scene by charting the way in which sexual equality and difference was viewed in late Soviet ideology, academic writing and the press. Soviet sex-role theory, just like its Western counterpart, combines a commitment to the interpretation of 'difference' as a product of social expectations and environment (the much discussed 'feminization' of men and 'masculinization' of women, for example, was blamed in part on the female domination of socializing agencies) with an underlying belief that difference is biological and essential. As Connell notes, this is sex-role theory's greatest failing, for it slips biology in through the back door; sex-role theorists assume that the female role and the male role are equal and thus substitute a theory of norms (based on a normative standard case) for an account of power (Connell 1987: 50–4). Unlike other social structures (race, class, etc.), sex is seen to be essential and the power relations between men and women are thereby obscured. By undervaluing the historical and social bases for gender relations, then, the sex-role paradigm reproduces the very problems it seeks to understand (Kimmel 1987b: 13).

In order to address the issue of power, therefore, it is essential to chart the changing nature of the sexual contract and state-sponsored and organized sex-role socialization into the 'different' roles of men and women on which the sexual contract is pinned. This is undertaken by Lynne Attwood, in the introductory chapter, in which she makes clear the great continuity from the past. Gender difference is understood in post-Soviet society often as biologically rooted sex differences and, as such, natural and necessary. Differences between men and women are essentialized and hypertrophied whilst the space for adopting genuinely alternative gender and sexual identities remains extremely limited; homosexuality may have been decriminalized but it has certainly not been de-stigmatized. Indeed, Attwood argues, the move to the market has not strengthened plurality and individual freedom but has reinforced essentialist sex roles, since the market is seen to require just those masculine characteristics smothered by what is portrayed as the 'feminized' Soviet culture of the past.

Two chapters in this part of the book directly address the question of how young people will negotiate the sexual contract for themselves. This is done by eliciting their imagined relationship with a future sexual partner, including how this correlates with their anticipated balance of familial and professional lives. Natal'ia Shalygina and Mariia Kotovskaia, from their study of value orientations amongst young men and women in Moscow, suggest that young women have more flexible attitudes to sex roles and that these are shaping changes in attitudes amongst young people as a whole towards love, sex and marriage. Although they discern three very different 'types' of young women, they focus in their chapter on that type (constituting half of their respondents) who show a strong orientation towards professional success and prioritize this over domestic life in their ideal images. Although, as they note, the 'strong woman' is no newcomer to Russian culture, the continued prevalence of traditional sex-role norms in post-Soviet Russia means that such women experience considerable psychological discomfort as they seek to implement their chosen life-path. Lynne Attwood's chapter on young people's attitudes towards sex roles and sexuality (based on small samples of student teachers in Moscow and Piatigorsk), discusses the whole range of views suggested by Shalygina and Kotovskaia. Attwood argues that there is still considerable adherence to essentialist notions of difference and complementarity between the sexes; state ideology has thus been relatively successful. Although their emphases are different, both these chapters explore the contradictions between young women's ideals of and desire for education and professional advancement and their familial orientation. Encouragingly, they both also find a good deal of tolerance towards alternative sexuality among young people.

Central to a positive feminine identity, of course, is confidence in one's body and health, and Anne Murcott and Annie Feltham in Chapter 9 of this volume focus on women's attitudes to their bodies, health and especially reproductive health. The excessive reliance on abortion for birth control in the past in the Soviet Union is now well known, but this may in fact obscure some of the wider issues concerning women's reproductive health in general. The experience of repeated abortions has had a catastrophic impact on women's health, and gynaecological illnesses in Russia are of epidemic proportions; reportedly one in ten women in Russia is infertile and 17 per cent of girls are already suffering from some gynaecological illness (Kodzaeva 1993). One area in which state ideology was never effective was in convincing young people that they should 'restrain' from pre-marital sex; surveys suggest that by the age of 17 the vast majority of young women have had their first sexual experience (Potekhina 1992). Thus, young women, and young men, need to be fully informed about contraceptive methods and have access to consultation services so that they can make informed choices best suited to their own bodies and situations. Murcott and Feltham suggest that, despite high rates of abortion, termination of pregnancy is not seen as a desirable means of birth control by Russian women, or even acceptable except in extreme cases. In this and in relation to more general health beliefs, the authors point to wide similarities with young women's views about their health in Western countries. At the same time, they note a peculiarly extensive use of home-made remedies and a striking essentialism in Russian views on the distinct psychologies and social roles of men and women.

The power relations involved in the sexual contract become most clear when it is enforced, not through consent but violence and, in the last chapter of Part II, Tat'iana Zabelina explores the way in which sexual violence directed towards women facilitates their subordination and oppression. It is recognized, even by the authorities, that the decrease in rape noted in statistics in the early 1990s is a false trend and that in the first half of 1993 the number of reported rapes was up by 15 per cent over the same period in 1992. Nevertheless, reported rates in Russia remain exceptionally low and thus absolute rates of rape appear equally so; official statistics show that 13,600 people were raped in 1992 (Yakov 1993). Not surprisingly, Zabelina notes the need to establish real rates of sexual assault by using survey methods now widely adopted in the West; the first such survey in the UK, conducted across London and published in 1985, revealed that two out of every five women had experienced rape (including marital rape), attempted rape or other serious sexual assault (Hall 1985: 32). The culture of non-reporting in Russia is partly due to fear of publicity and revenge, but is associated also with the sympathy with which rape offenders are treated, and which is reflected in the decreasing rates of conviction for sex crimes (a tendency which is also apparent in the UK) (Greer 1995). This is despite the fact that the crimes themselves are becoming more brutal and increasingly orientated towards young girls, children and old women (those whom it is impossible to accuse of being 'provocative') (Yakov 1993). Yakov also notes that three quarters of rapists in Russia are under the influence of alcohol, almost half of reported rapes are gang rapes, one out of three offenders are re-offenders (of sex crimes) and one in four is a juvenile (14–17 years old) (ibid.). In this volume Zabelina explores the similarities and differences between sexual violence and responses to it in Russia and elsewhere, and links this to a discussion of the concept of violence in general in Soviet and post-Soviet society. She also examines attitudes among legislators towards the problem of domestic and sexual violence and the concrete measures which have been taken, primarily by non-governmental organizations, to intervene and help victims of such violence.

GENDER, IDENTITY AND CULTURAL PRACTICE

If accounts of mainstream youth activity rarely consider the experience of young women, when it comes to youth cultural, or 'subcultural' activity, women have been even more absent. However, despite the invisibility of female actors, Western discourses of the teenage consumer and of working-class subcultural resistance, which became prominent in the post-Second World War period, have been deeply gendered. Both posited women as objects of the cultural processes considered: girls existed outside or on the periphery of subcultural groups as the objects of sexual desire or consumption by male members, or were viewed as the central targets of gender-aware market manipulators. In the introductory chapter to this final section of the book the present author first of all charts the Western debate on youth cultural formations and feminist interventions into this debate, which sought to uncover women's cultural practice, before proceeding to discuss the changing nature of Soviet and post-Soviet debates on youth cultural activity. The chapter suggests that although in late Soviet and post-Soviet society young men's cultural practice has been criticized, it has been increasingly accepted as a necessary expression of masculinity, which, it is suggested, had been severely limited in the 'feminized' society of the past. Young women's cultural practice, however, has been persistently sexualized and used to illustrate the degeneration of morality and of society as a whole. The tracing of these discursive contours acts to set the scene for the empirical chapters which follow, each seeking to bring to light the centrality of gender identity in different aspects of urban cultural practice.

One of the ways girls have been discursively positioned is as victims of sexual abuse, specifically by provincial male gangs. The high rates of gang rape by juveniles is confirmed by Tat'iana Zabelina in this volume as well as by police statistics and press coverage (see Antonian, Pertsova and Sablina 1991: 97). However, positing girls as 'common girls' (for sexual use) does not adequately describe their experience. Elena Omel'chenko's study focuses on provincial gang formations in one of the Volga cities particularly plagued by the problem of youth gangs, Ul'ianovsk. The author traces the changing nature of such gangs in the context of marketization and the extending web of organized crime, and discusses the positions held within the gangs by girls. Her analysis points to differentiated and distinct positions taken up by girls in gangs which, in mixed gangs, reflect male positions. By reference to style, mannerism and behaviour, Omel'chenko also uncovers part of the 'alternative' strategy adopted by girls in such gangs. Participation in gangs may, she argues, provide protection from other predatory males while all-girl gangs, like male gangs, often provide a mutual defence system.

My own chapter focuses on a very different youth cultural form: the central gatherings (*tusovki*) of the capital city. I explore the impact of post-Soviet developments (in particular marketization, Westernization and the heightening of ethnic tension) on the youth cultural scene in Moscow. The youth cultural careers of a group of young men and women first interviewed in the period 1988–91 are traced in order to explore how their youth cultural strategies have changed in the post-Soviet environment and to what extent they have retained a gendered profile. The author concludes that both individual life changes ('growing up') and the changed environment in which they act, have raised new questions about gender identity for the young people concerned. Although very different styles have been adopted (those studied in the chapter being bikers and skinheads), their strategies reveal a gender vulnerability and a search for workable masculinities and femininities in the post-*tusovka* world.

Unlike the other chapters in this section, Tat'iana Shchepanskaia's 'urban subculture of mothers' is 'invisible' except to the initiated. This does not mean it is 'underground', illegal or subversive, but nor does it seek expression in style or street position. This renders it immediately different from those youth cultures described in the other empirical chapters in this section of the book, but at the same time helps illuminate some key issues about urban cultural activity. The first of these is that distinctly female 'subcultures' are largely ignored and indeed rendered 'invisible' as a result of preconceptions about the resistant or delinquent nature of subcultures, which, when combined with a *Sturm und Drang* theory of adolescence, makes them appear essentially masculine. The second, and perhaps more important issue is that the symbols and meanings of subcultures are encoded on the body, and the study of their significance must take place on this level. To this end Shchepanskaia carefully traces her own and others' experience of first pregnancy and the role of bodily symbolism in initiating new mothers into not only a new part of their life-cycle but also a new, and distinctly female, cultural code.

GENDER, GENERATION AND IDENTITY IN POST-SOVIET RUSSIA

In considering contemporary British society, Angela McRobbie notes that recent macro changes have created a 'discursive explosion around what constitutes femininity' (McRobbie 1994: 158). The question linking all three parts of the current volume might be whether the acceptance of Russia into the post-Cold War global community has had the same effect on gender discourse in post-Soviet Russia, resulting in more space for women and men to form or re-form identities in a liberating way. Some would not hesitate to claim that, in the post-Soviet period, at last, both women and men have been released to rediscover and celebrate their 'difference':

> The concept of woman is much broader than its sexual basis . . . it includes the performance of a certain social role . . . the continuation of the species, the upbringing of children, the transfer of moral experience, the aestheticization of the domestic sphere. The desire to have a family, to bear and bring up children is instinctive in a woman. A woman who does not have this instinct, or who gives it only minimal priority, is a nonsense, a mistake of nature, a social hermaphrodite . . . emancipation understood in the most ridiculous way. If family and children are put first, then we have before us a real woman.
>
> (El 1990: 2)

The ideal man has been reduced [by women] to how much money he has. What is a real man? What is his social role? He also takes part in continuing the species, but his function is different. Fatherly instinct is in the creation of the necessary economic base for successful female activity in the family. This is why his efforts are directed towards the outside world. A man must be honest, clever, courageous – ready to oppose evil, defend principles and even die in the interests of his family. This type of man has been totally destroyed.

(ibid.)

It is, the authors of the present volume would suggest, difficult to celebrate this kind of 'difference', for its presence does not ensure but inhibit diversity, release and exploration. Difference, for the author cited above, is securely rooted and fixed. Or rather, the security of the author requires that this difference be rooted and fixed.

This is not to say that this view prevails in contemporary Russia. It is increasingly the case that women are talking about femininities, and strong and 'alternative' female images are in evidence. The press has carried an increasing number of articles about successful female pop singers (Cherkasova 1993), women who chose to marry men much younger than themselves (a feature no doubt inspired by Alla Pugacheva's new, young husband!) (Avdeeva 1993) and about young women who pursue traditionally male professions or hobbies such as women bodyguards (Tikhonova 1992), women soldiers (Bualvintsev 1994) or women kick-boxers (Bykanova 1992). The West is used also to suggest alternative versions of femininity (Boguslavskaia 1992), especially by providing Western, including feminist, 'expert opinion'.

For men, meanwhile, there has been an open recognition of the 'crisis of masculinity' hinted at before the collapse of the Soviet Union.[1] The 'men's page' ('Kto vy sudar'?') in *Moskovskii Komsomolets* over the last few years suggests that considerable attention is paid to defining the 'real man' and providing images to follow. This has been reflected in the reporting of 'Man of the year' and body-building competitions, the presentation of role models such as Arnold Schwarzenegger, articles on new aftershaves and male fashion and interviews with successful businessmen. There has even been discussion of contraception available to men.

The *MK* rubric, though, has failed men in their search for new masculinities in that it has ignored the real problems experienced by a majority of young men who are threatened by more aggressive masculinities, in particular via bullying, gang activity and hierarchial subordination in institutions, especially the armed forces. Women have also been failed – by articles which, whilst criticizing men for their shortcomings, do so without challenging the fundamental patriarchal premises of society. Those press articles dealing directly with the creation of the 'new, new Russian woman' thus are concerned primarily with skilling women to *use* their femininity to get what they want out of (family) life. This perhaps reflects concern with what Shalygina and Kotovskaia refer to as the 'masculinity complex' of strong Russian women, the double-bind of ambition and ability within the context of a general social adherence to traditional sex roles. Themes of such articles include:

- Courses run by a woman for women on how to be 'women'. Such courses, it is claimed, have successfully allowed women to get back their wayward husbands, achieve harmony in the family or trick reticent boyfriends or lovers into marrying them (Tiurina 1994).
- Advice on the best strategies in the hunt for husbands in increasingly short supply (summed up perhaps by the advice that 'it is best to entice men into marriage with a tasty morsel and do everything to make sure that for as long as possible they do not notice the bars of the cages you are constructing for them') (Barabash 1994).
- Advice on how to win, keep and, if necessary, get rid of men (the advice here is that women should always look as if they 'have just got out of a cold bath') (Kornilovskaia 1994).
- Warnings of the 'types' of people who will be unfaithful in marriage (Mashkova 1992).

Thus, in contrast to the unified ideal 'mother and worker' of the Soviet period, there are now a myriad of masculine and feminine types, perhaps even a 'discursive explosion' around gender identity of which McRobbie talks. Despite the plurality, however, there remains an underlying conviction that there exists, nevertheless, an 'ideal woman' and an 'ideal man' whose essential differences are fixed and normatively correct. There is, for example, a current fascination with constructing these ideal portraits via opinion polls. One such survey conducted in Russia by the VTsIOM (All-Russian Centre for the Study of Public Opinion) in February 1993 suggested that beauty is more important than brains in the ideal woman; whereas first in both men's and women's ideal of a man is 'intelligence' (Dzhaginova 1993).[2]

The very talk of the social construction of masculinities and femininities suggests a growing importance attached to gender difference.

However, the debate still often takes the form of providing 'solutions' to an identified problem; the issue is to re-create the 'ideal' or 'real' man and woman rather than to explore difference, diversity and cultural richness. Given the normative content of the 'ideal woman', it becomes clear that it is important to locate the 'real woman' not only for women themselves, but for the moral health of society.

This is not a uniquely Russian problem born of a pre-feminist consciousness or cultural peculiarity, however. As Seidler notes, it may well be a weakness in postmodern (and in this sense perhaps postfeminist) conceptions of difference in that 'we learn to think about difference as a way of not having to think about oppression and subordination.' (Seidler 1994: 209). In contrast, Seidler suggests, the power in recognizing difference is its ability to illuminate the 'particular relationship of reason to a dominant form of masculinity' (p. 200) and expose 'liberal visions of freedom and equality' and 'unified visions of humanity' as something conceived in terms of men (p. 209).

The authors of the current book are not seeking to break new ground in theorizing the complex relationship between structure and agency, difference and equality, or poststructuralist theory and feminist practice. Rather, they have tried to explore the actual experience of difference which lies at the heart of the debate yet is often subordinated to more abstract conceptualizations of its nature. The book aims to provide concrete case studies of the way in which the social institutions, modes of thought and individual subjectivity which make up 'discourse' (Weedon 1987: 41) position women and young people in post-Soviet Russia, and how these discourses are intertwined. It also aims to show the ways in which the subjects of our research form and re-form individual and collective identities to negotiate and challenge this positioning. In so doing, we hope that readers of the book will gain an impression both of common structures shaping the (post)modern world and also the diversity of ways in which we experience these structures and of strategies we develop to negotiate them.

NOTES

1 See, for example, the interview with Sergei Stankevich in which he associates the rebirth of 'real politics' with the re-emergence of a space for truly masculine activity (independence, responsibility, leadership and rationality) (Fopov 1989).

2 Both men and women place appearance first in their image of the ideal woman, although many more men (59 per cent) than women (46 per cent) do so (Dzhaginova 1993). A survey carried out by students of MGU-Ul'ianovsk branch amongst their peers on the ideal man found that the majority of young people surveyed, especially in the age group 16–20, could not construct a portrait of the ideal man. Among the young men surveyed, the independent and emancipated woman was not a popular ideal; only about 30 per cent gave a positive answer while 60 per cent were wholeheartedly against, seeing in emancipation a direct contradiction of female nature. When asked 'Are men the stronger sex?', 70 per cent of surveyed girls said that the moral decline of the male population and growing weakness among them meant they were no longer the stronger sex. However, all 100 per cent of surveyed lads said they were the stronger half of humanity (Sadykova and Gorobtsova 1994).

Part I

Surviving the new social environment: strategies at home, work and school

2 Gender and generation in the new Russian labour market

Sue Bridger and Rebecca Kay

The economic reforms which have accompanied Russia's emergence as an independent state have reintroduced the concept of officially acknowledged unemployment for the first time in some sixty years. At the same time, the price liberalization which kicked off the period of transition to a market economy in Russia has produced a massive drop in living standards for many families. It is, however, generally recognized that, in the chaotic period of change which has followed the demise of the USSR, women have been the major losers.

From the very beginning of this period, women have formed an absolute majority of the officially registered unemployed. Whilst their proportion amongst this group nationally has hovered around the 70–75 per cent mark, at a regional level the situation has often been far more severe, with women making up over 85 or even 90 per cent of the unemployed in a range of cities and regions across the length and breadth of Russia. A considerable degree of controversy has, however, surrounded Russian unemployment statistics throughout this period. Official unemployment has remained staggeringly low: less than 2 per cent of the work-force were registered unemployed through the first three years of transition, reflecting, in the main, the low level of benefit they might expect to receive.

The number of people actually laid off from work is, however, far greater than this. In part, the discrepancy is due to people not registering as unemployed and simply finding their own means of survival. Of greater significance, however, have been the rising numbers of workers on either short time or 'administrative leave' – periods of prolonged enforced idleness through which the employing enterprise pays little or no compensation but continues to hold out the carrot of a possible return to work at a later date. By the beginning of 1995, government officials were acknowledging a combined total of both official and 'hidden' unemployed at around 13 per cent of the work-force. An ILO survey in late 1994, however, had already placed the figure at nearer 40 per cent (Luce 1994; OMRI 1995). Whatever the true state of affairs, what is not in dispute is the disproportionate impact on women.

The Soviet legacy of 'protective' policies towards women and the family produced a situation in which responsibility for the extensive range of child-care-related benefits rested with employing enterprises at the same time as a prolonged media campaign sought to persuade women to place greater emphasis on home and children. For enterprises dealing with uncomfortable new economic realities, the result was to mark out women as a potentially expensive and troublesome work-force. Where cutbacks have occurred, therefore, women have immediately been targeted for redundancy or for 'administrative leave'. At the same time, many of the sectors in which women were heavily concentrated, such as health and education, remain primarily publicly funded and, given the parlous state of the economy overall, have seen a massive drop in pay relative to other sectors. Taken together, these factors have contributed to a steadily growing feminization of poverty in Russia.

The initial wave of redundancies primarily affected women in the defence industries, research institutes and ministries, and targeted first of all those approaching retirement age or with young children. Engineers and economists were therefore heavily represented amongst the first band of enforced job seekers in the transitional economy. With the passage of time their numbers have been swelled by new graduates, especially in these same specialisms, school leavers and, more recently, skilled workers across a whole range of industries. The fundamental problem women face in seeking alternative employment is the mis-match between the skills they have and the jobs on offer. During the first three years of transition, the majority of unemployed women have had a higher or specialized secondary education. Meanwhile, most of the available vacancies have been for manual and/or less-skilled work: sewing machinists, secretaries, shop assistants, cleaners and other unskilled jobs in the service sector. It is scarcely surprising, therefore, that surveys on unemployment have found women expressing reluctance to change profession or seek retraining when opportunities for other forms of professional work appear so limited (Rzhanitsyna 1993: 81). This situation is not, however, simply the product of a lack of suitable vacancies: where opportunities are available employers have a clear and well-documented preference for selecting men.

Attitudes such as these are not new. Discrimination in selection and promotion was rife in the former USSR and, although briefly debated in the era of glasnost, was never seriously tackled. Indeed, the economic and social policies of perestroika itself through the latter half of the 1980s effectively gave official sanction to a view of women as a subsidiary work-force to be eased out of employment as necessary for the good of society. It was in this period that a reluctance to employ women began to be voiced quite openly: a 1990 survey of enterprise managers, for example, found that 79 per cent would only select a woman if the job 'was not suitable for a man'. (ibid.: 105).

The combination of market forces and a lack of legal safeguards has, since 1992, simply given free rein to attitudes which were already well established. Job advertisements commonly express a preference as to the sex of applicants and, in the case of a clear majority of professional vacancies, especially those involving management skills, it is baldly stated that male applicants only are required. Where vacancies are notified directly to Employment Centres, employers expect that their stated preferences for male or female job applicants will be acted upon. Whatever the view of the Centres on this issue, particularly in the light of the fact that most of their clientele are women, they are evidently unable to combat this trend in the current climate. Women, therefore, have been facing a dual disadvantage as the new labour market has developed: unwanted skills and overt discrimination on the grounds of sex. To this, for so many of the new unemployed, can be added a further significant obstacle: discrimination on the grounds of age. In the pages which follow we will be drawing on material from Russian surveys and from the press as well as from interviews which we conducted with women in Moscow and Moscow region in 1993–4.[1]

OLDER WOMEN – PROSPECTS AND RESPONSES

Where employers are actively seeking women to fill vacancies it is commonly stated that applicants should be under 30 or, at most, 35. As this is precisely the age over which most redundancies have been occurring, the situation is extremely threatening for older women who lose their jobs. A willingness to employ women even up to the age of 40 is almost never expressed. The few job advertisements which specify women in the 30–50 age group must make utterly depressing reading to former scientific and technical staff whose maturity and experience are scarcely required for selling cigarettes outside metro stations, or other unskilled, casual labour of this type.

The massive degree of de-skilling implicit in this wholesale rejection of older women for both the new professional and clerical jobs is underlined by the retraining opportunities which women of this age have been offered. A whole range of private training courses has sprung into existence since 1992 apparently providing women with the chance to find their niche in the new labour market. The courses on offer, however, reflect very closely the limited opportunities currently available for women. Courses in bookkeeping, typing and office skills, computing and foreign languages prepare women primarily for subordinate clerical positions, if they can avoid being barred from these jobs on the grounds of age. Training in childcare, arts and crafts, hairdressing, beauty consultancy or even domestic service offer, at best, a move into low-paid service sector employment or, more probably, home-based casual work – the home being a place women of this age are still expected to be.

From the very beginnings of the market reforms, women have been urged to take responsibility for their own survival by using domestic skills to make money. Women made redundant from the defence industries, research institutes and former USSR Ministries have been encouraged to think in terms of setting up small businesses providing tailoring, knitwear, embroidery, catering or a whole range of other domestic crafts. Quite apart from the near insuperable problems involved in formally setting up in business in Russia, there has been virtually no discussion either of how economically viable such a move might be when engaged in *en masse*, or of how socially desirable it is to write off the experience of a generation of women in this way. Given the lack of alternatives, many older women who lose their jobs are forced into attempting to make money either from existing hobbies or newly-acquired handwork skills.

State and voluntary organizations which offer women courses in skills such as these make no bones about what they are doing. The Union of Russian Women, for example, with its courses in hairdressing, dressmaking and a range of traditional crafts talks about 'survival', and expects these skills to be used as a means of economizing, bartering or trading. Certainly, only a tiny minority of their trainees have found formal employment as a result of retraining, and it would appear optimistic to assume that this situation might improve given the growing numbers of women involved and the generally depressed state of the economy. Nevertheless, it says a great deal about falling living standards and the dire situation in which so many women find themselves that even courses such as these may have a four- or five-year waiting list.

Rather more popular with older unemployed women who have higher education have been courses in accountancy. Of all the opportunities for retraining regularly available, accountancy is virtually the only one which appears to offer the hope of remaining in professional employment. Accountants are much in demand in new commercial firms and it might well be hoped that, in a highly skilled area such as this, the age barrier would operate far less rigidly. Unfortunately, it is over the question of their level of skill that women who have taken this route have experienced difficulties. Most accountancy courses last just one or two months and cannot hope to provide even highly educated women with a grasp of the job's complexities. Moreover, the alacrity with which state, voluntary and private organizations have seized on the idea of accountancy training as a cure for all ills has led to a glut of ill-trained and inexperienced women faced with vacancies demanding a minimum of three years' experience or of particular specialist transactions. As one unemployed ex-engineer put it:

> You know what it's like in this country, all the engineers have turned into accountants! We've all done one-month courses – we studied for fifteen years to become engineers and in a month we've turned into accountants!'

(1)[2]

Where longer courses have been offered and trainees carefully selected, success rates may be much higher and the problem of age discrimination to some extent overcome.[3]

Nevertheless, this does not overcome the question of sex discrimination. Although women dominated the world of economics and finance under the Soviet system, with the opening up of the commercial financial sector in Russia new job opportunities have become highly attractive to men. Where well-paid work in accountancy and finance is on offer, women, even with appropriate skills and experience, find themselves in competition with men and may well face the same discriminatory attitudes prevalent in other professional spheres. It would be misleading to suggest, however, that women cannot make headway in professional employment in the new commercial sector: certainly, one of the areas where some women have become prominent is in banking. The relatively small number of women who have become directors of commercial banks may well employ a form of positive discrimination in their selection of staff, seeing women as potentially more efficient and committed. This remains, however, a development which serves the interests of only a small minority of women and cannot begin to combat the mis-match between the unemployed and the vacancies available or the degree of discrimination within the new labour market as a whole. Within the new commercial sector, only a quarter of employees are women (Khotkina 1994).

Even if employment were readily available after retraining, there is no guarantee that older women would automatically rush to take up places on courses. There has been no tradition in Russia of people changing direction in mid-career or of taking a variety of different paths through a lifetime of employment. A profession, for most people, was for life, with employment guaranteed from school or college to pension. It therefore demands an entirely new way of thinking about work to be able to accept the concept of retraining after perhaps twenty years of a working life. Understandably, older women who have been displaced from what they believed were secure jobs fail to see why they should be the ones to begin the experiment, as one erstwhile engineer commented:

> I'm 48, I can't retrain. I don't want to study any more. I've had study up to here. I've been in every higher education institution in Moscow, right up to Moscow State University!
>
> (2)

A large-scale Russian study of women and unemployment carried out in 1992 found that women were likely to be as negative about retraining as they were about accepting unskilled work (Rzhanitsyna 1993: 81–2). Perhaps more than anything else, women's attitudes to retraining reflect the suddenness of change: in contemplating the extraordinary state of the new labour market in Russia, older women might well be forgiven for remaining in a state of shock.

When older women discuss their reactions to the change which has so suddenly come upon them, their distress is often all too visible. The level of stress they experience in this situation is, of course, closely related to their domestic circumstances: women who are single mothers, for example, or who have large families, are faced with immediate practical anxieties about their own and their family's survival. Aside from financial worry, however, stress on redundancy may be due at least as much to a pronounced sense of loss, especially for those women who had been highly committed to their work and had seen it as a vocation or career. The assertion is often made that women who were classed as engineers, for example, in the former Soviet Union were not really high-level specialists. Amongst the women we interviewed there were certainly some who felt that this had been true for them; women who saw themselves as simply having marked time in a job which did not really exist or in which they felt powerless to make a genuine contribution. Others, however, described their love for their work, their high levels of education and their years of experience and were frequently unable to keep the emotion out of their voice as they spoke. It is, therefore, scarcely surprising that this combination of personal loss with anxiety for their future security produces significant levels of stress in women who may still be only in their late thirties or early forties yet see no future whatsoever for themselves in the new labour market.

The stress of unemployment is recognized by those working in the Employment Service and may be directly tackled by an Employment Centre as part of its overall programme. In a Centre where staff have incorporated this issue into their general approach, such as in Dubna on the northern edge of Moscow region, initiatives have been financed which may offer few prospects of employment but which provide an element of much-appreciated psychological support for older women. In addition, direct assistance has been given through the recruitment of a psychologist onto the staff able to provide direct counselling sessions. In the six months after the psychologist's appointment, nineteen older women had received counselling to help them cope with the stress of their situation. Whilst examples such as this remain a drop in the ocean given the extent of the unemployment problem, that such a service is provided at all is nevertheless of some significance given that counselling and support groups of all types remain in their infancy in Russia.

What none of these initiatives can do, however, is to bring women's jobs back. Many have undoubtedly been lost forever and future prospects of formal employment look very bleak indeed, certainly for women over 40. In the absence of realistic benefit levels, they get by on combinations of street trading, self-sufficiency and casual part-time jobs as cleaners or childminders or dog-sitters, a plunge in status which, for some, makes them acutely aware of their sudden invisibility:

All these women, they were better than the men – not better scientists necessarily, but more intellectual, on a different level. They were interested in art and music and literature. Now they're all working as cleaners and traders. We don't exist any more, no-one is interested in us.

(2)

Whilst age discrimination is rife in Western societies there is, nevertheless, a growing tendency for women over 40, especially those with older children, to be looking for new educational and employment opportunities for the latter half of their working lives. As the market has developed in Russia, women of this age, far from making a new start, are being immediately written off and pushed into what is effectively a very premature retirement from formal employment. In a country obsessed with women's maternal roles, the position of *babushka* (grandmother) with no concerns beyond the welfare of the family is, for many, the only vacancy now on offer.

YOUNGER WOMEN – OPPORTUNITIES AND OBSTACLES

If older women are experiencing great difficulty in coming to terms with the changes brought about by the market reforms, it could be expected that younger women would be more readily able to cope with the loss of the old certainties. Since the demise of the USSR, public opinion polls have, almost inevitably, found younger people more welcoming of change and prepared to tackle the unfamiliar. Younger women themselves may be very conscious of how much harder it is for their own mothers to adapt. Certainly, those we interviewed acknowledged very readily that it may be very hard for women of their mothers' generation to accept the end of Soviet-style job security and that this is scarcely surprising if the corollary is unemployment and increasing poverty.

For younger women, however, the loss of certain aspects of the former system may be seen as a positive development. The ending of automatic job assignment on graduation, for example, may come as something of a relief to young women who are less than whole-hearted about their choice of degree and see the potential for a move into something more interesting in the new job market. It is, however, a very different story for those who felt committed to a specialism in which there are now widespread redundancies. Recent graduate engineers and economists, for example, may find them-selves in a position which is little different from that faced by older women in these professions. Finding employment is likely to mean a complete change of profile and, whilst women under 30 have an undoubted advantage in the job market, this is not to say that the work on offer will appear acceptable. In a country in which a degree has been a vocational qualification leading directly to a job in one's chosen sphere, a considerable adjustment is required for even recent graduates to view it as simply an educational stepping-stone to the jobs available. Moreover, if the work on offer to women does not require high qualifications then a degree looks increasingly like a waste of time.

As the job market changes, the entire system of higher and further education is increasingly called into question. In the meantime, the training opportunities which are being developed by both state and voluntary organizations for unemployed school leavers and graduates reflect women's exclusion from the new professional jobs. In the main, courses on offer to younger women differ little from those provided for older women and may similarly lead only into casual employment, especially for the group of young women who have been hardest hit by change. Young women who already have small children, and it should be remembered that women in Russia have commonly had their children in their late teens and early twenties, frequently during the course of their higher education, have been particularly disadvantaged with the advent of the market reforms. The loss of child-care institutions and the unwillingness of employers to take on women in this situation has made them especially difficult to place in alternative formal employment once out of work. Job advertisements habitually specify that, if women are required at all, they must be unmarried and/or without children. Courses in child-care with a view to employment as childminders or nannies may, therefore, be seen as the most realistic option for women in this group, yet such training scarcely offers a future of anything other than a low-paid and insecure existence.

Younger women should not, therefore, be seen as a homogeneous group: those with young children may be substantially disadvantaged even in a situation which generally favours younger women whilst, in addition, differences in attitude remain between older and younger women within the under-30 age group. The effects of growing up under the former Soviet system come into play here very visibly. Women who are already in their mid-twenties would have begun their post-school education before any of the significant social and economic changes of the Gorbachev period took place. As a result, the notion of changing direction and finding an entirely new niche for themselves may be as alien to them as it is to older women who now find themselves out of work. Women of this age in insecure or poorly paid jobs may therefore express great indecisiveness about moving into a new area of work or the same reluctance even to think of change as older women do. As two women in their mid-twenties, both extremely poorly paid librarians, put it, 'It's too late for us to learn something else. What would we do?' (see Appendix: 3).

The problem that underlies attitudes such as these is the nature of much of the work on offer. A higher education, particularly in an area such as civil engineering, is certainly not essential for many of the subordinate office jobs currently available to younger women. Far from being grateful that the job market apparently works in their favour, young women may be scathing in their assessment of what is available to them and see the widespread disregard of their talents and skills as the most blatant form of discrimination:

> Men have taken over all the best-paid jobs and women get a pittance. The men have seized hold of everything, whilst the women are at their beck and call – 'get the tea, get the coffee'.
> (4)

This perception that women are required only as decorative append-ages to male 'professionals' is based not only on personal experience but also on statements made in the popular press by successful entrepreneurs. When the new breed of millionaire expresses the view that women in business should be no more than glorified waitresses, it is made very plain to young women that the new commercial opportunities are not for them (Posadskaya 1994b: 171).

A glance down the situations vacant columns immediately makes the position clear and explains the strength of feeling on this issue. Job advertisements effectively state that many employers, particu-larly in commercial firms, are not looking primarily for brains:

> Secretaries required: attractive girls with office experience, aged 18–22, at least 168cms tall.
> (*Reklamnoe prilozhenie* 1993:6)

> Secretary/personal assistant required with knowledge of English, pretty girl under 25.
> (*Priglashaem na rabotu* 1994:2)

This requirement that women, if they are employed at all, should be good to look at as well as young places an additional burden on women seeking employment. Where employers can afford to pick and choose there is pressure on the overweight to be slim, on the slim to be well-groomed and on the well-groomed to be beautiful. It is a short step from here to the addition of expectations of an overtly sexual kind.

Whilst sexual harassment was neither discussed, investigated nor tackled in the Soviet Union, there were widespread assumptions that it might well come into play when women were looking for promotions or other 'favours' from management. It should be pointed out that the definition of sexual harassment employed here is far removed from the elements of 'display of pin-ups/unwanted touching/use of innuendo' which form a major part of the catalogue of harassment in Western experience. In the Russian context, harassment, most frequently referred to by women as 'sexual aggression' or 'sexual terror', refers directly to sex in exchange for employment and continues to be a major taboo. Breaking the silence on this issue in the newspaper *Delovaia zhenshchina* in 1993 produced such a response from readers that an attempt was subsequently made by journalists to set up a support group for women who had suffered sexual harassment. As one reader observed, the situation had not been improved by the advent of the market reforms:

> Nothing has changed . . . only the added fear of losing your job. This particularly affects women who are the sole breadwinners for their families. It is these women who are transformed into office prostitutes. Those who refuse any proposition are simply chucked out.
>
> ('Ia k vam pishu' 1992)

Our interviews with Russian women suggest that there is a great deal of truth in this statement and that, for younger women seeking work, sexual harassment is a constant consideration. Returning to the situations vacant columns the importance of this issue becomes apparent. Whilst the growing sexualization of the workplace is suggested by the frequent emphasis on physical attributes rather than skills, no potential employer is likely to advertise the fact that sex is part of the job. It is, rather, the occasional advert which adds 'no sexual services required' which gives some indication of how widespread an assumption it is that women should provide whatever their boss demands.

Women we interviewed described job interview questions with a sexual element and expressed concern that there was often a hidden agenda of sexual favours, even in firms which had initially appeared above board. Whilst, by its very nature, it is extremely difficult to assess the extent of the problem, the anecdotal evidence is suggestive of a widespread concern. Certainly, young women themselves perceive the problem as a significant one:

> Sexual aggression is the main reason why Russian women cannot fulfil their potential. All my friends have met with this when trying to get jobs or once they were working. When a woman has been in her job for say three months and she is just starting to settle in and feel good about herself, suddenly she starts getting all these propositions and she has to leave.
>
> (5)

By the same token, some courses providing advice for young women entering the labour market have seen fit to make the issue of sexual exploitation a central element in their programmes.[4]

The key to this disturbing situation is, of course, the catastrophic fall in living standards which has accompanied the drop in employment. Taking a principled stand on the question of harassment is easy only when acute material need does not form part of the equation. Both young women themselves and some of those providing advice on negotiating the employment minefield tacitly acknowledge that there is a decision to be made on this issue. As one woman in her mid-twenties put it, 'If you're looking for something yourself, you have to know the rules of the game and decide whether you want to play.' (6) There is, in effect, an acknowledgement that, once wise to the situation, women may not necessarily be free to reject it.

This introduction of an overtly sexual element into the new labour market undoubtedly has a bearing on women's direct involvement in the glamour and sex industry. If an emphasis on personal appearance has become a common element in mainstream employment, it is scarcely surprising that women who fit the bill may seek to employ their physical gifts more lucratively. When sex may be expected of the humble office assistant, far better prizes may appear to be on offer for the same sexual favours elsewhere. When the gulf between rich and poor is growing ever wider, when the 'good life' available to the few is highly visible to all and when women's employment prospects are so dire, young women can scarcely be censured for regarding selling their bodies as a smart move. This is, moreover, a logical outcome which, far from reflecting a kind of youthful deviance, appears to be very widely accepted in society at large and, certainly, in what has been termed the 'pro-prostitution propaganda' of the media.[5] Here, surely, lies the origin of the notorious survey which found that 60 per cent of Moscow girls leaving school thought prostitution the most attractive profession. Whilst this tells us little about their personal aspirations and attitudes, it provides a very stark picture of their assessment of current job opportunities for women.

With the demise of the USSR, the sex and glamour industry which had been developing apace under perestroika was given an added fillip by the advent of the market reforms. An ending of controls and a growing constituency of Russian men with money, and of women without, ensured the rapid development of glamour modelling, pornography and both overt and 'undercover' prostitution.[6] Amongst young women keen to enter this world of apparently glamorous opportunities, the boom in beauty contests has provided an ostensibly safe stepping-stone to the much-sought-after foreign modelling contract. A notable feature of Russian beauty contests, and one which underlines the problems women face in employment, has been the high proportion of entrants with higher education employed in low-paid, public sector jobs.

However, in a country where the office junior may find that her job contains a hidden agenda, it is scarcely surprising to discover that the same is true of activities with a primary emphasis on physical attributes, such as beauty contests and modelling. The revelation that entrants in certain beauty contests, or at least those serious about winning, and photographic models expecting any kind of a career were commonly prevailed upon to grant sexual favours to photographers, agents and the like, was given some serious treatment in the media after an unexpected event in August 1993. Photographic and fashion models created a diversion in central Moscow by unfurling placards announcing, 'Models get paid, not laid!' in an effort to challenge the 'sexual terror' which they saw as endemic in the industry. Their seriousness can be gauged by the fact that they spent much of the subsequent winter attempting, unsuccessfully in the prevailing political climate, to form a models' trade union. That some modelling agencies are indeed, as they asserted, thinly disguised prostitution rackets, is made clear by reports in both the Russian and foreign press about Russian women trapped in prostitution after accepting modelling contracts. The most highly publicized cases have inevitably involved a traffic in women, controlled by Russian criminal groups, across Europe. The involvement of police forces in a range of countries, notably Germany, Turkey, Greece, Cyprus, Italy and, ultimately, America, has rescued some of the women involved and, usually, returned them to Russia. The women have not, however, always been willing to go, even after one disastrous experience. The lure of foreign travel and the chance of earning 'real money' abroad is enough to make some young women prepared to take the chance more than once, even if it means that would-be dancers have to be strippers and aspiring models become topless hostesses.

The key issue for women who become involved in this work is whether they are able to remain in control and, ultimately, to get out as easily as they got in. Though receiving far less publicity, the situation on home territory may clearly be little better for women working in the brothels disguised as escort agencies and massage parlours which are controlled by organized crime. However, in a climate in which prostitution is habitually described as 'the only way for women to make a lot of money', increasingly the ultimate goal in Russian society, it is small wonder that so many young women are undaunted by the possible consequences.

Considering prostitution merely as the largely indiscriminate provision of sexual services for payment does not, however, do justice to the range of options currently presenting themselves to young women in Russia. A popular alternative is to become involved in a much longer-term sexual relationship for the purpose of acquiring access to a lifestyle which their education and training could not hope to provide. When so many doors remain closed to women in Russia today it is not surprising if those who are young and attractive see the option of what might be termed 'undercover' prostitution as a career move. Although women may well embark on a relationship such as this through an acquaintance made in the normal way, the business element of the deal is underlined by the many personal ads in which men offer financial security in return for a full-time sexual relationship, or a more casual affair in the case of those who are already married or simply wanting to brighten up regular business trips.

Another option in this category are the advertisements placed by Westerners in the Russian press. Mail-order brides, a well-established feature of the traffic in women between South East Asia and the West, has come to Russia as a growing indicator of the new poverty. Russian women in search of security, especially those with young children, for whom prospects are particularly bleak, are in demand as accommodating, non-feminist wives to predominantly ageing, divorced Western men.[7] Declaring their solvent financial status, men such as these seek attractive women ten, twenty, even forty years their junior. In the West, men in their fifties and sixties with glamorous companions in their twenties are usually in possession of a very fat wallet indeed. The fact that Mr Average from an uninspiring provincial town feels he can aspire to a partner such as this, especially when so many of these potential Russian brides are highly educated, says a great deal about the buying power of Western currencies in Russia and gives the lie to all the talk of romance which surrounds this issue.

The problem in all of this for young women is that a substantial element of risk is involved. Remaining in control may be extremely difficult when it is the men in all these relationships who control the purse strings. It is a situation which is wide open to abuse of all kinds. Nevertheless, it is clear that many young women are prepared to take a chance. When conventional employment prospects are so poor, ordinary jobs are by no means risk-free and the spectre of years of poverty haunts millions, they may well feel that they have very little to lose. As Larisa Bogdanova, describing the phenomenon of 'undercover' prostitution in *Rabotnitsa* magazine within months of the start of the market reform process, summed up the situation:

> Today thousands of girls are calmly and calculatedly selling themselves. The stupider ones do it just for money, those with more brains and bigger plans do it for a prestigious job and a place to live. In the name of this main aim they say to hell with sentiment.
> (Bogdanova 1993: 28)

The sexual pay-off in return, not even for the enticing lifestyle of the new rich, but simply for a job, a flat, a measure of financial security has been firmly established as an all-too-common currency.

CONCLUSIONS

Faced with the growing threat of mass unemployment, Russian policy-makers have differed little in their overall approach from their equivalents in the West. People fearing redundancy, predominantly women, have been urged to reassess their abilities, develop self-presentation skills, set up their own ventures and, generally, to 'get on their bikes' in a repeat of the familiar Western pattern of placing responsibility for continued employment firmly with the individual. Russian women have been urged to appreciate that times have changed and that it is no good expecting the state to solve all their problems. New attitudes and new skills, especially in relation to job search and selection procedures, have to be acquired if they are to withstand competition in the new labour market. Whilst it would be frankly astonishing if women who had never had to face competitive situations in gaining employment were now experiencing a trouble-free adjustment, none of these suggestions for individual solutions tackles the key issue of discrimination.

Although the overall approach to dealing with unemployment may be familiar, attitudes held towards the future employment of women from the Minister of Labour down are marked by an open hostility which would generally be regarded as unacceptable in Western Europe and North America.[8] The crude and blatant discrimination women face in the new Russian labour market is not a factor which can easily be overcome by improved interview technique, especially where this is likely to involve positive answers to excessively personal questions. Taken on its own, the problem of matching vacancies to job seekers would be bad enough; with the added factor of the wholesale rejection of women as employees, the situation cannot be improved by the efforts of individuals alone. Small wonder, then, in such a climate, that older women may despair of what the future holds.Yet, if younger women are apparently better able to cope, psychologically at least, the prospects open to them may not be much brighter and may well propel them into situations over which they have little control and in which they face blatant victimization.

One of the few positive observations which can be made about this state of affairs is that, if nothing else, the gloves are now off and women can see exactly what they are up against. So many of the social attitudes which underpin the present discriminatory climate were established well before the period of market reform began. Policies which promoted an image of women as mothers and homemakers, ultimately to the detriment of their hold on employment, have their roots firmly in the Soviet legacy, in Stalinist family legislation and in Brezhnevite pronatalism. Finally, under Gorbachev, this view of women arguably attained its apogee, persuading women themselves that they could choose to spend more time with their children and still have safeguarded employment rights even as the edifice of the planned economy was being dismantled. Now, at least, the realities of Soviet-style discrimination can be seen for what they are: the failure to promote women, to grant equal pay, to tackle sexual harassment at work and chauvinism in society at large, all these have left their mark in the current shocking dismissal of women as 'bimbos' and *babushki*. Now, with increasing family poverty, continuing political rhetoric about the 'protection of motherhood' rings so hollow that it can no longer be used as a smokescreen to excuse women's inequality at work. Perhaps here, at last, there are some grounds for optimism that women may be able to combat the social attitudes and stereotypes which have produced the present catastrophic situation. Though the basis of a new women's movement in Russia remains very small, if women, young and old alike, have any energy left from the demands of survival, there is undoubtedly plenty to fight for.

APPENDIX: LIST OF INTERVIEWEES

1 40-year-old unemployed engineer, March 1994.
2 48-year-old unemployed engineer, March 1994.
3 24- and 26-year-old librarians, March 1994.
4 24-year-old unemployed engineering graduate, September 1993.
5 22-year-old final year student and part-time accountant, March 1994.
6 29-year-old music teacher, March 1994.

NOTES

1 The interviews with women, most of them unemployed, who had used voluntary agencies set up to deal with the changing situation in the labour market are discussed in greater detail in Bridger, Kay and Pinnick (1995). We would like to thank the Leverhulme Trust for their support of this project.
2 Hereafter the interviewees will be referred to by number only. A full list of interviewees is included as the Appendix to this chapter.
3 At Dubna Employment Centre, Moscow region, for example, which we visited in the summer of 1993 and in March 1994, an unusual ten-month accountancy course including a one-month work placement was being offered to unemployed women and was recording far higher rates of success in placing women in work on completion than recorded elsewhere in the region.
4 This is true, for example, of the Moscow-based Image Centre, run by fashion designer Elena Evseeva. See Bridger, Kay and Pinnick (1995), Chapter 8.
5 This term has been employed on numerous occasions by those, such as Elena Evseeva, who are critical of the exploitation of women in the media. It can also be found in parliamentary documents on discrimination against women.
6 The term 'undercover prostitution' has been used to denote a situation in which 'a woman contracts to sell her sexual and other services to an individual man in exchange for economic security and/or protection from other men', a definition which is particularly useful in describing the current situation in Russia. See Lindsey (1979: 4).
7 A recent survey of Russian women emigrating to Italy for the purpose

of marriage found that 40 per cent cited a desire to secure their childrens' future as their primary motive (Tiuriukanova 1994).

8 In February 1993, Minister for Labour, Gennady Melikian, made the observation that, 'It is better that men work and women take care of children and do the housework. I do not want women to be offended, but I seriously don't think that women should work while men are doing nothing', a remark which received more comment in the Western than the Russian press (Martin 1993).

3 Employment strategies and the formation of new identities in the service sector in Moscow

*Marta Bruno**

In his recent film *Window to Paris*[1] (1994) the Russian director Yurii Mamin gave an insightful interpretation of the issues currently affecting young people in Russia as they form new work and family relations. Nikolai Nikolaevich, a penniless but inspiring music and literature teacher, obliged to work in a school for the children of the business community (whose classroom walls are dominated by giant foreign currency notes), discovers in the wardrobe of his new room in a communal flat, a door that leads straight from St Petersburg to Paris. He decides to share his secret with his pupils and take them on a unique day-trip to Paris. After various adventures, in the course of which he becomes separated from the children, he discovers that the magic opening will soon close for the next twenty years. After a frantic search, he stumbles upon the children, who are earning money by dancing in a square. Having savoured the delights of Paris, they declare that they have no intention of going back to miserable St Petersburg:

N. N.: Children, I'm telling you, we must all go home, back to St. Petersburg. The window is about to close.
Child: Okay, let it close.
N. N.: The window will close for twenty years. Don't you understand?
Child: We understand.
N. N.: Then let's get a move on!
[Children laugh]
Child: We've decided to stay.
N. N.: Stay?
Child: Yes, stay.

N. N.: OK, OK, you've decided to stay. And your parents? Has anybody thought about them?

Child: We've thought about them. It will be better for them. There are always problems with food aren't there?

N. N.: You are being downright silly! They adore you, they will go crazy without you.

Child: Yes of course, because they'll think that something terrible has happened to us. But we've written to them; yes we've written. And when they realise that we are in Paris they'll be happy of course. And when we grow up we'll bring them over so that they will be okay too.

N. N.: Nastia, what will happen to your granny? You love her a lot don't you? She will die without you.

[Nastia starts crying]

Child: Leave her alone, Nikolai Nikolaevich, don't put pressure on her. You know very well that her grandmother is ill because there are no medicines at home, in Peter,[2] to cure her. We will buy the medicines here and then she will recover.

N. N.: [laughs] Okay, that's great. But what will you buy them with, the medicines? Have you thought about what you're going to live on?

Child: See this, Nikolai Nikolaevich? It's 248 francs. It's what we've earned today.

N. N.: So, you're going to wiggle your bottoms with your hands stretched out, hippity, hippity, hop, for the rest of your life?

Child: Why for the rest of our lives? We'll do something else.

N. N.: What?

Child: We could work in McDonald's.

Child: We could even wash dishes.

Child: ... or cars.

Child: There are lots of jobs ...

Kriuchkova [second child]: They say that beauty is appreciated in every city.

French woman: Come on children, are you not ashamed of yourselves? Your teacher has organized a little party for you and this is how you thank him. You've sent him to hospital. You are cruel and ungrateful.

N. N.: OK, you are right. You were born at the wrong time and you live in a country that is on its knees, but it is still your country. [music] Is it impossible to improve it? So much depends on you, children, believe me. But you don't even want to try? Can you really not care at all?

As the economic crisis and the processes of restructuring unravel in Russia, new stratifications and groupings of society are taking shape and becoming increasingly visible to the outside observer. In this chapter, some of the social groupings, stereotypes and cultural norms that are interacting in the formation of new labour markets in Moscow will be explored. The aim is to offer some insights into the formal and informal construction of discourses and practices which are redefining workplace cultures and the kinds of counter-cultures which are emerging.

Gender and age represent two of the determining factors in individuals' ability or inability to mediate between change and continuity with the past. Being victims or survivors of new social and economic realities in present day Russia depends not only on exogenous economic conditions and government ideology and policies, but also, as argued by Pilkington, on the role of the individual (*lichnost'*) in bringing about social change (Pilkington 1992). The formal acceptance of a market economy has created a set of expectations and rules that are shaping economic behaviour and defining conditions and constraints in accessing new labour markets. It is generally accepted that these conditions do not favour certain social groups, notably women, the old and the very young. This is mainly because state and dominant ideologies seek to make women take the strain of rising unemployment and the breakdown in the social safety net by increasingly pushing them back into the home.

This chapter attempts to address the question of how individual women, or groups of them, are responding to these pressures and constraints and whether they are altering the contours of the curious hybrid capitalism which is taking shape in Russia. It also asks whether appurtenance to a specific gender or generation automatically disadvantages individuals in the new labour markets.

While it is fundamental to analyse general systemic constraints limiting women's rights and options, it is also important to see how these constraints manifest themselves and are perceived in specific situations. Thus, this chapter also draws on a micro-level study of the experience of women working in joint ventures and foreign firms in Moscow. This study reveals a variety of attitudes and cultural spin-offs in response to both exogenous and endogenous employment and workplace characteristics and constraints. Individuals are trying to survive, and make the most of, the current economic crisis and in the process they generate and adapt to new relations of production. For foreigners, working in Russia constitutes a complex experience made up of economic interests, cultural colonialism and charitable intents; for Russians, working in foreign firms offers real-life 'schools of capitalism' with social, psychological and economic benefits and drawbacks. It is in workplace interactions between Russians and foreigners that the transfer of skills, technology and culture takes place. In this context, women of different generations are finding their own ways of responding to constraints and demands put upon them by the state and the firms for which they work. They are also, it will be argued, finding means to covertly challenge these systems.

NIKOLAI NIKOLAEVICH: DECONSTRUCTING THE STATE AND THE NEW LABOUR MARKETS

The state

Recent literature has documented the *cahier de doléances* of the cultural values and socio-economic burdens which the Russian state, backed up by writers, journalists and other members of the establishment, has sought to impose on women (Buckley 1991, 1992; Funk and Mueller 1993; Posadskaya, 1994b; Rai, Pilkington and Phizacklea 1992; Sedaitis and Butterfield 1991). The state and dominant culture invade all spheres of women's lives with their images of femininity and sexuality, promoting their preferred patterns of behaviour in the familial and employment spheres and openly demanding that women shoulder the responsibilities of the disintegrating welfare system. Furthermore, it is expected that women welcome what the state is asking them to take on. This is an able exercise in propaganda and is fully in tune with past approaches of the Soviet state to women. Indeed, the current Russian government displays many elements of continuity with its predecessor; what it lacks is the same capacity for coercion in order to implement its policies.

The new so-called democratic institutions are still very weak. Executive authorities are not in tune with legislative ones and society is governed more by the unwritten rules of common economic and bureaucratic practices than by a clear-cut sense of civic rights and duties and of the constitution and functions of institutions. In theory, one of the most important functions of the new institutional infrastructure should be that of aiding former Soviet citizens in the transition process from one political system to an entirely different one. Although clearly this is not an easy task, it could be tackled by promoting education and information on the new political and economic structures and encouraging political and civic awareness and the development of a civil society. Instead, however, the government, and political leadership in general, appear intent on constructing gendered notions of citizenship. Cultivating a symbiotic continuity with the past, the state is trying to turn the former *Homo Sovieticus* into a new Russian man, while women are being asked to rein in their own identities in order to provide space for this renaissance of the masculinity of men. Women are thus second-class citizens whilst providing the background against which men can define themselves and develop their new identities as men and as members of the new Russian nation. If women are asked to conceive of themselves as carers whose natural realm is the private, then men, by contrast, are told that they should be providers and take the leading role in mediating between the private and the public.

This notion is also deeply rooted in dominant culture. In political life, the emergence of a political bloc such as 'Women of Russia' shows to what extent new notions of femininity, as a social and cultural category, separate but supportive of what Peggy Watson defines as the rise of masculinism (Watson 1993), are finding widespread consensus. But, as Pilkington argues:

> although the culturalist approach does allow us to see the way in which women are involved in crucial areas of decision-making outside the public sphere, it does not help us evaluate how important these areas have been – that is, it allows us to see women as having a separate sphere of power from men, but it does not say anything about the relative nature of that power.
>
> (Pilkington 1992: 114)

By emphasizing the silence around the relative nature of gendered power Pilkington reveals a fundamental inconsistency of the social/ sexual contract: while it shapes the dominant system of values of a great majority of Russian men and women, as far as women are concerned it does not necessarily determine their behaviour. Russian women often seem to be unaware of the apparent (at least to the Western feminist eye) contradictions between their beliefs and their everyday actions. Political, economic and personal conditions and constraints take women constantly beyond their assigned sphere of influence and, for the most part unknowingly and almost despite themselves, lead them to generate patterns of resistance to the dominant gender ideology that they apparently support. These contradictions are particularly apparent in the work environment, where what is at stake is economic survival in the private sphere. In the private and joint venture service sector the majority of women still claim that, ultimately, they work for the family (be they mothers or daughters) but engaging in a completely new environment and dealing daily with new practices and values cannot but alter their identities. In what ways, with what outcome and with what degree of awareness this occurs are the key questions to be addressed.

The labour market

Labour markets in Russia are being shaped and governed not so much by official policies (despite intense government legislative activity) as by common practices and the interests of the economic elites. Business and work patterns, whether technically legal or illegal, are legitimized more by informal networks than by law enforcement. This is true also of that section of the labour market dominated by foreign firms or joint ventures.

The formation of a new managerial or capitalist class in Russia is characterized more by continuity than by any break with the late Soviet system. Privatization, considered the core element of the introduction of a market and of capitalism in Russia, seems to have mainly reinforced the position of power and ensuing economic capacity of the industrial *nomenklatura*. In Simon Clarke's words:

> Privatisation is not about selling state property, since the state has long lost control over its property, nor is it about the transformation of the social relations of production, since such transformation has barely begun. At its crudest it is about the legalisation of theft, the process of *prikhvatizatsiia* – 'grabbing' . . . it is the equivalent of the colonial plunder which financed the lavish consumption of a parasitic ruling class, and left the plains of Bengal littered with the bleached bones of a generation of peasants and artisans.
>
> (Clarke 1994)

While it is certainly the case that there were few changes in distribution of power amongst the top layers of Russian society, what Clarke's, and indeed most analyses of the spread of corruption amongst the new Russian entrepreneurial and managerial elite, fail to mention is the distinctive gender dimension of the phenomenon. Corruption and what is increasingly becoming known as the 'wild East' business environment are closely associated with masculinity. Part of this phenomenon is structural and a direct inheritance from the Soviet period, when very few women held top positions in production or government. As a consequence while older men who did hold key positions now have access to and control of materials, goods and production opportunities (as well as the Russian equivalent of 'old boy' networks'), very few women find themselves in that position.

Cultural and gender stereotypes further reinforce the notion that women should not, as a rule, occupy top economic positions. The pervasive halo of corruption and semi-criminality which so strongly characterizes the Russian business environment requires aspiring business 'people' to display toughness, authority and aggressiveness, all characteristics alien to the 'new Russian woman', feminine and in search of patriarchal protection both in the economic and romantic sphere.

Despite these dominant cultural attitudes and inherited constraints which considerably restrict women's access to elite economic activities, women do not necessarily comply with the role assigned to them by government ideology and societal pressures; the strategies employed by them in this process are discussed below. What needs to be mentioned here is simply that the majority of women cannot afford to leave employment and, if they are made redundant or their job no longer guarantees enough to live on, then they resort to survival strategies. These may include cottage industry work and street vending, working as domestics for foreigners or the new rich, sub-letting flats and renting somewhere else in order to live off the difference, and growing their own food on small garden-plots in the outskirts of urban areas. Women also constitute the healthier part of the labour market since, when involved in the informal sector, they rarely personally engage in criminal or violent activities.

Generational differences in the labour market

Finally, the impact, if there is any, of generational characteristics of the gendered labour market must be considered. Is Posadskaya correct in arguing that the market is taking a higher toll on older generations, since they find it harder to adapt whilst younger women's opportunities of a career are severely curtailed by gender stereotypes as either non-employed wives or as secretaries in mini-skirts (Posadskaya 1994b: 170–1)? Although in general one might talk of a hierarchy in socio-economic stratifications which posits older women at the bottom and younger men at the top, nevertheless this is not applicable indiscriminately. In the case of the foreign firms' service sector in Moscow, for example, there are significant numbers of older women in positions other than secretarial ones, and even in management positions. Of eighteen department heads employed by the American publishing firm Interperiodica in autumn 1993, twelve were women, most of whom were in their forties and fifties.[3] On the other hand, Sadko Ltd, a Swiss–Russian joint stock company running one of Moscow's most expensive, Western-style shopping malls, has an explicit policy of only employing young people without previous 'Soviet' work experience.[4] Of those retained after undergoing training, the overwhelming majority are women because 'they are more suitable for service sector jobs and have less of a problem of general attitude towards work' (Interview with Peter X, Marketing Manager, Sadko Ltd, Moscow, July 1993).

While it is impossible to obtain comprehensive data of employment patterns for this sector by gender and age, observation suggests that companies sharing Sadko's approach are a minority and that in most foreign and joint venture firms in Moscow it is possible to find significant numbers of older women holding a wide range of professional positions. Thus, the crucial point about the interaction of work and gender and generational characteristics is linked more to individual attitudes and responses than to *a priori* economic characteristics. Belonging to a specific age group *per se* is not a meaningful category; what places people on one side or the other of the victim/survivor fence is the ability or the opportunity to decode the new economic and social environment and the mental flexibility to learn how to operate within it. This 'skill' depends partly on individuals' inclinations and character and partly on exogenous socio-economic conditions. As far as the latter are concerned, an older woman living in Moscow and with an average education is exposed to both an intellectual and a practical experience of the new so-called market. In theory, she may possess more information and instruments to survive or even succeed employment-wise than a young male from a rural area with no access to information or first-hand experience. This argument may smack of truism but it is something that is very rarely considered when exploring labour market characteristics in Russia. I would argue that generational factors are, in terms of employment and economic survival, a constructed and variable cultural category[5] meaningful only within specific contexts.

Gender, employment and unemployment

The current literature on labour market characteristics offers little more than general quantitative data (rarely broken down by age, gender or region) occasionally illustrated by rather superficial explanations of socio-economic phenomenona. Unemployment, a crucial issue which is rightly receiving widespread attention is one such case. According to mainstream arguments put forward by World Bank experts, the Russian Federal Employment Bureau and other Russian and Western governmental agencies, unemployment rates are always surprisingly low but mass unemployment is always presented as imminent. According to a World Bank publication, there were 472,040 unemployed in Russia on 1 January 1992 and by September of the same year the figure had reached 904,259, 'of which 33 per cent were registered unemployed' (Fong 1993: 18). According to another World Bank publication (in an annexe by the same author) in the first six months of 1992 440,400 men and 673,900 women were seeking employment (Fong 1994: 98). The sum total of these two numbers would appear to be 1,114,300, which contradicts the estimates above. The same publication also states elsewhere that 'open unemployment has been allowed to emerge, but amounted to only about 1 per cent of the labour force by the end of the year [1993]' (*Russia: Social Protection and Beyond* 1994: xiii). Since no estimate of the overall labour force is provided it is difficult to know what this 1 per cent may mean in real terms. A more serious approach is taken by Aukutsionek and Kapeliushnikov (1994) who rightly argue that, depending on what factors one takes into consideration when estimating unemployment, the numbers may vary from 0.85 per cent to 6 per cent. They stress the ambiguity of the concept of unemployment and the need to analyse its social and cultural aspects.

The same uncertainty characterizes estimates of women's unemployment. There seems to be a general consensus on the fact that women make up the majority of redundancies, especially in certain sectors of industry, services and health-care which were traditionally feminized. The World Bank report claims that women make up 71 per cent of overall numbers of unemployed, with the curious one-off addition that they make up 89 per cent of the unemployed in the Nenets region in 1992. Forty per cent of unemployed women, it is stated, have higher or secondary specialized education (Fong 1993: 18). Another estimate for 1992 places women at 78.3 per cent of all unemployed with secondary specialized education (Posadskaya 1994a: xii).

While the basic assumption that women constitute the lion's share of the unemployed would appear to be correct and hard numbers on women in the labour market are very welcome indeed, quantitative data in their present state are not meaningful unless combined with thorough qualitative research on the nature, cultural perceptions and hidden aspects of both employment and unemployment.

NASTIA: FROM THE OLD SOVIET WOMAN TO THE NEW RUSSIAN WOMAN?

Taking a qualitative approach to unemployment, therefore, it must be recognized that this is a new concept in Russian society, and as such, is imbued with significant cultural and generational meanings. Elsewhere I have analysed the phenomena of hidden unemployment and downwards re-deployment as well as considering the situation of women whose wages are lower than day-care fees for their children or whose long working hours prevent them from shopping within their means (Bruno 1995). In general, women are more willing to register as unemployed, because for them it carries no social stigma. The women I interviewed stressed the utilitarian nature of receiving unemployment benefits:

> I work anyway. Shopping, looking after my children and doing housework takes up most of my day. Why should the state not help me? . . . I also knit sweaters for a friend who sells them on the street. That is how I survive.
>
> (Interview with T., 31 years old)

Working in the informal sector or in a cottage industry is a frequent characteristic of officially unemployed women.

However, interviewing women working for a large American publishing company, there emerged a noticeable difference in how older and younger women related to their *husbands'* work status. Older women had no difficulty in admitting their husbands' unemployment while younger women appeared much more reluctant to do so.

Q: What does your husband do?
A: He . . . well, he works.
Q: In what field?
A: I don't know. . . . he works with a friend, they are businessmen.
Q: What do they do together?
A: Well, they go out sometimes. I'm not sure what they do when they go out.
Q: Did your husband have another job before?
A: Yes, he worked as an engineer but they shut down his section about a year ago.

Q: Who earns more, you or your husband?

A: Well, we live on my wage. I earn more now, but he will be earning more.

Q: When his business gets started?

A: Yes.

(Interview with I., 19 years old)

Older women seem not to have imbibed capitalist and patriarchal concepts of 'productivity' and 'laziness'. Although labour productivity was a fundamental concept of Stalinist and Soviet ideology it was weakly translated into everyday work culture and practice, especially in the era of stagnation. Thus, for older women, these concepts have little meaning, and having an unemployed husband is more of an economic inconvenience than a social shame. Many are very supportive of their husbands. Since they retain the notion that men's work is, in the *public sphere*, inherently more valuable and important than women's, they tend to construct their husbands as innocent victims of a crooked system. As one woman put it:

My husband has been cheated by them [i.e. the authorities or political class] much more than I have. All our men have. Women haven't so much because they put their energies into the family.

(Interview with M., 53 years old).

It is worth noting that both husband and wife had been made redundant at about the same time.

Younger women have a much stronger sense of gendered responsibilities. Men's work is still considered more valuable and important than women's, but in the *private sphere*; men should be responsible for women and thus be employed and earn more, even earning a family wage. For younger men, therefore, unemployment presents a real menace to their newly found market masculinity and is anathema to many younger, educated Muscovites.

Examining employment scenarios within foreign companies, one finds very similar notions of the innately gendered worth of work. This, it is argued here, is a direct legacy of some fundamental aspects of the Soviet social contract. As Linda Cook points out:

the Brezhnev leadership sought universal full employment, but was more active and thorough in assuring this outcome for cadres of young urban males, whose discontent could threaten stability, than for isolated groups of unemployed women in provincial towns.

(Cook 1993: 202)

The subjects of the social contract for the state were men; it was men who should be exempt from real productivity and job efficiency, as long as they observed social and political quiescence. They were authorized, almost encouraged, albeit informally, to be lazy. If they grew accustomed to the link between laziness and being provided for by the state they would not relinquish it for political strife or increased control over their lives. Women had no such option. They too were allowed not to be productive and to informally take time off their jobs. But this spare time was mostly devoted to activities connected with domestic labour and consumption: queuing, shopping, sewing and knitting, exchanging information and building those informal networks which ensured survival in times of economic crisis. Women guaranteed, through traditionally unrecognized and invisible work, the social reproduction of labour. Most of them failed to see that the popular saying 'we pretend to work, they pretend to pay us' did not apply to them. Being allowed practices of resistance to authority in the workplace through non-productivity did not translate into laziness for them.

It is interesting to see what happens when these gender-differentiated work ethics are confronted with Western capitalist values of efficiency and productivity. As one respondent pointed out, when asked if she resented the intensive labour productivity required by foreign firms from their employees:

> I really like the way that foreigners work. You can do things and get them out of the way. My work is appreciated and I have more time to do the shopping and housework. I don't think I work more than in my previous job but everything is better organized. You work at work and do all the rest outside it. I wouldn't take time off when I'm on the job, but then I never did. Me and my friends, we never spent much time drinking tea or smoking because there was always something else to do.
>
> (Interview with T., 35 years old)

In terms of labour-intensiveness women have little to learn about capitalist modes of production. For most of them, working for a foreign firm entails learning a new job and adjusting the organizational balance between employment and domestic work but does not necessarily entail changing the nature of their productivity. Having to work in exchange for a salary is something they can relate to. In addition, women's experience in developing survival solutions via careful domestic organization has made Russian women very efficient managers. This trait is widely recognized by foreign employers, who frequently exploit their abilities. Many of the foreign firms in Moscow where interviews and participant observation were conducted have well-developed means of using women's organizational abilities to their best advantage. By assuming (or pretending to assume) that Russian women are innately responsible and organized, they automatically give them heavier burdens than Russian men. The expectations made of them are determined more by their gender than by individual character. Men, on the other hand, are permitted mistakes and failings. Since it is accepted that the transition from a totalitarian system and a command economy to the free market is a long and painful one, if a man gets drunk on the job, this, to a certain extent, will be 'understood'. It is a systemic fault, not a personal one. If women fail to fulfil expectations or if they break the unwritten rules, however, they are seen to be deviating from their gender role and thus the fault or mistake will be a personal one, not excusable on the basis of some wider category. In this context, age is a significant determinant for men but not for women. The more men are perceived to belong to a 'Soviet' generation, the more they will be 'let off'. Women, whether young or old, however, are seen, above all, as women and thus outside 'Soviet-ness' or 'new Russian-ness'.

KRIUCHKOVA: JOBS AND NEW SEXUAL IDENTITIES

This mixed blessing is generating different responses and patterns of resistance amongst women, in some cases almost despite themselves. Within the boundaries of the cultural resources of their assigned femininity, women in the job market are not just silent victims of ideological and labour market constraints, they react resourcefully and actively, often creating what World Bank experts might call models of proactive femininity. In inventing these new roles older women are often more self-assertive than younger ones. This is because their experience of systemic change is more intense. They have learned from their lives having been turned upside down and they are aware of how to construct a public persona which conforms to the system and possibly even turns it to their own advantage. To them, 'Soviet-ness', or at least reactions to it, are meaningful, if not necessarily conscious, categories:

> I was pregnant but I did everything to hide it. At the time we were closing a very tough deal with some Americans and I didn't want them to think that I was not going to be on their backs

because I was having a baby. When the baby was born I spent one day in hospital. After giving birth I asked for a telephone and rang the Americans up to make sure that everything was under control. The next day I was back at work. When the Americans asked me where I had been the day before, I told them I'd had a baby. They were amazed. They hadn't even noticed I was nine months pregnant. After that they signed the deal the way I wanted it.

(Interview with M., 37 years old)

In this specific case, the attributes displayed are all perfectly in keeping with the construction of appropriate gender categories: childbirth and motherhood, organization, reliability and efficiency. The outcome, nevertheless, might be considered unorthodox.

Another respondent was more conscious of the scope for different behavioural models, both covert and resourceful, that being a woman in business entails:

We've had to act for so many years under the Soviet system and devote so much thought to constructing a public face. Interactions in a market system are just the same; you just have to study the rules and write a different part for yourself. The difference is that before you always had to play the same part and now you can be more inventive and change your role according to your business interlocutors. Some days I am very feminine; I dress accordingly and do my make up to look more feminine. You realise how important dress-codes, tone of voice and acting are. It is easy for me because I studied acting. Other days I become a tough manager if I have to. Most of our partners and clients are men and a woman can tell at a glance what is the best way to make them listen and respond to you. But you always have to be caring, especially with your colleagues and employees, and being a woman this comes naturally.

(Interview with M., 43 years old)

Older women retain a much stronger sense of the supportive and sociable dimension of the workplace. Many female managers are very concerned about the morale and atmosphere among the work collective and some of them have succeeded in transmitting a similar concern to foreign employers who, in general, tend to be completely oblivious to it. A woman working for a large American publishing company as personnel manager was particularly proud of how manipulative she had been:

Somebody told me how the Americans love the fourth of July holiday. I knew that a lot of our employees were complaining about the fact that the company offered them no facilities or recreational activities. So I went to see the management and convinced them to have a fourth of July picnic. For Russians it has no meaning whatsoever but it was a good excuse.

(Interview with M., 47 years old)

The picnic took place in a squalid bottom-of-the-range *Dom otdykha* (holiday home) two hours' drive from Moscow and the food was provided in a *stolovaia* (canteen). However, all the participants, mainly older employees with their families, were enthusiastic about the day and many of them said later that they hoped that more such events would be offered by the firm – it would make their work more pleasurable.

When some of the younger employees, both men and women, were asked why they had not attended the picnic they answered that they had enough of their job as it was. All said that their colleagues were very nice but they preferred to spend their days off with their own friends and families. This attitude appears to be a common characteristic of younger age groups but specifically of younger women. While younger generations have grown up at the very end of the totalitarian era, when many forms of social control and dichotomies between public and private life were waning, very young women are one of the groups which have been more shielded by the protection of the family and private sphere from the Soviet system. Because of gender stereotypes in socialization and education, young men were more exposed to public and, to some extent, political life (via military service, if nothing else). Young women were the group that most consistently claimed, in interviews, that nothing had changed in their lives or their system of values over the last decade apart from external economic conditions; political change had not affected them at all. There was no experience of ideological and political collapse of a system and of disclosure of a new reality. This seems to result in lack of engagement with the political sphere which, according to them, also enables them to cope better with the new system and especially with the new labour market. Working for a foreign firm is an almost obvious option.

Many young women are aware of the fact that they constitute one of the most sought-after groups in the foreign firms' sector of the labour market. They are more adaptive to new skills and, in particular, to new technologies and can reproduce Western role models with greater ease than older women. They have a better relationship to authority than the other groups. Their boss can be anybody, of any sex or age, while older women tend to resent having younger people of either sex above them and men tend to resent having women bosses. Women in general, are perceived to pose less threat of an increase in training costs due to labour turnover. Although older women are seen as being by far the safest bet, they also take longer to train and are seen as 'less malleable'. Younger women, on the other hand, offer less stability, although they are seen to be more stable than men and are considered to have more flexible 'learning' abilities.

Many younger women interviewed have been fast to latch on to the characteristics attributed to them and have been actively using them to enhance their professional 'desirability' and increase their 'indispensability'.

A: After you have worked for a couple of years with a foreign company you can know more about your job than your bosses. Maybe they know more about telecommunications back at home but they never really bother to learn how the Russian market works. They think they do, but most of them don't even speak Russian. They would never be able to get by, if we left.

Q: What about your male colleagues?

A: Russian men have a problem – there are certain things they would never lower themselves to do. I am a manager [*nachal'nik*] but I don't mind having to type a letter, make the coffee or perform tasks below my level. You have to be flexible in all situations. That is what makes you a professional. I would be able to take on anybody's job in the company. I could stand in for my boss or for the secretaries, and when I pass my driving test, even for the drivers!

Q: Does the company want you to stay with them?

A: Yes, I think they do.

Q: And are you going to stay?

A: Well . . . no, probably not I think.

Q: Why not?

A: Well, we'll see [laughter].

(Interview with O., 24 years old)

These new models of assertiveness and flirtations with forms of resistance are extremely widespread. Returning to the argument about gender differences in the values of work and unemployment (or rather lack of employment) women can afford, at least in theory, to threaten to undermine workplace control. The worst that can happen is that they lose their jobs and, as already shown, although in economic terms this is hard, it carries no real social stigma. Thus, although their real bargaining power might be small, and very few actually follow through their threats, nevertheless the process of voicing to each other their preparedness to resign, and the knowledge that this will trickle through to the management, is a means of surviving the authority and behavioural codes governing production.

CONCLUSION

At the end of the film *Window to Paris* the children, headed by Nastia and Kriuchkova, follow Nikolai Nikolaevich back to St Petersburg as he plays an enchanting tune on his flute, invoking the Pied Piper of Hamlyn. Will new Russian women also follow and conform to the magic tunes played by dominant culture, state ideology and capitalist demands into their prescribed categories of gender and generation? First of all, I would argue, these different magic tunes do not necessarily coincide with each other and are characterized by inherent contradictions. Moreover, any attempt to impose a given ideology automatically generates adaptive strategies of resistance. Russian women, both younger and older, who work for foreign companies are, and see themselves as 'being in the know'. They are not just passive victims of yet another bout of adverse economic and political conditions. In the context of employment many women are constructing their identities for themselves, and whether they are resisters or accommodators, they will do so on their own terms. The endorsement of the capitalist market culture will not happen without their consent and without their challenges to its rules. Generational characteristics might result in different responses to workplace cultures and create different identities, but all of them contribute to keeping the window to Paris open.

NOTES

* I would like to thank Paul Willis and the participants in his workshop (Wolverhampton 1994–5) for many enlightening and controversial discussions as well as Barbara Sorgoni and the Chiqui for their support. I dedicate this chapter to my parents, Sergio and Teresa.
1 The original title of the film is *Okno v Parizh* (1994).
2 St Petersburg is often referred to in Russian as 'Peter'.
3 In total the firm had 583 Russian employees on site (of whom 357 were

women and 226 men) and approximately another 500 working from home (many of whom worked part-time).

4   Sadko employed a total of 1,050 Russians in summer 1993.

5   As Bernard and Meade point out in their introduction, 'growing dissatis-faction with chronological definitions [of age] has led to an emphasis on functional definitions and status constructs which are based on positions in the social life structure' (Bernard and Meade 1993: 6).

4 Women's career patterns in industry

A generational comparison*

Irina Tartakovskaia

This article takes a focused look at one example of the wider problem of 'women's careers', which is a problem far from unique to Russia. A wide literature on the issue of 'women in management' already exists and documents the fact that across the world, managers at the highest levels are predominantly male. Moreover, if women do achieve top positions then it is usually not as line managers, but as narrow specialists in specific areas; in the West this is usually work in personnel or public relations, whereas in Russia it is generally economics and finance.

A number of hypotheses have been proposed to explain the difficulties faced by women managers. One might divide them preliminarily into three groups. The first, to simplify them slightly, suggest that women's failure to get on in management is connected to the behaviourial models generated by society which socialize women into emotionality, gentleness and, most importantly, dependence. This, it is argued, contradicts the basic image of a top-level manager which assumes harshness, individual independence and pronounced aggression. For this reason, women themselves feel uncomfortable in such positions and prefer not to seek them (Homer 1970; McClelland 1975; Putnam and Heinen: 1976; Schein 1973). Those putting forward this hypothesis assume that women's career problems are explained by the peculiarities of women themselves and thus posit the solution as being the development and implementation of a new concept of management which would replace pressure with dialogue, tolerance and co-operation.

The second hypothesis, put forward above all in feminist literature, argues that explanations must be sought not in women themselves but in the organizational structures created by men for the realization of men's goals – structures which have resulted in a 'hegemonic patriarchal ideology' (Andrew, Coderre and Denis 1990; Fagenson and Horowitz 1985; Kanter 1977).

The author's own research rests on a primary hypothesis that women in Russia have been hindered in their careers by both sets of reasons cited, and that these have been thoroughly integrated into a 'Russian type of organizational culture'. For a similar methodological approach see Martin, Harrison and Dinitto (1983) and Terborg (1981). The research draws on a small number of in-depth interviews with women managers, including both line managers (heads of shops, enterprise management) and specialists (heads of groups, sectors, departments) who were either working or had worked previously in machine-building plants, defence complexes, light industrial enterprises or scientific planning organizations.[1] The latter were included in order to analyse the possibilities for 'alternative careers' for qualified women engineers.

This article will draw on interviews conducted as part of two case studies of the large machine-building enterprise *Kol'tso* and the garment factory *Kometa*. The conclusions are preliminary and are intended to provoke discussion as well as to generate more focused hypotheses. One of these hypotheses concerns differences in the practice and professional identity of female industrial managers of different generations which, it will be suggested here, are due more to changes in patterns of socialization than to changes in the organization of industrial production.

THE PATH 'TO THE TOP'

The first factor that must be mentioned in exploring the conditions facilitating the careers of women managers is their preference for diversity in their work. The overwhelming majority of women occupying top positions in the enterprise structure have changed their job frequently, moving either vertically or horizontally. Virtually all respondents who had made more or less successful careers in the enterprises researched had changed their jobs five to seven times during the first seven years of work. Moreover, they had not been shifted between jobs like pawns, but had made their moves consciously and voluntarily. This is how they expressed this themselves:

> I worked in back-up. That meant that I was constantly transferred
> to different operations, five to six times a day. I liked this very

much because I wanted to learn everything as quickly as possible. I also began to earn well relatively quickly. Now with the younger girls it is more difficult, they object to being moved ... But I learnt everything relatively quickly and the quality [of my work] was fine.

$(2)^2$

I worked as an operator for about six months probably. The operator and the controller work in combination, you could say, that is you have an operator and above him/her a controller. So I worked as a controller when someone went on leave, on sick leave, that is unofficially. Then I worked for probably about six months or a year in ready-made clothing.[3] Then I worked as an engineer doing preparatory work. And then I went on maternity leave and when I came back I also worked in ready-made clothing, I worked again as an engineer doing preparatory work, here again, it was simply a transfer. And [now] I have been working for eighteen months in this job ... I wanted myself to do all these jobs ... As soon as anybody went on leave, I took on these jobs; I wanted to find out as much as possible. I think now that I have been through all the operations in this department and I can talk as an equal to every one of our specialists because I have done it all myself.

(3)

One of the respondents, the director of the factory, made a similar observation:

I have noticed also, that if a person stays in the same job for five years, even if they work well, if they are not transferred either horizontally or vertically, they are stifled. They lose their interest in work, in acquiring new skills.

(1)

There is no real reason to think that this is true only for women's careers; a comparative analysis would have to be conducted to test this. However, for women managers the ability to 'master the field', to be competent in all aspects of the work entrusted to them has a particularly important significance, since women as a rule feel themselves less confident in leadership positions (this will be discussed in greater detail below).

The second important career factor is early acquisition of educational qualifications, preferably before starting at the enterprise or during the first two or three years there. Women who return to study after attaining considerable work experience tend to experi-ence slow career development, being kept in primarily subordinate positions and being promoted only where there is no competition.

To a certain extent this constitutes a generational difference; this second type of career is more common among older women amongst whom higher education for workers of industrial enterprises was relatively rare. On the other hand, now that virtually all young women coming to engineering and technical (ITR) or white-collar positions (*sluzhashchie*) have a minimum of secondary technical education, their starting positions are to a certain extent equal whilst for older managers, especially women, education remained a kind of 'cultural capital' which had great advantages. This is how one respondent explains her appointment to the position of chief accountant at 24 years of age (unprecedentedly early in Soviet enterprises):

> Of course not everyone was delighted, especially those who hoped to be appointed to this job themselves. But I had a technical college (*tekhnikum*) certificate and then, in the sixties, even this was rare; accountants were employed generally with secondary education followed by a training course.
>
> (4)

A CAREER 'THROUGH TEARS'

Socialization and socio-cultural stereotypes do indeed play an important role in the behaviour of women working in Russian indus-try. With very few exceptions respondents admitted that they had been promoted to management positions against their wishes:

> Of course, I did not want to take on such responsibility. I did not agree to it for a long time, but then they could always use the Party to force you.
>
> (4)

> After a year or two they appointed me deputy head of the depart-ment. I stuck out a long time. I am a gentle person, I find it difficult to keep discipline, I can't pressurize people. The boss put a lot of pressure on me: 'If you don't agree we will give it to someone from outside[4] and you will have to work by his rules!'
>
> (5)

It took a long time to persuade me to become the head of the planning department. I refused persistently. Then they made me ... Maybe I was afraid, frightened that I would not manage, even though I had been doing the job effectively already.

(9)

In part such a reaction was a reflection of social norms which suggest it is unseemly for a woman to push herself forward. However, many respondents were, it would appear, completely genuine, and even those who are now confident in their management posts accepted their appointment, if not against their will, then nevertheless with severe reservations:

I was so afraid, I even had nightmares about things falling on me.

(2)

It was terrifying, the first time they called me in and offered it, I refused. I simply had not expected it and it had never been part of my plans or thoughts. I had never had such desires or aims ... Then, nevertheless they persuaded me but I set one condition; that they left my old job open for me to return to if I couldn't cope.

(6)

This attitude is relatively peculiar to women; men, especially in industry, are much more ambitious and confident and extremely rarely refuse promotion (unless it entails a wage cut). Women are much more inclined to settle for the job they are in and to gain satisfaction from the labour process itself and from interaction with their colleagues. As one woman (the deputy head of the economic administration of a large enterprise) said:

You know, I really enjoyed working on the assembly line, it was so nice, pleasant ... I never wanted to get on the ladder.

(5)

However, the research suggested that attitudes towards careers are changing among the new generation of women industrial managers. Young women managers related to career development opportunities much more naturally than their older colleagues. From an interview with a 35-year-old head of a shop:

In the shop they were worried, and when I arrived to take up the job the [female] head who was retiring actually hissed at me 'How could you accept it?'. And I said, 'It will be fine, you managed, so I will manage.'

(2)

In general, there are significant differences between different generations of women managers. Young female managers, as already noted, do not hide or suppress their ambition and do not fall into careers by chance but pursue them consciously. Among the older generation, however, it is common for women's careers to come about 'automatically' as a result of the absence of male competition.

THE PRICE OF SUCCESS

However, women's reluctance to 'get on the ladder' was not only influenced by negative associations attached to female ambition. Movement up the career ladder often entailed tangible difficulties and even sacrifices. In particular, this concerned the degree to which such jobs were compatible with family life.

Without exception, all respondents noted that they had to stay on at work after the end of the official working day, sometimes till 8 p.m. or 9 p.m. Naturally, this meant that family responsibilities had to be re-negotiated and the traditional patriarchal family model, still dominant, modified. If other members of the family do not cooperate, as is often the case, women are faced with a real dilemma: career or the family. Moreover, if the wife is promoted higher than her spouse, the latter often takes this very badly: one respondent – a chief engineer of a defence enterprise – admitted that her marriage had broken down precisely because of this.

Thus, single women and those whose families had been destroyed by their careers are the ones with the real career opportunities. As the director of a garment factory noted:

> usually a woman moves up the career ladder when there are problems in the family ... Because, in these jobs, you can't combine work with serving a family ... My husband and I divorced and I lived on my own for eleven years and ... I was promoted very quickly during that time because I was occupied only with work.

(1)

However, a single or divorced woman with children is in an even more difficult situation:

When I was studying, even part-time, I had to travel. My daughter was independent – it was in the second and third class (8–9 years old) – and she stayed on her own. Once she was on her own for two weeks – my neighbour kept an eye on her a bit.

(1)

This tendency may lead to assumptions that an unsuccessful personal life is some kind of guarantee of the 'reliability' of managerial staff. As the former editor of the factory newspaper testified:

If anybody in the factory had a good, outstanding family, they hid this. The former director tried to promote 'the unlucky ones'

(7)

The problems of women managers cannot be reduced to their domestic problems, however. If they work in a mixed enterprise, where men dominate in management, then the virtually exclusively male environment in which they find themselves means they have to adopt or, at best, tolerate specifically male approaches to problem-solving. Moreover, it is accepted as a social norm that management is 'men's business' and that men should set the tone:

The whole administration consists of men. I have a lot of complexes because of this, I don't like going to meetings. They feel more restrained as well, some are not embarrassed to speak their minds in front of us, but others do get embarrassed!

(5)

Swearing and the use of crude language is the basic form of communication in factories and this is cited by enterprise administrations as a key reason for excluding women from management; not only is a woman herself incapable of adequate communication with male workers, but she also inhibits them from talking among themselves. In practice the presence of women rarely embarrasses anybody, and women workers are equally well-equipped in terms of vocabulary. However, at management level many male administrators have complained that women prevent them 'talking normally'.

Women managers in mixed work collectives also frequently have to adopt other peculiarities of the 'male way of life'; in particular the frequent oiling of events in production with large quantities of alcohol. It is very important to be present at these informal meetings since many questions are resolved at them, including questions of personnel transfer. Although drunkenness is widespread at all levels of the industrial enterprise, managers have the advantage of having personal offices which can be utilized for such purposes. The consequences for women of participating in these events are sometimes very serious:

> *Respondent*: It is interesting that it was only the two women – the deputy of the department in our institute and a woman chief accountant – who were subsequently fired for drunkenness.
> *Interviewer*: And were men fired for drunkenness?
> *Respondent*: Extremely rarely.

(8)

Factors affecting career development cannot be discussed without raising the question of intimate relations with higher management. The problem of 'sexual harassment' remains virtually unresearched and is rarely discussed publicly in Russia and this made it very difficult to raise the issue with respondents. However, this does not mean that the problem does not exist. On the contrary, this path of career development is relatively widespread. One specialist who had resigned from the garment factory recounted:

> Before, when the director was a man, he had his own 'harem' – a certain circle of women whom he liked and got close to. In general, promotion to managerial posts took place on the basis of personal intimacy.

(7)

FAMILY OR CAREER: AN IRRESOLVABLE DILEMMA?

In contrast to men, whose personal circumstances have little impact on their careers, women's domestic arrangements were a key factor in determining career prospects. However, in addition to single women, a second group of women had significantly improved career opportunities – those whose families were founded on a 'partnership' model in which the husband or other members of the family were prepared to take on a significant proportion of domestic responsibilities. Such instances are not all that uncommon. This is a fragment of an interview with a 53–year-old head of a planning department:

Interviewer: When did you get married?
Respondent: Very early, at 18. But I think that my husband has got used to me studying and working. We had one child already and

he looked after it, I studied whilst he stayed at home. It was him that failed to graduate in the end. He has probably got used to the fact that I am either at work or at the institute. We didn't have any particular problems. When I was studying he helped me a lot and even drew up draughts for me ...

Interviewer: And weren't you bothered about overtaking him on the career ladder?

Respondent: No, everything is fine, I think. At home I never show that I work as a manager there ... We somehow decide everything together.

Interviewer: Do you have one child?

Respondent: Two. The first came along straightaway, when we were really young. And then a second daughter. Of course my husband did not do everything on his own, my mother was also still young, and worked shifts. So either my mother, or he, or I were at home depending who was on what shift.

(10)

This was an extremely propitious situation and in general it is met more often among married women managers than, for example, among lower management or white-collar workers (clerical staff). This is explained very easily – those women whose familial situation did not facilitate career promotion as a rule refused such promotion. However, the cited interview is more or less unique in so far as it was with a woman of the older generation. As a rule, patriarchal approaches to family life are much more deeply rooted and wide-spread among men and women over 40 years of age in Russia and thus a woman being dragged away from the 'domestic hearth' had painful consequences:

Interviewer: Did you have problems at home because of your work?

Respondent: Yes, of course. [unwillingly] But that is a different issue.

Interviewer: Was your domestic burden lightened – after all you had such a responsible position?

Respondent: No, nothing of the sort happened. Everything was left and is left to me.

(4)

This woman, who did not want to talk in detail about the reaction of her close family to her being late home from work, is the enterprise's chief accountant (54 years of age). When asked if she would wish her daughter to carry on her profession, she answered decisively:

No, never. It's enough what it's done to me, I've had enough.

(4)

Discussing the double burden on a woman manager, the director of the garment factory (about 45 years old) said the following:

A male director comes home. His wife says to the children: be quiet children, Dad is resting, Dad is tired, Dad has to read the papers, he must watch the television, he must eat well and he must have cleanliness and order, right? Because otherwise he would be in a bad mood. I am a director and I come home. I have to make the supper, I have to tidy up in the flat, right? I also have to read the papers, watch the news because I have to interact with people. Thus I do all this in parallel, I have a double burden. Apart from that I have to give the children attention ... This is the difference between a man and a woman. A man is only occupied with that which he is doing; the family does not exist for him.

(1)

At the same time, among the new generation of women industrial managers – who can approximately be defined as those between 25 and 40 – the 'partnership' model of family relations is found much more frequently. This changing attitude to the distribution of domestic responsibilities improves the conditions for women's professional activity. The 30-year-old head of a shop, for example, noted:

My husband has a good attitude, he helps. I have been able to train him. He is really a typical mummy's boy, he couldn't do anything. But he has learned from me. At first he prepared food for the dog; now he can already cook for himself. My mother-in-law of course interferes a lot: how can my son iron? But I say to him: never mind, shut the door into the front room and iron. I say to him, 'Serezha, peel the potatoes for when I get home.' I come home and see that the old woman is peeling them. I gave him such a telling off! The next day he said: 'Today I peeled them myself!' But generally he helps a lot. When our child was ill with antritis and couldn't go to nursery, he left work and stayed at home with him for a year.

(2)

It is characteristic that, in this, as in many other families, the conflict is more generational than marital. Incidentally, this respondent's in-laws, with whom the couple (not having their own flat) have lived for two years, still do not know about her appointment to the position of head of the shop.

In other cases, however, the child sometimes stays with one or the other sets of in-laws (if they are retired) and this 'insurance' is essential to any woman (with a family) seeking a career in industry. However, the very need to have this kind of 'insurance' puts male and female managers in unequal positions since men, as a rule, free themselves from domestic responsibilities (if they have any at all) as their workload increases.

INDUSTRIAL MANAGEMENT: A FEMININE STYLE?

Because a woman manager in a Russian enterprise is still a relatively atypical phenomenon, the majority feel under intense observation from colleagues and, consequently, generally behave less confidently than a man in the same job. This has lent the 'feminine style of management' certain peculiar traits. First among these I would include the desire to devote a large amount of attention to and keep total control of the situation in the sphere under their management. Above all, this relates to personnel issues and was manifest among women heads of shops in a desire to resolve all personnel questions personally and not via the foremen (10). In comparison with male heads of shops, women of the same status also took a much greater interest in the individual lives of their subordinates and strove to influence them:

> Not long ago a girl came asking to borrow money. I said, 'Tat'iana, I will give you the money but tell me what it is for?' She said, 'I need 25,000 for an abortion'. I said, 'I won't give you money for an abortion. Okay, so you have had a row with your husband! Make it up. If you have an abortion now, you won't have children! Even it it's only one child, have a child. My cousin even decided to have a child without a husband and then married, just imagine, now they have three children and live very happily. And you have a husband! Tomorrow you will make up, I'm telling you'. She came back and just as I knew: 'We made up.'
>
> (2)

It is worth noting that this is not even a manager from the 'old school' speaking, but a young, successful working woman. She is also waging an active campaign against women smoking in the shop which she believes is a habit girls learn from the city girls when they go there to study:

> I tell those who come on work experience: 'If you smoke we won't take you into the shop! We don't have time to have smoking breaks here. And anyway you are future mothers, you can't smoke surely!' They say, 'we will stop.'
>
> (2)

Thus, subordinates are expected to modify their behaviour in ways which far exceed their functional obligations. The former editor of the factory newspaper confirms that the personal life of all workers of the garment factory were subject to scrutiny and might influence a person's place in both the informal and the formal career hierarchy (7).

The second peculiarity worth noting is the greater employment of psychological tactics and manipulation of colleagues:

> You need to be able to manage everyone ... Sometimes if you want to get something done, the best way is to say something to a third person. And everything will be done in the best way!
>
> (1)

Women managers are also more inclined towards self-reflection and a playful approach to work, renaming the controllers department the 'marketing service' or the 'trade centre' so that the job became more interesting, for example (1).

However, in making claims about the existence of a 'female' and 'male' essence of management a number of points must be borne in mind. First, some of the traits of women industrial managers outlined are the product of the reality of their working environment and, if this environment should change significantly, then their managerial strategies could also undergo a significant metamorphosis. Second, Russian organizational culture *per se* is characterized by a significant degree of 'personification', whether that manager is a man or a woman. Third, although the majority of women workers in industry, especially of the older generation, are prone to take a more 'hands-on' approach, be more conservative and be drawn towards paternalistic managerial strategies, those rare women managers who really have outstanding personal qualities and are able to 'swim against the tide' often have great innovational potential which allows them to push their concerns ahead of others.[5]

One should note also the relatively significant changes in the female management styles which the new generation of industrial managers is bringing with it. In order to describe how significant the differences are between managers of the old and new schools, it is necessary to give a relatively long quotation from an interview with the head of a shop (36 years old):

> Before ... everything was done by shouting. When some issue had to be sorted out – those who shouted the loudest, those who put others down strongest, those were the ones who were right. And it was difficult, because even when I began working in ready-made clothing, when all the heads of shops were that kind – older – they often almost reduced me to tears because I am not that kind of person myself, not aggressive ... now I have Nelia here – the chief controller also many of the heads of shops in the sewing shops as well are young ones and technologists, it is already easier. It is easier among ourselves, even though the same problems occur, of course people are all living things, production, something happens, some violation occurs somewhere ... But among ourselves we can solve it, we can correct it without a lot of fuss, without shouting, without resorting to some kind of drastic action, or any mutual pretensions ... maybe [because] we are all the same age, it is easier to understand each other.

(6)

The authoritarian style of management, characteristic of the classical 'Soviet model' sometimes took on somewhat hysterical tones in its female variant and these were reproduced via the work collective. However, it is interesting to observe how the situation is changing with the arrival of new, young female managers:

Interviewer: Are there conflicts in the shop?
Respondent: You can't avoid conflicts. The meetings are very lively. But I have trained them here, at first they all shouted, everything was done by shouting. But I said 'Girls, why are you shouting? Do you want to show your lack of culture?' And now I have noticed that they have already started to speak calmly, in turn.

(2)

Finally, the context of women's management styles must be considered. The majority of those interviewed are managers who had been promoted in the course of radical economic reforms conducted by the director of the garment factory, *Kometa*. Thus, it may be assumed that the peculiarities of the 'new management' are connected not only with its generational characteristics but with a concrete management policy which, given previous problems with the former generation of workers, had placed the emphasis on the employment of 'progressive workers' (3). However, the very fact that the director in her transformations emphasized youth says something about her ability to gain support among young women. A 26-year-old woman – an acting deputy director for production – said:

> I think that if it had not been for Galina Nikolaevna, I would not be working here. Why? Because she is unusual in that she takes notice of young people . . . not all managers welcome this, on the contrary, many prefer not to take you on if you are still young, but she is the opposite . . . I think that she took quite a risk in putting me in this position straight away, because I had worked a relatively short time and you know how many people here look at it: I had not worked in the shop, so, in the eyes of many people, I was not a pure production worker, it's like it was before here – you have to pass through all the stages: foreman, technologist, head of shop . . . But now I think that my heads of shops do not think like that.

(3)

Thus, many of the changes in the management style of young women managers may be explained by the fact that many of them did not come to management positions 'from the bench', after gradually passing through all the stages of the hierarchy. A more or less rapid career pattern allows them to identify less directly with the positions of rank-and-file workers and concentrate more on resolving global management tasks – as many put it 'to work for the future'.

SEGREGATION AND 'EQUAL OPPORTUNITIES'

The results of the research conducted suggest that the promotion of women in Russian industry is not only hindered by the peculiarities of their personal make-up or their family circumstances. The segregation of women both in production positions and in departments of scientific and technical institutes is an everyday practice and is accepted by the majority of participants in the labour process as the norm. One often heard such statements as 'Well, if the last man goes, maybe they will appoint me sector head' (11).

In general, the career pattern of women in 'women's enterprises' (light industry) significantly differs from that in enterprises where there is competition from men. In the latter industries establishing a career is more difficult and slower:

Respondent: I don't remember any women chief planning engineers at all.[6] The first woman to head the personnel department had worked as acting head for a very long time; they did not confirm her in the job for two years. Those who wanted a career had to move somewhere else.
Interviewer: Where?
Respondent: In recent times into commercial structures, where they did not use their specialist training.

(8)

Numerous fragments from interviews could be cited describing instances where male specialists are appointed to vacant managerial positions over women candidates better qualified. Thus, even those women who seek fulfilment in industrial management despite difficult family situations have to overcome quite difficult hurdles in their way:

before this interview I had not really thought about it, but now I recall that women really could not get promotion . . . they were at the most superintendents.

(8)

In practice, an increase in the number of women in management positions always indicates that an enterprise or organization is undergoing a serious crisis; wages are low, leading the majority of men to resign.

In appointments to the top positions, women in women's enterprises face the same problems. Historically this has been linked to the personnel policy of the CPSU (Communist Party of the Soviet Union) which was the chief regulator of the value-normative system which infused the organizational structure of Russian industry. Women never played any serious role in party committees; they could rise to the post of ideological secretary at most, and even then in a committee at a low level. Except in purely women's enterprises there were practically no women secretaries of party committees (women in general simply collected party dues). The personnel policy was also conducted from within the 'male club of managers'. As a result, the position of director of the garment enterprise had been given to a reprimanded secretary of the district committee, then a former deputy director of a defence-complex chemical enterprise and finally the director of the driving school who had no previous experience in production, let alone in garment production. It was only after the enterprise had got into deep trouble that a woman specialist, who had worked for many years there as the chief engineer was 'appointed':

Interviewer: Who took the decision to transfer you to this position?
Respondent: I did. Because I had acted for both the director and the chief engineer. And I sensed that they were looking for a director again and that once again it would be of the *nomenklatura* type. And when they confirmed this at the city party committee Sergeev, Vladimir Petrovich, was there, who also now heads some enterprise here in Samara. They thought that I would not be able to get the factory out of trouble, they had not even considered me as a candidate. It was a significant time and then I went to see him and said that they should appoint me because nobody would do the job better. He, of course, was very surprised.

(1)

In general, it must be noted that in production organizational structures there were numerous bases on which women were discriminated against which were not necessarily connected directly with any particular post. Thus, in the field of 'social work', men retained control over the distribution of any real wealth: housing queues, for example, were traditionally controlled by a man, whereas women as a rule distributed only sanatorium and holiday trips (8, 11). Business trips abroad, at those enterprises which had such contacts (usually with socialist bloc or developing countries) were regulated in the strictest way; women managers in enterprises with a mixed staff practically never went on such business trips.

CONCLUSION

The observations made here have intentionally not been illustrated with statistical material; the aim has been primarily to present simply a 'preliminary diagnosis' of a very deeply rooted socio-cultural phenomenon. This phenomenon, it has been suggested, has influenced managerial strategy in industrial production as well as the reproduction of some norms and patterns of family and gender relations.

The material presented suggests that above all the promotion of women in Russian industry is a social process involving a multitude of problems. This process is linked, on the one hand, to the peculiar type of organizational culture (and aggravated by patriarchal and authoritarian traditions), and, on the other hand, to the fact that in the years of Soviet power the much higher rates at which women were brought into industrial production than in the majority of the countries of the world meant that these women possessed significant potential. There remains, therefore, a significant imbalance between the role which women play to this day in the system of material production in Russia and the way this production is managed.

The new strategies which a new generation of female managers is introducing, and the changes they inspire, give grounds for a certain optimism. However, it must be remembered that this group of women – industrial managers who, by definition, challenge the traditional image of woman as the 'defender of the hearth' – is far from typical, and the conclusions drawn cannot be extended to the attitude to women's work as a whole. In general, the socio-economic changes taking place in Russia are having a complex and contradictory impact on gender relations, often reviving archaic and more patriarchal models than those of the Soviet era. Thus, behavioural models may differ more significantly within the generation of women of the new Russia than between different generations.

APPENDIX: LIST OF INTERVIEWEES

1 Galina, director of the garment factory *Kometa*, 45 years of age.
2 Margarita, head of shop, 30 years of age.
3 Nelli, head controller, 26 years of age.
4 Paifar, chief accountant, 54 years of age.
5 Evgeniia, deputy head of the planning-economic department, 53 years of age.
6 Liubov', head of shop, 36 years of age.
7 Elena, editor of the factory newspaper, 43 years of age.
8 Liudmila, retired, former head of laboratory, 62 years of age.
9 Alevtina, head of the planning department, 52 years of age.
10 Galina, head of shop, 48 years of age (interviewed by G. Monusova).
11 Larisa, chief engineer, 50 years of age.
12 Tat'iana, head of the economic office, 40 years of age.

NOTES

* This work was conducted as part of the project 'Restructuring of Production Relations and the Management of Enterprises in Russia', headed by Professor Simon Clarke, University of Warwick.

1 In all, twenty-nine interviews were conducted with women of different ages. The interviews were conducted personally by the author between May and October 1994. A life-story approach was adopted although in the course of the interviews various more detailed questions were asked about the organization of production and changes taking place at the enterprises.

2 For a brief description of respondents see the Appendix to this chapter. In subsequent references to respondents only the respondent number will be given.

3 The position held is that of *konfektsioner*, that is, a person responsible for ensuring that suitable material, thread, buttons, etc. are selected for a particular garment.

4 The term used in the original Russian is *variag*, literally meaning 'Vangarian', which relates to a term used in early Russia to refer to foreign princes occupying the Russian throne. Here it is used to suggest an appointment from outside the factory.

5 The garment factory *Kometa*, for example, being headed by such a manager became the first privatized enterprise in the light-industry sector in the Samara region and, even before the passing of the laws on shareholding and privatization, it was the first to start working with Western firms.

6 The staff list of the institute, however, shows that there were women in these positions, at a ratio of about 1:10. Women in total constitute more than 70 per cent of the planning institute's staff.

5 Orientations, re-orientations or disorientations?

Expectations of the future among Russian school-leavers

Elena Dmitrieva

'Those who continue their education, now do not earn very much.' This is how one participant in the focus groups summed up the attitude of young people today towards higher education. Indeed, as a result of the changes which have taken place in Russia as a whole, there has been a noticeable shift in the attitudes of young people towards higher education. It is generally accepted that these changes began in 1985, although the most profound transformation in the education system came only with the introduction of market relations. It was only then, for example, that new educational institutions such as *lycées* and grammar schools (recalling pre-revolutionary institutions in Russia) as well as colleges and private schools appeared. It was then also that many higher educational establishments across the country began to offer courses on a fee-paying basis. Although these processes have been considered and analysed by a number of authors, the transformational period being experienced by former socialist societies presents us with a continuing stream of new issues for discussion.

One such issue is connected with the fact that the job market currently offers a completely different range of opportunities for young men and young women. There is no demand in the labour market for young women with higher education and they are offered positions below their level of education. This is linked to an emergent tendency in Russian society towards the return of women to the family. Girls are being orientated towards self-realization in the family rather than towards education and work.

This is reflected in the changing situation of women in education in Russia. In the higher education establishments of the former

USSR women traditionally constituted the majority of students. From the beginning of the 1990s, however, there has been a marked fall in the absolute numbers of female students: the number fell from 1,427,300 in 1990 to 1,331,400 in 1992. The same picture is forming in specialized secondary educational establishments (the number of women fell from 1,327,100 to 1,236,000 in the same period). Among students of full-time departments of higher educational establishments women made up 47 per cent in 1992. Thus, the dynamics of change in the proportion of women among students of higher educational and technical institutions shows a gradual tendency towards the reduction in the proportion of women studying in higher education. If, in 1985–6, the proportion of female students was 56 per cent, then in 1990–1 it was 51 per cent and in 1992–3 it was 50 per cent. This pattern is even more marked in technical higher educational establishments: in the academic year 1985–6 the proportion of women in such institutions was 44 per cent, whereas in 1990–1 it had fallen by 9 per cent to just 35 per cent.

EDUCATION AND PROFESSIONAL ORIENTATIONS IN SOVIET SOCIETY

Attitudes towards education among young people are far from static, however, and have changed over time. As Golovakha suggests, the problem of education was particularly acute in the 1960s when the vast majority of school-leavers aimed to enter higher education. In the 1970s and the beginning of the 1980s, however, there was a definite shift in the structure of professional orientations among youth, as a result of which higher education became less of a priority (Golovakha 1988: 65). Sociological data show that whilst at the end of the 1960s 80 per cent of school-leavers aimed to enter higher education, in the mid-1970s only 45–55 per cent had such intentions and by the beginning of the 1980s the proportion had fallen to just 34.3 per cent (Tartsan 1992: 131).

The fall in interest in higher education is explained by the fact that education was seen to be a value in itself and people treated it formalistically; for most people it was having a certificate of higher education which was important, not what they actually studied. Education in the USSR, therefore, was not seen as a step towards a career (since the latter was interpreted negatively) and this is reflected in the work of Soviet researchers who, unlike their Western counterparts, did not consider education as a necessary step in developing a career, choosing a job or achieving professional status.

Thus, Millicent Poole's apparently straightforward proposition that 'Upper levels of education are usually associated with higher occupational expectations and opportunities, lower levels of education with lesser expectations ... Education is fundamental to individual life-chances' (Poole 1983: 110), does not hold true for the former USSR.

In contrast to the Soviet period, the attitude towards education among boys and girls today is characterized by greater pragmatism. Before turning to the results of the research conducted by the author, however, a brief outline of existing published literature concerning the former USSR and Russia will be presented.[1]

One of the first sociologists to consider this question was V. N. Shubkin (Shubkin 1970; Shubkin 1978; Shubkin 1992). In his research – which was begun in the early 1960s – school-leavers (as well as their classmates, teachers and parents) were asked how they saw their immediate future, what profession they would choose and where they would work or study. In the course of the research a number of related issues were studied: the social problems associated with the transfer of young people from education to work; the influence of socio-economic demographic and other factors on their choice of profession; the changing prestige and attractiveness of various professions among school-leavers; and work motivation. Research into the life plans of school-leavers has been conducted by E. I. Golovakha in Kiev. Golovakha employs the term 'life prospects' (*zhiznennaia perspektiva*), which he explores via life priorities, desired profession, status, family and economic position. This research is particularly interesting, since the author subjects his findings to a gender correlation and, on the basis of this, concludes that girls are more likely to be orientated towards acquiring higher education than boys (in 1985 73.4 per cent of girls and 60.7 per cent of boys). His research suggests that girls aim to achieve their goals in life earlier than boys and the author explains this by the greater significance of the family and private sphere for girls and the fact they seek self-realization primarily in this sphere. This is confirmed by their attitude to work. In the professional sphere girls prioritize job satisfaction over salary. They are 'prepared to accept low-paid but interesting work ... For girls good working conditions are also important' (Golovakha 1988: 88). Golovakha also notes the lack of correlation between what is wanted from life and what is actually achieved, especially among girls.

The connection between the professional orientations of boys and girls living in Moscow and their social background was ascertained in the course of their research by Mkrtchian and Chirkova (Mkrtchian and Chirkova 1986: 162–7). In their research, based on longitudinal methods of study, the changes in value orientations of youth as they chose their professions at various stages of life was studied. The data was gathered in Moscow using a questionnaire survey and content analysis of answers. On the basis of the data obtained the following basic motives in the choice of profession were discerned: the broadening of one's horizons, the creative character of the work; and the prestige of the profession. The researchers also concluded that:

> in general those young men and women who are oriented towards continuing their education after school have parents with higher educational qualifications. The proportion ... among children of white collar workers [*sluzhashchie*] is on average 26 per cent higher than among the children of blue collar workers [*rabochie*].
> (Mkrtchian and Chirkova 1986: 163)

This is not, of course, an exhaustive survey of all the research in this area, but should at least provide an impression of the directions Soviet and Russian sociological work has taken to date. The key issues have been: professional orientation, work motivation, the prestige of professions and the connection between social status and the choice of profession or education. This differs from the research conducted by Western sociologists. First, in the West the phenomenon of youth has been studied using a variety of quantitative and qualitative methods. Second, the gendered experience of youth has been naturally integrated into a number of academic studies.

In Christine Griffin's *Typical Girls? Young Women from School to the Job Market*, for example, a detailed qualitative analysis of all aspects of young women's lives, including study at school, family life and how they spend their time, is presented. The influence of social stereotypes and the social environment as a whole on how young women live their lives and form their plans is also described (Griffin 1985). Given that such extensive research into so wide a range of aspects of girls' lives has not been conducted in Russia, this book might well act as a core text and methodological guideline for those working in this area.

The work of the Australian researcher Millicent Poole is devoted to the expectations and plans of young people who have finished school and it employs quantitative methods. In particular, the author focuses on the problems associated with young people who drop out of school. Given the domination of the ideology of secondary education for all in the USSR, such problems could not even be studied or described by sociologists. Poole explores the problem of the correlation between what society expects of young people and young people's own expectations. Analysing the ideas of girls about their future profession, the author describes the socially circum-scribed choice foisted on girls as well as the relationship between girls' educational plans and starting a family. 'About half the girls in the sample', she writes, 'specified the effect of marriage on their career' (Poole 1983: 248).

The majority of work conducted by sociologists in Russia is characterized by the use of quantitative methods and in particular the use of the survey method. This reflects the traditional predomi-nance of quantitative methods in sociology in the former USSR and Russia. The distinguishing characteristic of Russian work is the lack of attention paid to gender difference. Only recently has the term 'gender' begun to be used by sociologists and the first sociological articles to appear on this question (for example in the journal *Sotsiologicheskie Issledovaniia*). Thus, the attempt to conduct socio-logical research using a qualitative 'focus group' method undertaken by the current author has no precedent in Russia. The aim of the research was to describe the attitudes of boys and girls towards higher education and their future work and the attitude of boys to the education of girls. The focus group work was conducted within the framework of the project 'Youth and the Future'.[2] In the course of the focus group project, final year secondary school students were asked about their educational plans, their future profession, their views on the family and on the future economic and political devel-opment of the country. Eleventh year school students were selected as the object of the study, even though the problem of choosing a future direction is already encountered by boys and girls in their ninth year, when they choose between further study in school, moving to a secondary specialist educational institution or going out to work. After the eleventh year they can enter an institute, a university or a secondary specialist educational institution or they can seek work. Thus, in their eleventh year at school young people again encounter the problem of choice; at this stage, however, there are even more options open to them.

The focus groups were conducted with students in their final year at school in Moscow. The average length of each focus group was around one and a half hours and between six and eight people took part in each group (with equal numbers of girls and boys being represented). Within the framework of this project a focus group was also conducted in which school-leavers from various towns took part. In all, ten focus groups were conducted between 1991 and 1994.

The relationship between attitudes to education and future work and the status of parents (material position, education, profession) is not discussed here, since it is anticipated that such correlations will be better discerned via the quantitative methods being used in the wider project. However, the significance of these factors was taken into account in selecting participants. Thus, focus groups were conducted in special schools where there is a focus on a particular foreign language (traditionally considered to be elite schools) and in schools in outlying districts,[3] whose residents are of low social status.

The focus group was chosen as the chief method for the gathering of material since it allows information to be gathered in the course of group discussion. This was considered to be important, since group dynamics and the discussion which arises in the group reduce stress for participants, ease any difficulties arising from the analysis of one's own observations and remove the oppositional status of the researcher and respondent. Questions were employed only to encourage participants to give more detailed and more grounded answers. It turned out that the focus groups provided not only the researcher but also the participants with new information as a result of listening to the opinions of their peers. Particularly interesting – for both boys and girls – proved to be hearing the opinion of the opposite sex. The focus group method also allowed the researcher to establish a good relationship with the respondents and thus to clarify issues in the course of the discussion itself. The project showed that the questions connected with future profession and family elicited much greater interest than, for example, those about politics. In general, the focus groups were very lively with the participants sometimes arguing amongst themselves. The young men and women felt themselves able to answer questions freely, although sometimes participants were reluctant to answer specifically about their own plans. For example, some felt that stating the future in advance might endanger the chance of success and doom their plans to failure. A typical response was 'I think you should never try and guess things in advance.'

MOTIVES FOR CONTINUING EDUCATION

The results of the research suggest that, just as before, a significant proportion of boys and girls want to continue their education. The participants of the focus groups cited numerous motives for gaining an education, but here only the most common ones will be considered. These motives include both traditional ones, relating to earlier ideas about education, and new ones, connected with the emergent images of education in post-Soviet society.

Education as a value in itself

First, education continues to be seen as of value in itself. For several decades it was 'accepted' that gaining higher education was to a certain extent prestigious and the majority of school-leavers sought simply to obtain a higher education which would lend them a certain social status. As research, in particular that of Mkrtchian and Chirkova (1986), shows, these young people begin to think about their future profession directly only in the course of their study. The continuation of this mode of thinking expressed itself in statements by participants such as:

Higher education is simply necessary.

(Andrei (m), 1991)[4]

Having higher education can't do any harm.

(Kostia (m), 1991)

You will get a higher salary in a state enterprise, that is if you have higher education you get an increment.[5]

(Olia (f), 1991)

Education as cultural capital

Second, education is seen as essential for young people to raise their general intellectual level and widen their horizons. There is an image that obtaining higher education is an indicator of the cultural and intellectual level of an individual. This motif was evident among school-leavers in the past and continues to be so today:

You need education for yourself.

(Ira (f), 1994)

Higher education is your level of culture.

(Georgii (m), 1991)

Education helps young people to orientate themselves better in an information society. This is particularly important today; in the past the absence of a wide range of ideological movements and ideas meant that people were not faced with the problem of choice. In post-Soviet society, however, education can help one survive the information flood.

Education as a safety net

Third, political uncertainty and the possibility of at least a partial return to the old order and behaviourial models influences young people when thinking about entering higher education. Their fears were expressed in such statements as:

It is not certain what things will be like in a few years time. Everyone is a bit wary. Time will tell what fate has in store for us.

(Oleg (m), 1991)

Nobody knows what things will be like in five years time.

(Mikhail (m), 1991)

Education as 'putting off the undesirable'

Entering higher education for boys is connected with the question of military service, since sometimes entering higher education means the possibility of avoiding military service. According to current Russian legislation those who are in full-time education may postpone service in the army or navy until they complete their studies, and are required to serve only twelve rather than twenty-four months. Thus, by choosing a higher educational establishment with a military department, young men release themselves from military service and this is clearly part of boys' motivational structure:

Why go to an institute, if in a year's time you are called up into the army? If they aren't going to call up from the institute then it would be worth starting this year.

(Tolia (m), 1991)

The lads all look for an institute with a military department.

(Vika (f), 1994)

Some boys simply don't want to go into the army and so go to an institute.

(Natasha, 1994)

However, students who work and study on a part-time basis are not released from military service. Over recent years the question of whether students studying in institutes should be called up for military service has remained under discussion and it is possible that legislation might be changed so that students in full-time higher education will also have to undertake military service.

Entering higher education may also help young people evade the responsibilities associated with entering the world of work:

Some people don't want to go out to work. We are simply not ready for it.

(Ania (f), 1994)

Thus, entering higher education for some young people is a continuation of their childhood dependency on their parents.

Education and 'getting a good job'

Relatively rarely did participants say that education was necessary to get a good job. This may be explained by the fact that at the current time no clear connection is made between education and future career or future life in general. In Soviet society the significance of a certificate of higher education was obvious. Now, as the nature of the labour market, the labour force and competition for jobs are changing rapidly, there is a demand for qualified specialists with real knowledge rather than formal certificates of such knowledge. Thus, as the labour market becomes more fully formed, education and knowledge will become increasingly important for an individual's job and career prospects:

Higher education is necessary in order to get a good job.

(Masha (f), 1994)

If you don't have good connections, you will need an education even more in order to find a job.

(Lena (f), 1994)

In most cases both boys and girls found it difficult to say exactly what they would study and to anticipate where and in what capacity they would work. Thus, currently, they only partially associate the education they receive with their future job prospects:

> I like working with numbers. Generally I would like to be a computer programmer.
>
> (Anna (f), 1991)

> I'll go and get a job. I'll find some kind of creative work. [*Question*: What kind of work exactly?]. Oh, I don't really know.
>
> (Oksana (f), 1994)

> I haven't really decided yet.
>
> (Volodia (m), 1991)

Girls are generally more likely to seek education for education's sake, regardless of its connection to a future profession or job. This might be explained by the idea that work for women is not as important as for men, since men are considered traditionally to be the breadwinners and their salaries to be the basis of the family budget. This lack of direction among girls is expressed in statements such as:

> I want to study. I'll choose some kind of arts subject, something like journalism.
>
> (Natasha (f), 1991)

Education as means to sexual equality

Some respondents expressed the relatively rare opinion that education is not only a contribution to personal, intellectual development but that getting an education allows the creation of a balance, an equality in male–female relationships

> She should have an equal position in the family, not be inferior to her husband.
>
> (Ania (f), 1991)

> You need education for yourself. If she doesn't know anything, they won't be equal.
>
> (Olia (f), 1991)

For some of the girls, however, it was more important to marry successfully and sort out their personal life than to get a good education and find well-paid work; a wealthy husband reduced the necessity of work and the acquisition of higher education:

> On the whole, in my opinion, you don't necessarily have to work at all.
>
> (Zhenia (f), 1994)

When asked whether they considered getting an education or getting married to be more important, the following answers were recorded:

> I think that it is more important to get married. If my husband was a rich business man I would cook and wash for him.
>
> (Natella (f), 1991)

> Of course personal life is more important.
>
> (Natasha (f), 1994)

These views are not surprising given that in the Russian media there is much talk currently of the return of women to the family and that one of the reasons cited for the fall in the birth-rate is the high level of employment of women. This discussion also indirectly propagandizes an easy life for girls and young women behind a rich business man or 'sponsor'.

Other girls who consider marriage a necessary step in life think about acquiring an education and then about combining work and running the household:

> For me it is more important to get an education. If you get married to a businessman, then you will be dependent on him and I wouldn't want to be.
>
> (Nastia (f), 1991)

> I want to study and when I have a family, we'll see what happens.
>
> (Iulia (f), 1994)

> If your work is interesting, then you can work full-time.
>
> (Olia (f), 1994)

Girls' job prospects are closely tied to their views and images of the family. All of them included having a family as part of their future, although they found it difficult, and rather embarrassing, to say at what age they planned to get married:

> When it happens, it happens.
>
> (Tania (f), 1991)

It is difficult to make any predictions in this sphere.

(Katia (f), 1994)

Not later than 30.

(Vika (f), 1994)

Education as 'the next step'

Some boys and girls were orientated only towards the achievement of the set goal, namely, being accepted into an institute. Such people could not even imagine what would happen if they did not succeed in entering higher education:

For me at the moment everything is geared towards getting in. If I don't have an education, then everything will be different.

(Dima (m), 1991)

Even though many girls were intending to go into higher education, none the less, few saw education as an integral part of a career. For a long time in the USSR anybody orientated towards climbing the career ladder was condemned and the word 'careerist' had a negative overtone. Thus, people in general had a negative image of anybody orientated towards making a career, and for some of the girls the concepts of 'woman' and 'career' were still difficult to combine:

I would none the less try to spend more time on the home.

(Zhenia (f), 1991)

A career is more for a man.

(Tat'iana (f), 1991)

I can't imagine myself as a woman-manager. A woman should concern herself with women's things.

(Iulia (f), 1994)

For this reason, many girls state a preference for part-time work.

THE ATTITUDE OF BOYS TO WOMEN'S EDUCATION AND WORK

In a period of such fundamental change in society it would be interesting to know how stereotypes associated with marriage, family and education for women are changing and, to elicit this information, a number of questions were asked. Unfortunately, it is difficult to compare the findings since there is very little literature on male attitudes to the role and place of women in society in the Soviet period. However, the results of the author's research suggest that, on the whole, young men retain traditional stereotypes of the role and place of women in society.

Educating women for the family

Some young men considered education to be necessary for girls, not in order for them to get a good job or for their individual development but for the family.

> A woman needs an education so that she is an interesting interlocutor.
>
> (Sergei (m), 1991)

> So, that if, for example, you invite guests round, she can chat, so that you are not ashamed of her.
>
> (Andrei (m), 1991)

> Culture is passed to a person via the family. Children are brought up by the mother and an uncultured person cannot bring up a child well.
>
> (Sasha (m), 1994)

> It is necessary for children to know as much as possible by the time they start school.
>
> (Ivan (m), 1994)

> An intelligent woman should not show off in front of a man.
>
> (Kolia (m), 1991)

These answers reveal clear stereotypes of patriarchal consciousness corresponding to a time when women were confined totally to the home and family and all their creative efforts were directed to this private sphere, especially to the education of children. The girls, in part, agreed with the boys, but not on everything and in some of the focus groups interesting discussions arose around the question of education for girls. One girl, for example, stated that:

> Children can be brought up excellently without higher education.

The most important thing is to love the child, education doesn't come into it.

(Ira (f), 1994)

'As long as it's not my wife': women and work

With regard to the question of women, work and careers, boys tend to see women as concentrating their efforts on the family and children and running the household, even if girls see themselves as combining work and family. If a woman works, according to the boys, then she should work part-time. The following answers were received to the question 'What would be your attitude to your wife working full-time?':

I would try not to choose such a wife.

(Georgii (m), 1991)

A woman manager? Let it be any woman, as long as it's not my wife.

(Viktor (m), 1991)

A woman who works full-time is not the best option.

(Andrei (m), 1991)

CONCLUSIONS

The motivations uppermost in the minds of school-leavers as they prepare to enter higher education revealed by the research cannot, of course, be extrapolated to the population at large. The focus-group method employed does not permit any conclusions about how widespread these ideas are; however it does allow the description, in their own words, of attitudes towards continuing education among school-leavers.

Above all, it must be concluded that the attitude towards higher education among boys and girls is ambivalent. Young people's views reveal a residue of old attitudes to education as well as providing evidence of new attitudes which are beginning to take shape. Although a significant proportion of participants of the focus groups continue to orientate themselves towards entrance to higher educational institutions, even Moscow school-leavers have been affected by the process of the devaluation of education.[6] Attitudes which predate perestroika and the emergence of market relations include:

the understanding of education as a value in itself, the use of higher education as cultural capital and the role of higher education in postponing entrance to adult life. Although the latter motivation is absent from existing, published literature, this is probably because it contradicted official ideology which assumed young people wanted to work and considered any other orientation to constitute 'deviant behaviour'. New motives for entering higher education include political instability and fears of an at least partial return to the old Soviet order. If the political situation was to stabilize it is possible that such young people would not consider entering higher education, since 'those who continued their education, do not earn very much'. A second new motivation for entering higher education is the desire to avoid military service. In the Soviet Union young men, regardless of whether they were in full-time or part-time higher education were required to complete military service. After the differentiation was introduced into legislation this became one of the significant motivations for entrance to full-time higher education. If the Russian army continues to embark on military actions then this motivation is likely to be strengthened.

It has been noted above that, until 1994, higher education was only infrequently embarked upon in order to improve job prospects. This is explained by the process of the devaluation of education which is a result of the knowledge that young graduates often work in positions for which they are overqualified; at the beginning of the 1990s, 4 per cent of those with higher education were employed in working-class jobs (Molodezh RFSR 1990: 74). Girls tend to link education with job prospects even less than boys. This is not surprising given that in post-Soviet society patriarchal attitudes which posit the man as the chief breadwinner and confirm the subordinate position of women still prevail. This is strengthened by the position of women in the new labour market, where they are offered jobs not demanding higher education (secretarial posts, sales assistants, models, etc.).[7] Boys talked more confidently about the connection between education and future profession since traditionally boys have been orientated towards achieving personal goals and gaining recognition in society whereas girls have been channelled towards self-realization in the family. Although girls remain orientated towards education, their professional and career horizons are limited by their anticipated future family role. Nevertheless, comparing the research completed in 1994 with that of 1991, it becomes clear that both boys and girls increasingly refer to the necessity of education for getting a good job. This is a result of the consolidation of new social stereotypes and behaviourial models, in particular in relation to the establishment of what constitute the new 'prestigious professions' and what place higher education has in the life of the individual.

During the research gender differences in responses were noted. Although girls' expectations of the future were just as high as boys', nevertheless, girls' responses revealed evidence of social pressure and stereotypes affecting their choices. Particularly prominent were notions about the necessity of getting married and having children and the preferability of working part-time. Heated discussions on the significance for and application of education by women which developed in the focus groups also revealed that male peers continue to hold patriarchal stereotypes of the role of women and of women's education and work. Boys, it emerged, viewed education for women in a utilitarian way: as enabling them to be good interlocutors and to bring up children well. Indeed, boys and girls were agreed on the fact that education aids the process of bringing up children (although they did not agree on the length of maternity leave).

It is important to note that the state, and society as a whole, is not promoting the formation of any other attitude towards the education and employment of women. On the contrary, current draft legislation – such as the new draft labour law wherein the responsibility for children is presumed to be women's, and numerous benefits to be granted to women (such as the right to stay at home to look after children even longer, the introduction of 'housework days', etc.) makes women unattractive employees. In society there is a persistent idea that women were created for the family and women's employment is blamed for depopulation and the fall in the birth-rate. In such circumstances girls will find it very difficult to realize their expectations, to continue to identify themselves with gaining higher education and to link their choice of higher educational establishment with a future profession.

The attitudes of young people towards education, work and the family reflect their life positions and strategies. If, in the course of future research, significant gender differences are found, then it should be expected that different behaviourial patterns among boys and girls will develop in the future. Knowledge of such gendered behaviourial models might help in the formation of a social policy in relation to youth which takes into account the peculiarities of the position of young men and women, especially in the period of transformation and change. Determining and analysing changing attitudes amongst the population is an interesting although difficult project. This is even more the case when the group under study is youth since young people are experiencing major changes in their own lives simultaneously. This article, therefore, aims to provide no more than a descriptive analysis of the attitudes of youth in the current period of transformation as young people pass from school to work which, it is hoped, will aid further study which takes into account gender difference.

NOTES

1 The literature survey here is confined to that concerned with the choices made by students in their final years at school (*starsheklassniki*), since it would be difficult, and not entirely relevant to the current article, to consider the literature on youth as a whole. Readers should also note that comparing the results of research is complicated by the absence of a single definition of 'youth' among sociologists evident in the lack of agreement as to what constitute the upper and lower age limits, let alone the social characteristics, of the category of 'youth'.

2 'Youth and the Future' is a joint American–Russian project led by Professor I. M. Slepenkov of Moscow State University and Professor John P. Robinson of Maryland State University.

3 These are the so-called 'sleeper districts' (*spal'nie raiony*) with extremely poor socio-cultural infrastructural development. For fuller explanation, see Chapter 12 by Elena Omel'chenko in this volume.

4 Respondents are referred to by first name only, followed by their sex (m [male], f [female]) and the year in which the focus group was conducted.

5 Salaries in Russia are linked to a grading system (*razriad*) of work. One may move up the scale through either work experience or educational qualifications.

6 It is important to note here that this research was conducted in Moscow, where the orientation towards higher education has always been high. In 1981, 81.3 per cent of those leaving secondary school intended to enter higher education (Rutkevich 1984: 25). This is due to the fact that Moscow has a particularly large number of institutes and universities.

7 For further discussion of the gendered nature of the post-Soviet labour market see Chapter 2 by Sue Bridger and Rebecca Kay and Chapter 3 by Marta Bruno in this volume.

Part II

The new Russian woman: feminity, sexuality and power

6 Young people, sex and sexual identity

Lynne Attwood

Despite its revolutionary origins, the Soviet Union was in many respects a staunchly conservative society. This was certainly the case concerning relations between the sexes, both social and sexual. Although men and women were theoretically equal, traditional notions of male and female personality and behaviour continued to prevail, with women persistently described as the 'weak sex'. Once the relatively loose sexual morality of the revolutionary era was brought under control, physical intimacy was supposedly confined to married couples and dedicated to procreation. Each new generation of young men and women was expected to fit in to the established pattern of gender and sexual relations without complaint or question. The Soviet Union claimed to have created a 'new psychology of the personality, the basic trait of which is collectivism' (Kovalev 1983: 38). This supposedly meant that everyone now acted in the interests of everyone else. In reality, it meant that everyone was supposed to act the same as everyone else.

This chapter begins with a discussion of the norms of gender relations and sexual behaviour which were promoted in the past in the Soviet Union and which continue to pervade the more conservative publications in post-Soviet Russia. It then turns to attitudes towards homosexuality, which clearly could not be accommodated within this staunch pro-family ethos based on traditional notions of male and female roles. Finally, the ways in which democratization and the move to the market have altered male and female relations will be explored as well as how this has been reported in academic literature and the press.

SOVIET WRITINGS ON GENDER RELATIONS AND SEXUAL BEHAVIOUR

Women in the Soviet Union formed an indispensable part of the work force, yet there was always a tension between their dual roles as workers and mothers. This was exacerbated by the perennial Soviet concern with the birth-rate. The Soviet Union linked its power with its population size, which had to be sufficient to sustain an enormous army and a labour-intensive industry. Accordingly, Soviet history is marked by periodic campaigns aimed at persuading women to have more children. One such campaign was launched in the last years of the Brezhnev era. Women's high level of involvement in paid work was said to have resulted in a gradual drop in their family orientation, and the balance in their lives between production and reproduction had gone awry. As educational specialist Liudmila Timoshchenko explained: 'Many girls in the final year at school cannot imagine themselves in the role of wife and mother. The majority of them connect their future lives only with study and work' (Timoshchenko 1978: 38). It was time for them to change their priorities and put their careers in second place. Teachers had a major role to play in this process. In the words of G. Belskaia: 'Our schools are to be praised for their success in bringing up girls to be good citizens, but it is time we paid more attention to making them feminine and housewifely, more kind, neat and gentle' (Belskaia 1977: 12).

Discussions about male and female personality and the nature of the 'real' man and woman began to proliferate in the general press and in specialist journals aimed at teachers and parents. In 1984, after a trial run in a number of schools in Russia and the Baltic republics, a new school course called 'The Ethics and Psychology of Family Life' was introduced in all schools for pupils in the ninth and tenth grades. It was described as a programme of 'sex upbringing' (*polovoe vospitanie*), or 'moral upbringing with regard to one's membership of one or the other sex' (Khripkova 1979: 3), and one of its stated aims was to help children 'become aware of... their special male and female roles' (Snegireva 1984: 12). In other words, it was a programme of overt sex-role socialization. The hope was that if men and women fitted into more traditional models of masculinity and femininity, they would also fit better into family life: they would be less likely to divorce, and more likely to want more than one child.

There was considerable debate as to whether the course should include explicit discussion about sex. Those in favour argued that most teenagers were given no information about sex by their parents, and if teachers were not able to provide it they would get it wherever they could, often in a distorted and unsavoury form. As a result, neither teenage pregnancy nor 'sexual hooliganism' had been eradicated from Soviet society. Opponents claimed that in those countries in the West where sex education did form part of the school curriculum there had been no positive results; on the contrary, 'a greater and greater number of boys and girls do not want and are not able to have normal family relations' (Afanas'eva 1988: 100). The opponents won, and the guidelines published for teachers of the course made no reference to what Afanas'eva has referred to as the 'technology of sex' (ibid.). The course did not ignore sex completely, however, but explored it from 'an ethical and psychological perspective' (Cherednichenko 1989a: 25). What this amounted to, in practice, was little more than a series of dire warnings about the consequences of premature sexual activity (see Attwood 1994: 269–70, 276–80; Cherednichenko 1989a: 25–6; 'Sut' liubvi' 1989: 122–30). The course ceased to be a compulsory part of the school curriculum in 1991, but articles and books have continued to appear offering teachers and parents advice on preparing teenagers for family life. These promote the same model of gender relations espoused throughout the last two decades.

The basic premise of these writings is that men and women are different but complementary beings, both physically and psychologically, and that these differences are essential both for their personal well-being and for the smooth running of society. These so-called 'eternally masculine' and 'eternally feminine' traits (Timoshchenko 1978: 6) are supposedly innate, but nature needs some help in bringing them to fruition. If people do not develop appropriate gender identities they experience acute mental turmoil and are likely to engage in anti-social behaviour.

There are a number of ways in which this can be achieved. Since children learn to a large extent through imitation, parents should exhibit appropriate gender stereotypes themselves, and make it clear to their children how much they value these in one another. If a father does not make his daughter aware that he cherishes his wife's femininity, for example, 'there is a danger that the girl will take on the characteristics of male behaviour' (Kamalina 1993: 63). Traditional rules of etiquette between men and women also help foster appropriate gender differences. Children should be taught that the man 'always holds out his wife's coat for her, allows her to walk through a door first, kisses her and pays her a compliment when he returns from work, [and] ... praises a meal she has cooked, or a new dress.' Girls should be encouraged to be 'above all concerned about the preservation of (their) charm and femininity' and learn how important it is to 'maintain high standards of hygiene in the home, ensuring, for example, that the bed-clothes are always clean and fresh' (Iagodinskii 1990: 64).

Given the concern about the birth-rate, great emphasis has inevitably been placed on preparing girls for motherhood. Eulogizing motherhood is nothing new in Russia. The 'Mother of God' was one of the most powerful images of the Orthodox Church; Aleksandra Kollontai, one of the main proponents of women's equality in the early years of the revolution, saw motherhood as a crucial feature of the 'new Soviet woman'; and despite its name, the magazine *Rabotnitsa* (*Woman Worker*) has been directed as much at women as mothers as at women as workers, insisting that having children is 'the most splendid and highest purpose of a woman's life' (Viukova 1968: 1–2). Propagandists have been able to take an existing glorification of motherhood, then, and insert it into a new programme of gender socialization.

The desire for maternity is said to be a gift from nature. It can be seen in girls of the youngest age, both in the way they look after their younger siblings and in their general inclination 'towards caring activities – looking after people, nursing, showing concern, and so on' (Khripkova and Kolesov 1981: 73). Boys have no equivalent paternal instinct, so it is the woman's task 'to turn her spouse into a loving father for his children' (Malenkova 1990: 68). The man's principal role in the family is to provide support and protection, and an appropriate model of masculinity for his sons. A boy growing up without a male role model 'forms his attitudes about all aspects of life through the prism of female awareness, and does not learn male behaviour' (ibid.). It is up to the woman to decide what other functions her husband should have in the household. One education correspondent, E. Krashennikova, advises:

> The husband can, of course, do work about the home, scrub the potatoes etc. But in my opinion, it would be more useful to make him 'head of supplies'. Give him the address of the shops, and a bag. And be diplomatic: 'Darling, this is absolutely astonishing: where did you buy these potatoes? They taste so good!'
>
> (Krashennikova 1990: 66)

In general, girls should be brought up to keep a steady stream of 'tender words' flowing, since husbands are happier and more sure of themselves if they are continually praised for their successes at work and for their help in the home (Iagodinskii 1990: 64).

In the interests of perpetuating the human race, nature has craftily ensured that men and women find gender-specific qualities the most attractive features in each other. A man likes shyness and modesty in a woman, and is turned off by 'mannish' behaviour: 'a cigarette between the lips, a harsh voice, a too-free, rather coarse way of conducting herself' (Khripkova and Kolesov 1981: 120). A woman, on the other hand, is attracted to a man who is resolute and decisive, and can 'only love a man who is stronger than her' (Kotliar 1986: 69–71).

It is hard to see how this promotion of traditional gender differences is compatible with the claim that equality had been established between women and men. All the same, the advocates of differentiated upbringing have insisted that they do support equality, but explain that it 'must not be understood as being the same in everything' (Timoshchenko 1992: 45). Nor does equality require an exact division of family chores. As V. V. Sorokin explained to readers of *Vospitanie Shkol'nikov*, 'If my wife, for example, picks up a screwdriver, I am insulted – this is my job. And a husband need not, in my view, put on an apron and cook cabbage soup' (Tarkhova 1993: 16)

In the past, the meaning of equality was misunderstood, and this had dangerous consequences. It led to a blurring of male and female roles and personality traits: women had begun to lose some of the essential aspects of femininity such as kindness, concern for others, tenderness, etc., while men had become increasingly indecisive and weak of character. Some women tried 'to take the reins of family life into their own hands', which was a disaster not only for society but also for individual families (Iagodinskii 1990: 64). Women were rarely happy without a man to look up to; as Tarkhova insisted, 'a happy, healthy family is unthinkable without any kind of cult of the father, the husband' (Tarkhova 1993: 17–18). The negative effect which the demise of the father's status in the family had on children was compounded by the fact that most school teachers are female. This reinforced the impression that women were active and men passive. Boys, then, were deprived of strong, positive male role models throughout the most crucial period in their development and this led to 'the manifestation of extreme, negative forms of behaviour in youth: aggression and depression'. Looking for ways of rectifying this situation, two educational theorists, as recently as

1990, have even criticized the fact that boys and girls 'work identically on lessons and are expected to meet the same general demands of the school' (Breslav and Khasan 1990: 64–9).

A number of reasons have been put forward for the importance of sex-typed personalities and behaviour. The Soviet Union placed great emphasis on the duties as well as the rights of its citizens, and if boys and girls were not brought up differently, it was argued, 'when they reach adulthood, such children often prove incapable of fulfilling the roles which society requires of them' (Belkin 1975: 60), the so-called 'eternal duties which they cannot escape' (Cherednichenko 1989a: 25–6).

Women's principal 'eternal duty' was, of course, the bearing and rearing of children. However, they were also expected to act as the guarantors of society's moral health. There have been repeated references to a distinctive female morality, virtue, honour and purity, both in the Soviet and post-Soviet literature. Feminine qualities soften and humanize society, and encourage men to be strong and protective. A demise in femininity hence leads inevitably to a demise in morals in general. As Tamara Afanas'eva puts it, 'if [the woman] refuses to be firm and correct [in her behaviour], then we say goodbye to [society's] moral foundations' (Afanas'eva 1988: 99). Despite the supposed commitment to equality between the sexes, concern has often been expressed about the danger it brings in its wake: in the words of Iagodinskii, 'the collapse of morals in the modern world is often considered to be an inevitable consequence of female emancipation' (Iagodinskii 1990: 61).

In some texts, this heightened female morality is interpreted in purely sexual terms. Writers have referred to a justifiable 'moral inequality' between the sexes. Women, they point out, are largely responsible for bringing up any children produced by casual relationships, and so society is bound to be less lenient about their behaviour (Agarov 1991: 61). They also have a greater influence over their children's behaviour and so they always have to set an excellent example (Afanas'eva 1988: 99). Accordingly, social opinion only respects girls who are modest and circumspect. Even the boys who seduce them 'do not respect girls who enter lightly into an encounter with anyone who wants them' (*Dlia Vas, Devochki* 1993: 236), and soon abandon them. Such girls find themselves permanently branded: they are unable to find husbands, but at the same time have to fend off the unwelcome advances of men who assume they are available to everyone. They are 'doomed to loneliness', deprived forever of normal family life (Cherednichenko 1990a: 68–72 and

1990b: *Dlia vas, Devochki* 1993: 236: 70–2; Iagodinskii 1990: 62–4). The only way to avoid such a tragedy is 'not to indulge in casual liaisons and to place at the head of loving relations not sex and licentiousness but maidenly honour and conjugal fidelity' (Iagodinskii 1990: 61).

This moral rectitude is easier for girls than for boys because girls are less troubled by sexual urges. Demographer Iurii Riurikov explains that the sex instinct is stronger in boys due to the presence of the male hormone, which gives them a greater physiological need for sex ('Sut' liubvi' 1989: 126). Cherednichenko asserts that a girl will usually enter into sexual relations only because of pressure from her boyfriend, who accuses her of not loving him enough if she refuses to sleep with him. The boy knows this is not true, but he 'is unable to control his [sex] instinct' (Iagodinskii 1990: 61). It is the girl's responsibility, then, to protect her 'maidenly honour', and she can do this simply by denying her boyfriend sex before marriage. Even if he does not realize this at first, it is in his own interests. Marriage is good for people, especially men: it leads to a marked improvement in general health, life expectancy, and emotional well-being. Indeed, 'a person is really happy only in a family' (Cherednichenko 1989b: 137; Dorno 1981: 18; 'Etika i psikhologiia semeinoi zhizni' 1983: 36).

There appears from this literature to be a major imbalance in male and female needs and desires. Women have maternal instincts; men have sexual instincts. Women put up with sex for the sake of marriage and children, men put up with marriage and children in order to have sex. Yet if women use the promise of sex as a carrot to entice the chosen father of their future children into matrimony, the logical conclusion is that once they have succeeded, they have no right to deny him the promised reward. V. Cherednichenko, a teacher on the school course entitled 'The Ethics and Psychology of Family Life', implicitly makes this point in an article in *Vospitanie Shkol'nikov*. When one of his pupils asked if he thought it permissible for a couple to have sex after they had booked their wedding date but before they were actually married, Cherednichenko answered with a cautionary tale. A young man thought he had persuaded his fiancée to sleep with him, but she changed her mind at the last minute. He forced himself on her, after which she went to the police and accused him of rape. He was sentenced to ten years in prison. His defence, that they were virtually married, was not accepted by the courts. To Cherednichenko, the crime clearly lies not in the fact that the man forced the woman into having sex, but that he did so before they were married. Husbands, it seems, can do as they like with their wives (Cherednichenko 1989b: 132–7).

A book aimed at pubescent girls, published in 1993, continues to portray sex as something that should only happen within marriage and, from the girl's point of view, for the sake of having babies. Pregnancy is still presented as an inevitable consequence of sex; there is no mention of the increased availability of contraceptives in post-Soviet Russia. The one concession to the changing times is a section on AIDS, but the refusal to discuss sex openly and frankly renders it absurd. Readers are given shock figures about the antici- pated spread of the disease, but no information about the causes of transmission, apart from a reference to intravenous drug use in the United States, and no advice on how they can protect themselves against infection (*Dlia Vas, Devochki* 1993: 253–4).

ATTITUDES TOWARDS HOMOSEXUALITY

The general approach to gender differences and sexuality has remained remarkably consistent throughout the past two decades, despite the enormous changes which have taken place in society as a whole. What has emerged from the literature is a highly conserva- tive model of gender relations and sexual behaviour which provides no space for alternative lifestyles, and which could hardly be expected to tolerate alternative sexual orientations. Society is por- trayed as a network of traditional family units, each consisting of a strong man, a nurturing woman and appropriately socialized children. Men and women are supposed to appeal to each other precisely because of their differences: as Sysenko put it, nature has 'made [them] for each other' (Sysenko 1980: 14–15). In the Soviet era, there could be no alternative to this way of life since everyone was meant to adhere to the 'psychology of the collective'. In the words of Elena Grigor'eva, 'we all had to walk in the same direction, always think of morality and "the well-being" of society' (Grigor'eva 1991: 14).

Homosexuality defied all this. It could not be confined to mar- riage, and was clearly not geared towards procreation. It involved sex for its own sake, not for the public good. It complicated the cosy image of men and women as two indivisible halves of a whole, drawn to each other as opposites. It was also a dangerous sign of individualism. Accordingly, it was vilified. It was variously described as 'anti-social behaviour' (Belkin 1975: 60), as a 'pathological devi- ation' (Kamalina 1993: 63) and as a crime. In a book aimed at teenage boys, male homosexuality was portrayed as synonymous with paedophilia:

> Homosexuals try by any possible means to win the sympathy of young boys; they buy them sweets and cigarettes and cinema tickets, they give them money, help them with their homework, and generally pretend that they selflessly love young children. But after such preparations, they sooner or later proceed to action. Don't allow them to touch you! Don't be shy of your parents and teachers, tell them immediately about any such attempts with yourself or with other boys! And parents and teachers will quickly and willingly help you. Homosexuality is a punishable crime, and homosexuals well know this; therefore being saved from them presents no problem.
>
> (Gyne 1960: 37)

Male homosexuality was indeed a crime in the Soviet Union, even between consenting adults. Article 121 of the Criminal Code made 'men lying with men' (*muzhelozhestvo*) punishable by up to five years in prison. Lesbianism was not against the law but was interpreted as a sign of mental illness, so lesbians were incarcerated in mental hospitals instead of prisons. The initial period of hospitalization generally lasted only two to three months, but after her release the 'patient' was required to continue seeing a psychiatrist on a regular basis, was likely to be treated with powerful drugs and, like other mental patients, was banned from certain types of work and forbidden to hold a driver's licence (Gesson 1994: 17–18). The strength of anti-homosexual feeling was such that parents often reported their own children to the authorities when they found out about their sexual orientation (Dukarevich 1993: 23–4; Gesson 1994: 17; Kruglov 1993: 25).

Gays and lesbians who were not imprisoned or hospitalized faced myriad other forms of discrimination. It was virtually impossible for them to set up home with their partners, since they had to be married in order to be considered for an apartment. Many did marry in an attempt to convince people (and sometimes themselves) that they were 'normal', and hence were forced to live a lie. Those who did not marry and continued living with their parents were often subject to the taunts of neighbours simply for not doing their duty as Soviet citizens: marrying and having children (Suvorova and Geiges 1990a: 12). If their sexual orientation was discovered, gays and lesbians would invariably lose their jobs, and often their friends.[1]

The legal situation has improved in recent years. Male homosexuality is no longer a criminal act since the repeal of Article 121 in April 1993 and lesbians derive some legal protection from a law passed in July 1992 outlining the rights of psychiatric patients and imposing strict limits on involuntary hospitalization (an attempt, no doubt, to restore the credibility of Soviet psychiatry after the human rights abuses with which it was associated in the past). However, the diagnostic manual which defines lesbianism as a personality disorder has yet to be replaced, and old habits die hard: according to a report by Masha Gesson, 'the vast majority of psychiatrists from outside Moscow... earnestly believe that homosexuality is a mental disorder or a symptom of one' (Gesson 1994: 53). Lesbians and gays are still dismissed from their jobs, although the reason for dismissal is now likely to be disguised. In some cases, however, employers would be able to dismiss a gay or lesbian member of staff without needing to find another excuse; a lesbian teacher in higher education told the author that she would be certain to lose her job if she were 'found out' since she worked with young people.[2]

A number of lesbians have reported that they feel more hostility directed towards them than towards male homosexuals.[3] There are several possible reasons for this. Lesbianism clearly defies the patriarchal model of family life which was promoted with such persistence throughout the literature we have explored, with its male head of the family and its 'weak', submissive woman. Kseniia Bogoliubova has argued that, while male homosexuality was perceived as alien and threatening, 'a woman who was not willing to tie herself to a man and accept his pre-eminence, his ' "patriarchal power", was even worse' (Bogoliubova 1991: 14). The idealized image of the woman, linked so inseparably to that of the mother, has always had a strong coating of selflessness and self-sacrifice; a man who put his own needs above those of his family was a disappointment, but if a woman did so this was 'an insult to the word 'mother', which is so dear to all of us' ('Syn soldata' 1965: 18–19). The acceptance of uncontrollable male sexual urges meant that male homosexuals could be excused on the grounds that they simply could not help themselves, but since the existence of female sexuality was virtually denied, lesbians had no excuse. Women were also held responsible for establishing and sustaining standards of morality in society as a whole, and so lesbianism was even more of a moral outrage than homosexuality.[4]

In an article in *Sobesednik*, Galina Toktalieva's refusal to accept lesbianism is clearly based on a notion of female duty and self-sacrifice. She tells readers about her meeting with a lesbian feminist called Ol'ga, who explained that she had two main reasons for becoming a lesbian. First, her profession as a photographer was crucial to her and she felt that women who were attached to men had little chance of developing their own careers. Society's encouragement of women's maternal instinct discouraged their ambition, with the result that they helped their men get ahead while they themselves were reduced to 'baby machines and washing machines'. Second, an unhappy love affair with one of her university lecturers had convinced her that men 'brought nothing but unhappiness' and that women were better human beings. Toktalieva agreed with Ol'ga that 'woman is indeed a higher being' but, she added, this is only the case 'if she pursues her lofty mission – the spiritual and wonderful mission of compassion and love. Without women's compassion and love, men and children would be terribly alone and defenceless in this world' (Toktalieva 1989: 11). In other words, women have a duty to use their moral superiority for the good of men and children, not for other women.

With glasnost and the move towards democratization, some more positive appraisals of homosexuality began to appear. Igor Kon called for an understanding attitude towards homosexuals in an interview with the newspaper *Literaturnaia Gazeta* in 1989. People had different ways of expressing their sexuality, he argued, and the Soviet Union was one of the few countries which did not recognize this as a human right. When pressed by the interviewer, he did suggest that there were ways in which parents could minimize the chances of their children becoming homosexual, linking it, for example, to excessive guardianship (Moroz 1989: 11); in other words, it was still a disorder, albeit one which should be treated with tolerance. All the same, given the social situation at that time, Kon's position was nothing short of courageous; not only was male homosexuality still illegal, but the arrival of AIDS had been used by some as a justification for increased homophobia (Burgasov 1986: 15). In his more recent work Kon argues that homosexuality is not an illness or a disorder but an inevitable and natural feature of human society, and that acceptance of difference is 'the only social policy which corresponds to the spirit of a democratic society' (Kon 1991b: 242).

Psychologist A. Grishin attempted a tolerant approach in a 1989 *Rabotnitsa* article when he told the story of a young patient who had discovered to his horror that he had homosexual tendencies. It began when he got talking one day to a lad in the park, and was invited back to his hostel room to drink wine. Afterwards they went for a shower together, and suddenly his new friend went down on his knees and began to kiss his penis. He tried to push him away, but felt such a strong surge of excitement that he could not help himself, and 'that which is against the law took place'. He was desperate to know how he could restrain himself in future. Grishin explains to readers that such 'misfortune' befalls many young men, especially if they find themselves in all-male environments such as the army or prison (he does not make it clear whether he means that the powerful male sex urge will find whatever outlet it can or that a dormant homosexual orientation can be triggered off in an all-male environment). They can be helped by a doctor, however, and if they voluntarily apply for treatment no legal action would be taken against them. Grishin does point out that one of the main problems for homosexuals is society's strong aversion towards them, but he does not call for a change in this attitude nor denounce the law which at that time made homosexuality a criminal offence. The limits of his understanding are particularly clear from the fact that the discussion appears in an article on 'sexual perversions' (Grishin 1990: 26–7).

Publications aimed primarily at young people have generally taken a more tolerant line. *Moskovskii Komsomolets*, now referred to by its racier abbreviation '*MK*', is the most widely read newspaper in the capital and has published a number of sympathetic articles on homosexuality (though some are couched in an ironic tone which is said to have offended gay and lesbian readers) (Gesson 1994: 37). An article in 1991 insisted that the country's continuing discrimination against lesbian and gays violated its claim to be moving in the direction of democracy. Contrary to popular Russian belief, it argued, it was not possible to 'cure' people of attraction to those of the same sex; moreover, most lesbians and gays did not want to be cured. 'They . . . consider their attraction not a deviation from the norm, but one of its variants, which has a right to exist' (Mladshii 1991: 4).

A recent *MK* article told of a Danish family which consisted of a gay couple, a lesbian couple, and their 5-year-old son, conceived by means of artificial insemination. The author, Elena Egorova, contrasted Russia's rigid understanding of the family with the more varied possibilities permitted under Western laws. While much of the article was clearly addressed to a heterosexual readership, at the end she turned directly to lesbians and gays and commiserated with them: 'You are not able even to dream of the possibility of entering an official marriage, and the new law on marriage and the family which is now going through the Duma does not give you any ray of hope' (Egorova 1994: 2).

The publication one would most expect to take up the issue of homosexuality is *SPID-info* (*AIDS Info*), a monthly newspaper which began appearing in 1989 with the professed aim of providing young people with enough information about AIDS to enable them to enjoy a relatively safe sex life. However, even though gay men remain the principal 'group at risk' (to use the Russian term), *SPID-info* is geared firmly towards a heterosexual readership. Even articles about homosexuality present them as 'other', and are generally far from supportive. In a sample of eight copies of the newspaper appearing between 1991 and 1994 there were nine articles either about homosexuality or which included reference to it; of these, only two articles took an unambiguously positive position. One of these looked at the ways in which popular music could be used to heighten social awareness, and mentioned with approval a Berlin rock concert aimed at defending the rights of sexual minorities (Veselkin 1991: 6–7). The other challenged the prevalent notion that most male ballet dancers were gay, explaining that it only seemed this way to outsiders because dancers tend to be sensitive and emotional and these traits are generally perceived as feminine. In any case, 'it is not the world which is divided into two halves, it is each of us: we are all bisexual' (Volskaia 1992: 5).

This was not a view shared by most *SPID-info* correspondents. One recurring topic is how one can determine whether a person is homosexual, which implies that one either is or is not. A medical expert, Sergei Agarkov, explained that one could not tell with any certainty from a person's physical appearance, but if a man had long hair, a 'soft' or coquettish manner and wore make-up or jewellery 'in such a case there is a fifty per cent chance that he is'. A more accurate, scientific way of diagnosing homosexuality, he continued, involved measuring people's physiological reactions to films to which 'those with homosexual feelings would not be indifferent'. Such tests were important because 'many sexual disorders are linked to concealed homosexual attraction,' and accurate diagnosis was essential for treatment (Podkolodnii 1992: 8–9).

In another article, Georgii Khlebnikov made it clear quite how dangerous 'concealed homosexuality' could be when he suggested that Hitler suffered from the condition. Hitler's desperate attempt to suppress his homosexual desire, and the self-hatred this produced, resulted in his intense cruelty. To back up his hypothesis, Khlebnikov pointed out that Hitler was quite feminine both in appearance and manner, being short with narrow shoulders and a hairless body (Khlebnikov 1992: 10–11).

A letter purportedly written by a gay reader (though this is a society with a strong tradition of ghost-writing 'readers' letters') describes an unhappy secret life of furtive meetings in hired rooms and a terrible sense of shame 'that I am a "blue"[5] and that I do something that has put other people behind bars'. The editors offered the author no reassurances nor, indeed, any word of comment, leaving the reader with the impression that homosexuality is inevitably squalid and shameful ('Pochta *SPID-info*' 1992: 5). The same impression is conveyed in an article by Fedor Podkolodnii about the hidden functions of the Russian *bania* or bathhouse. The author explains that as well as providing special 'family' rooms for heterosexual activities the bania also serves as a gay meeting place and he relates the experience of an acquaintance of his who was approached by an unknown man offering to massage his back. He innocently accepted, but was given more of a massage than he had anticipated. He had not had sex with a woman for a month or so, and his body responded involuntarily, but now he was disgusted at what he had done and had not been to a *bania* since (Podkolodnii 1991: 10).

There is a rather different approach to lesbian sex. In another 'reader's confession', the author, Marina, explains that as a teenager she spent some time in a detention camp, and was forced into lesbian acts by the older inmates. These were her first sexual experiences, and despite her initial resistance she came to develop a taste for them. After her release she started going out with boys, but she could never forget the excitement of those camp embraces. She eventually confessed to her sister what had happened, and then introduced her too into the joys of lesbianism. The sex was described in considerable detail, and the story illustrated by a photograph of two women engaged in a sexual act ('Na voliu vyshla drugoi' 1993: 14). Lesbianism, then, is being used for the purpose of sexual titillation. It is presented as something naughty and forbidden, its 'wickedness' emphasized by the associations of criminality and incest. We can be certain that the tale is not aimed at lesbian readers – nor, for that matter, at women at all. The pornography and sex industry in the West has long recognized that lesbian sex can be sexually arousing for men, and the Russian industry has followed its example.[6] Lesbianism becomes an item in men's sexual arsenal; what is really concerned with women identifying with women is distorted into spectacle for men.

Intriguingly, only one article in eight issues of *SPID-info* mentioned any link between male homosexuality and HIV infection. This came in a news brief in July 1991, which noted an increase in HIV infection amongst Moscow's gay community. This was due, apparently, to gay men's lack of concern for each other: 'It is highly characteristic that many who are infected by the virus do not take care to protect their partners.' To knowingly infect another person with HIV was a criminal act in Russia, but since homosexuality itself was illegal, a gay man would be unlikely to go to the police. Accordingly, those with HIV did not have to worry about legal repercussions if they infected others ('Assotsiatsiia informiruet' 1991: 31).

Such unsympathetic portrayals of the gay community, combined with the lack of information about AIDS for gay men, makes it clear that homosexuals are not seen as, or encouraged to be, part of the newspaper's readership. Discussions about AIDS focus firmly on the risks to heterosexuals and how these can be avoided. Accordingly, readers are warned that heterosexual sex is now responsible for 90 per cent of new HIV infections across the world ('Tselii chemodan novostei' 1992: 3). They are told about the dangers of intravenous drug use (Pokrovskii 1991: 3) and about buying sex from prostitutes ('Deshevka-2' 1992: 5–7). Reference has been made to unsanitary hospital conditions and to the children who were infected by contaminated needles in hospitals at Elista and Volgograd ('V teni kryli tvoikh ukroi menia' 1991: 7). Visiting Africa, and getting intimate with Africans, is portrayed as foolhardy: a report on the first Soviet citizen to die of AIDS mentioned that he had been in Africa some years before the disease appeared ('Assotsiatsiia informiruet' 1991: 2), while an actress is quoted as saying that a friend of hers used to fantasize about having sex with a black man 'before she knew about AIDS, it goes without saying . . .' (Nevskii 1992a: 29). AIDS is not a 'gay disease', of course, and *SPID-info* is right to point out that heterosexuals should not be complacent. However, it is indefensible for a publication supposedly aimed at helping the population protect itself from AIDS to ignore the section of that population which is most at risk. This is particularly the case since the publication and distribution of a specifically gay literature has encountered enormous financial and legal impediments.

There has been a small but organized gay and lesbian movement in Moscow and St Petersburg since around 1990, when the short-lived gay newspaper *Tema* was launched in Moscow (Gesson 1994:

56). Two years later, in July 1992, an international conference was held, first in St Petersburg and then in Moscow, aimed at promoting the rights of lesbians and gays. All the same, gay and lesbian organizations still have difficulties getting official registration, without which they face severe restrictions on what they can do. As Gesson points out: 'Far from a mere formality, registration is required to open a bank account and to be able to conduct basic operations necessary to the functioning of an organization' (ibid.: 40). Registration is apparently denied in accordance with a law against 'the creation and activity of civil unions that aim to harm the health and morals of the population' (ibid.: 41).

Despite such difficulties, a gay infrastructure has begun to develop in the major cities. A number of cafés and discotheques have opened in Moscow and St Petersburg, though patrons have to contend with the distinct possibility of being attacked when they leave, a practice known by the perpetrators as *'remont'* ('repair work'). Accordingly, most clubs stay open until morning and discourage people from leaving until then (ibid.: 42). The official lifting of censorship in 1991 enabled the gay community to begin publishing its own magazines and newspapers. A number of publications have been launched, but financial problems mean that few are able to appear on a regular basis. With limited access to desk-top publishing, publishers have to pay large sums of money for expensive typography. There are few places where such literature can be touted openly,[7] and since publications do not appear regularly it is difficult selling them through subscription. Making money from advertising will not be possible until gays and lesbians cease to be such a marginalized and low-status group. The situation has been compounded by the high inflation rate. At present, those attempting to produce gay or lesbian publications can only do so with the help of Western sponsors.[8]

The financial problems are compounded for lesbians attempting to produce their own publications. Given the pressures on women to marry and have children, many lesbians do so before they realize, or accept, their real sexual orientation. Accordingly, a high proportion of lesbians are single parents, while lesbian couples are likely to be bringing up children from both previous marriages. This, combined with the fact that women in general earn less than men, means there is little surplus money in the lesbian community. While material of interest to lesbians is included in gay publications such as *Ty* (*You*), at present there are no specifically lesbian publications.

The development of a gay and lesbian press is crucial in breaking down the isolation currently experienced by most gays and lesbians, particularly those living outside the major cities who have no access to gay meeting places such as cafés and discotheques. However, if attitudes in general are to be improved, homosexuality needs to be given wider and more sympathetic coverage in the media as a whole. In recognition of this fact, one Moscow lesbian organization, MOLLI (Moskovskoe ob"edinenie lesbiiskoi literatury i iskusstva, the Moscow Association of Lesbian Literature and Arts), was established in 1990 with the aim of providing 'humanitarian education'. Its members hope eventually to publish their own journal, *Adelfi*, which will be a forum for women writers and artists, but they are also attempting to improve the public perception of lesbianism by means of art exhibitions, concerts, television appearances and interviews. The idea, as explained by MOLLI's director, Mila Elenovskaia, is that if a person likes a work of art or a performance, the sexual orientation of the artist will seem irrelevant. At the same time they make it clear by their name that they are lesbians, and so hope to persuade people that lesbians are people like anyone else and are no less capable of producing talented work.[9]

Resistance to that notion can be acute. Nadezhda Popova wrote a report for the newspaper *Rosiiskie Vesti* on a concert organized by MOLLI in November 1994, at which the author of this article was also present. The audience consisted of a mixture of lesbians and heterosexual women with a smattering of men, but in Popova's article it was dominated by predatory dykes who leapt on her even though she had brought a man along for protection: 'I had to clutch hold of my escort's arm; this flirting was just too open'. Those gathered in the theatre buffet, who were for the most part chatting in groups, were described by Popova as a parody of heterosexual coupledom:

> the 'man' was, as a rule, taller, short-haired, and with somewhat abrupt movements. He looked after his lady according to all the usual rules: blew fluff off her jacket, put a stray hair back in place for her, and poured wine into her glass.
>
> (Popova 1994: 8)

Out on the street, after fleeing the concert before the end, Popova did wonder: 'Do we have the right to judge them? Or is this strictly a personal matter – who one loves, and why?' All the same, she gave thanks to God for dividing most of the population into 'weak women' and 'strong men' (ibid.). Popova's use of these terms bring us back to the point made at the start of this chapter. As long as the stress on traditional gender roles and sex-typed personalities continues, there is little chance that people with alternative sexual orientations will find acceptance.

THE MARKET AND ITS IMPACT ON GENDER RELATIONS

Although the mainstream publications have continued to endorse an unchanged model of male and female relations, the transformations in Russian society have had a considerable impact on gender relations. The market economy is said to require just those traits which have traditionally been ascribed to men – entrepreneurship, individual responsibility, activity, initiative, rationality, courage, a willingness to take risks – and the demise of state socialism has been accompanied by a celebration of masculinity.

The move to a market economy has fuelled the old calls for a more differentiated upbringing. An article by Iu. E. Aleshina and A. S. Volovich, appearing in the scholarly psychology journal *Voprosy Psikhologii* in 1991, discusses an Academy of Sciences' research project concerned with 'Socio-psychological problems of the socialization and learning of sex roles'. This report suggests that gender-differentiated socialization continued to be sponsored by the state throughout the Gorbachev era. Although Aleshina and Volovich do not insist that traditional male and female personality traits are innate, they still see them as essential. This is especially the case given the new economic situation, the authors explain, which requires traditional masculine entrepreneurial traits. Under the old Soviet regime, boys were confronted with a fundamental contradiction: they were told from childhood to 'act like men' but were given no legitimate ways in which they could do so, since socialist society had 'a negative attitude towards being active, competitive, and showing aggression in other ways', all of which were typical masculine forms of behaviour (Aleshina and Volovich 1991: 76). Even in the workplace, the traditional male arena, men were not able to manifest masculine qualities because the Soviet Union's planned economy was based on 'feminine' qualities: 'collective responsibility, implementation (of state decisions), an instrumental attitude towards work, conservatism, etc' (ibid.) Denied positive outlets for their masculinity, many boys turned to negative forms of activity.[10] The market economy now requires exactly those qualities boys were not able to exhibit in the past, and which are still lacking in most Russian men. Aleshina and Volovich call for a yet more determined programme of gender socialization to help overcome male passivity and develop in boys traditional masculine qualities.

The authors are not explicit about what role they envisage women playing in the market economy. They do, however, suggest that domestic work is a major component of the female role, and call on parents to make it seem more palatable to their daughters by involving them from the earliest age in such tasks as tidying up, cooking, and doing the laundry (ibid.: 79). They acknowledge that at present working women are under physical strain because of the double burden of paid work and domestic responsibilities, but they seem less concerned about this in itself than that about the possibility that it might undermine the status of men: if children see their mothers doing everything, this will enhance their perception that women are the active sex and men the passive. Their proposed solution is not that men take on half of the housework, which would ease women's burden at the same time as making men seem more active, but that they do more 'masculine' tasks around the house (ibid.). Since the market economy apparently has no use for the feminine qualities that parents and teachers are still being urged to inculcate in girls, it is difficult to avoid the conclusion that women are expected to play a largely domestic role in the new Russia.

The Sex Industry

One area of the new Russian economy which clearly does have use for female workers is the sex industry. A full range of sexual services is now on offer to 'new Russians' – pornography, prostitution, erotic massage, striptease shows, 'telephone sex' – which have a clear significance for gender relations.

Glasnost initiated an explosion of soft pornography which was not confined to specifically pornographic publications but extended into publications aimed at youth (most notably *Sobesednik*, the weekly supplement to *Komsomol'skaia Pravda*), current affairs magazines (such as *Ogonek*) and even some publications ostensibly aimed at women (for example, *Zhenskie Dela*). Advocates of this 'erotica' have claimed that it is part of the reform process, a reflection and extension of Russia's new social freedoms. As Rosamund Shreeves explains, it is 'presented as the literal embodiment of a radical challenge to authoritarian and conservative political structures' (Shreeves 1992: 138). Andrei Maksimov argues in *Sobesednik* that those who oppose pornography are unable to accept the transition to democracy. Their anger stems from a rejection of anything that is natural, a fear of feeling or doing what has not been sanctioned by the state. 'We are ashamed to admit that we are excited by the naked female body,' he explains, 'because there is no [official] position, no ideology behind this excitement' (Maksimov 1992: 15). Although pornography involves the display of naked female bodies for male consumption, its supporters have argued that it is liberating for women as well as men since it gives them the chance to discover their suppressed sexuality (Shreeves 1992: 139).

Officially, prostitution did not exist in the Soviet Union, since its causes – private property and female poverty – had been eradicated. In the new Russia, however, at least according to the press, it has become one of the biggest growth industries. It has been portrayed both as a result and a symbol of Russia's rampant new consumer orientation, a side-effect of the 'shady' business dealing which characterizes the Russian market, an indication of the nation's general state of moral decline. The media has concentrated particular attention on women at the top end of the profession who ply their trade amongst foreigners and, increasingly, the 'new Russians', and are able to enjoy the expensive clothes and lavish lifestyles of which most women in Russia could not even dream. This has prompted some critics to argue that the new Russia has produced a new breed of prostitute, motivated by greed rather than poverty (Meliksetian 1990: 87). The results of a magazine survey amongst Russian schoolgirls supposedly found that even they saw prostitution as one of the most desirable professions they could enter, a 'fact' repeated again and again as an indication of Russia's moral collapse (Shlapentokh 1992: 175). Once again, then, women were used as the touchstones of the nation's morality.

The morality of the male clients who bought the services of prostitutes received scant attention. Since men had stronger sexual urges than women, they had to satisfy them in whatever way they could. The worrying thing was that female morality was in decline.

Some attempted to pathologize prostitution. A. S. Meliksetian, for example, suggested that 'a great many women ... give themselves over to prostitution because of depraved inclinations, because of a genetic, psychological, or inherited disposition' (Meliksetian 1990: 89). In this way prostitutes, like lesbians, could be seen as abnormal women, psychological degenerates. Moralists could reassure themselves that society, with its patriarchal family structure, was not under threat.

Given the past emphasis on purity as one of the principal traits of femininity, any evidence of female sexuality could be interpreted as a sign of depravity by the more conservative commentators. This did not escape the attention of some of the men involved in the sex industry, who were able to claim that prostitution, like pornography, was liberating women from sexual repression. One pimp told readers of *Gazeta dlia Zhenshchin* (*The Women's Gazette*) that the women who worked for him derived considerable sexual satisfaction from the job but that this had nothing to do with perversion. Some were single mothers who would otherwise have little opportunity to find sexual partners, while others were simply 'not, according to their natures, created for family life'. Prostitution gave them both economic independence and sexual satisfaction. This positive image collapsed, however, when he was asked how he protected his employees from drunken and violent customers. The prostitute was a professional, he answered, and 'has to be able to please any client . . . Unless he is a criminal, the client is always right.' Violence generally occurred only 'on account of [the prostitute's] non-professionalism'. In other words, men only beat up prostitutes who fail to please them. As paying customers in a free market economy, they apparently have the right to express their dissatisfaction in this way (Efremov 1994: 6–7).

'Telephone sex', which has been available in Russia since 1992, is clearly a less dangerous area of the sex industry than prostitution. Again, advocates have argued that it is as satisfying for the women who provide it as for the men who buy it. An article in *SPID-info* told of a woman who was too unattractive to find sexual partners and could only masturbate by herself until she had the idea of advertising sex phone calls. Now she had three regular 'lovers' and a great aural sex life. The author concluded that telephone sex was 'not dirty, not psychotic, but above all an antidote to loneliness' for women no less than men (Nevskii 1992b: 7–8).

Sociologist A. Iu. Zotova conducted a participant observation study of 'telephone sex', working as a 'sex-telephonist' from August 1992 to January 1993 (Zotova 1994: 59–68). Her colleagues ranged in age from 19 to 50 and half were married with children. Most had taken the job because they needed the money, but several told Zotova that they also wanted to satisfy their curiosity and fulfil their own erotic fantasies. Three even hoped to find a partner from amongst their clients, despite the company's rule forbidding face-to-face contact. Many said they wanted to 'help other people'.

The service was originally advertised as 'psychological help for men', and Zotova's description of the job makes it sound like a form of social work – 70 per cent of the callers only wanted to talk about sex, but 30 per cent wanted more than this, and 14 per cent were not interested in sex talk at all. Many were lonely and depressed; some were newcomers to the city, had recently been released from prison or were suffering the loss of a loved one. The overwhelming majority, however – 90 per cent – were young businessmen so intent on moving up the corporate ladder that they had no time for real relationships. Zotova's implication is that the service performs a valuable and positive function for these people.

It turned out to have offered little to the women, however. The work was extremely hard, with twelve-hour shifts not uncommon. More than forty calls could be taken in one shift, 65 per cent of which required the simulation of sex. Most of the women were soon complaining of exhaustion and several of deteriorating health. As with prostitution, the customer was always right. It was entirely his decision what form the conversation took, and he could demand that this be changed at a moment's notice. Male administrators listened in on the conversations periodically to make sure that the women achieved a sufficiently high 'professional level'. Because of the high inflation rate, the price of a call was constantly increased, going up ten times between September and December 1992; in the same period the women's salaries were only doubled. By the time she left the company, Zotova estimates that the women were receiving only 3 per cent of the cost of each call (ibid.).

In short, what telephone sex really amounts to is not, as *SPID-info* suggests, an antidote to the problem of loneliness for both men and women. It is, like pornography and prostitution, about women providing a sexual service for men, for the financial benefit of other men. There is nothing equal about the transaction. Far from liberating women from the old confines of the Soviet state, the sex industry takes onto a new plane the submission and self-sacrifice which Soviet writers have always insisted were essential female traits.

DISCUSSIONS ON TEENAGE SEXUALITY

When the attention of commentators is turned to young people (and in particular teenagers), however, far from liberating female sexuality, the market (and its origin, the West) has been seen to have led young women astray. Viktoriia Molodtsova, deputy editor of the newspaper *Uchitel'skaia Gazeta* (*Teachers' Gazette*) has claimed (with rose-tinged nostalgia) that when the Soviet Union was a closed society governed by its own set of morals and values young people did not even have sex before marriage.[11] Now, influenced by the flood of Western films and videos which have poured into the Russian market replete with images of sex and violence, they have embraced a very different morality (Arshavskii and Vilks 1990: 57–65; Molodtsova 1994). Moreover, it seems that girls do not necessarily have sex for the purpose of sexual gratification. Psychologists Alena and Aleksandr Libin conducted a series of interviews with promiscuous girls and found that few knew what an orgasm was, let alone ever experienced one. They determined that most of the girls had a pronounced lack of self-esteem and were convinced that sex was the only thing they had to offer (Klimova 1994: 36). A similar point was made in a study on teenage sex crimes by V. L. Vasil'ev and I. I. Mamaichuk who describe how a 12–year-old girl was found to use sex in order to make friends when she moved to a new town (Vasil'ev and Mamaichuk 1993: 66).

V. Eremin has suggested that teenage boys also use sex to gain acceptance and to overcome feelings of inadequacy (Eremin 1990: 25–8). Participation in gang rape, it is suggested, is one way of gaining peer approval: five or six boys commit the act, while others encourage and applaud them. Rape can also be used to overcome feelings of inferiority, derived, perhaps, from a poor relationship with their parents, lack of progress at school or college, or low status within their gang. By taking out their frustration on a girl, they are able to transform themselves from victims into violators. Whilst Eremin sees sex as a way of achieving status and power for boys, he portrays girls (especially those in gangs) as weak and vulnerable. Such girls need the boys in their own gang to protect them from attack by other boys, but in return they have to provide 'their' boys with sexual services, being passed round from one boy to the next.[12] Despite the picture Eremin paints of rampant aggression and nihilism amongst post-perestroika youth, he seems less concerned about the kind of adults these young men will turn into than the kind of women these 'common girls' will become, and especially 'what kind of wives and mothers' they will make. The implication, once again, is that boys will be boys. Only a collapse in female morality will have disastrous consequences for society.

The general press therefore continues to suggest that sex still has very different meanings for boys and girls. While girls offer it to boys in the hope of earning their affection, boys use it for the purpose of male bonding and enhancing their own status. The sense of inadequacy Eremin refers to in relation to boys stems from personal failure while girls seem to have a more generalized sense of low value which could be said to reflect society's attitudes towards them. Not only have Soviet and post-Soviet writings consistently referred to men and women as the 'strong' and 'weak' halves of humanity, but the move to the market has enhanced male status by glorifying 'masculine' characteristics. At the same time, women find themselves in an increasingly precarious financial position. Sex has always been portrayed, however implicitly, as the means by which they can ensnare men. The old stress on 'maidenly virtue' and the importance of preserving it until marriage implied that this was all men would want from them. However much pornography and the sex industry goes against the notion of 'maidenly virtue', it could be said to reinforce the same message. In the past women were told to secure the economic support of a man by denying him access to sex until he agreed to marriage; now they can guarantee their economic independence by selling sex to men. Either way, sex is their only marketable commodity.

Publications geared towards young people portray sex in a rather different way, as something that can be equally fun for both participants. *SPID-info*, for example, puts forward an image of women as passionate beings who are capable of enjoying sex no less than their male partners. To help ensure that they do so, it includes regular features on female sexuality which explain to male readers how they can help their girlfriends reach orgasm (Podkolodnii 1992: 16–17). However, even if *SPID-info* purports to recognize that female sexual desire exists, it makes little real attempt to actually cater for it. Although it referred to an article on male strippers performing for female audiences and quoted a psychologist endorsing the fact that women were increasingly able to enjoy their own sexuality and get pleasure from looking at nude men (Belaga 1994: 11–12), the newspaper continues to carry pictures only of women's bodies, or couples arranged in such a way that the man's genitals are concealed. One is left with the impression that the idea of female passion and sexual arousal is being used, like lesbianism, for the purpose of male titillation.

CONCLUSION

This chapter began by exploring the conservative attitudes towards gender and sexuality first espoused in the Soviet era, moved on to attitudes towards homosexuality and ended with a discussion of the sex industry, teenage promiscuity, gang rape and writings on male and female sexuality in the new Russia. Despite the apparent contrast in these topics, there is a consistent strand running through the literature. Women are cast by the more conservative writers as modest, kind, and self-sacrificing; advocates of the new morality also place them in a secondary role and have them putting the interests of others above their own. It could be argued that the new sexual culture which has replaced the official puritanism of the Soviet period has not challenged but has reinforced many of the old stereotypes of masculinity and femininity.

The easing of the tight controls on people's behaviour and the greater acceptance of difference has made it possible for a gay and lesbian sub-culture to develop. However, the stress on gender difference continues, and has even been boosted in some respects by the move to the market. This makes it unlikely that gays and lesbians, who challenge many of the traditional conceptions of gender, will, at least in the near future, cease to be a marginalized minority and will come to be seen as a legitimate part of a genuinely democratic, pluralist society.

In short, if the old monolithic patterns of behaviour have to some extent unravelled in the new Russia, there is still a long way to go before people can, without hindrance, experiment with more flexible gender roles, engage in egalitarian sexual practices, and opt for alternative sexual preferences.

NOTES

1 Interviews with members of MOLLI (the Moscow Association of Lesbian Literature and Arts).
2 Personal discussion with a member of MOLLI in Moscow, November 1994.
3 Personal discussions in Moscow in November and December 1994.
4 One of the members of MOLLI noted that much of the press coverage of lesbianism has portrayed it as something immoral.
5 A derogatory slang word for gay.
6 In an article in *SPID-info* on the burgeoning striptease industry, a female stripper refers to a lesbian act she performs with a colleague for the gratification of her male audience (Belaga 1994: 11– 12).
7 One stall-holder at the Pushkin metro station continues to sell gay publications, despite repeated harassment.
8 Personal discussions with Gennadi Kremenskoi, publisher of the gay magazine *Ty* (*You*) and members of MOLLI, Moscow, November–December 1994.
9 Interview with Mila Elenovskaia of MOLLI. (This surname is a *nom de plume*.) See also Balon 1993: 4.
10 For Aleshina and Volovich's argument here see Chapter 11 of this volume.
11 Talk given by Viktoriia Nikolaevna Molodtsova, deputy editor-in-chief

of *Uchitel'skaia Gazeta*, 29 November 1994 to the 'International Club' organized by the Union of Women of Russia, attended by the author.

12 For a more detailed discussion of actual roles of girls in such gangs see Chapter 12 of this volume.

7 Love, sex and marriage: the female mirror

Value orientations of young women in Russia

Mariia Kotovskaia and Natal'ia Shalygina

The issues considered in this chapter have wide academic significance for those analysing intra-family relations. Of all the frame-
works used in the study of the contemporary family (economic,
social, ecological, etc.) the 'humanistic' one – by which is meant
that which takes into account the personal make-up of the individual
located in whatever familial structure – is acquiring increasing rele-
vance. This is understandable; as academic knowledge about the
individual deepens, so the demand increases for the application of
more differentiated concepts and categories which will be more
adequate for understanding the complex nature of the individual.

One such concept is that which will be referred to here tentatively
as 'value expectations'. The period in the life of an individual
immediately before they enter marriage and start a family is saturated with the symbolism of stereotypical images about the meaning
of this act. These stereotypes are peculiar to particular ethnic (ethno-
confessional) groups and, within this group, influenced by social
stratum, age group and sexuality. The ethno-cultural diversity of
family value expectations itself has always created a problem for
anticipating the development of intra-familial relations. The proportion of 'pure' marriages (for example, intra-elite marriages) in
developed societies is small in comparison to 'mixed' marriages
in which various value systems become intertwined, and as a result
are difficult to predict. If, in addition, the peculiar pace and nature
of the historical development of each value system is taken into
account, then the study of such a complex phenomenon as intra-
family relations appears even more fraught with difficulty.

As part of its general programme of research (into the ethnic factor in the evolution of sex-role behaviour), the Centre of Ethno-Gender Research at the Institute of Ethnology and Anthropology of the Russian Academy of Sciences (hereafter TsEGI) has sought to construct a value scale of expectations among young women in Russia at the time of the country's transitional period from totalitarianism to democracy. This current period is characterized by a new diversity of value positions hitherto untypical for Russian society, which directly influence the attitudes of young people to marriage and the family. It is highly probable that the degree of success achieved in uncovering and taking stock of the new elements in family orientations among young people will determine both public reactions to their behaviourial models and thus also the formation of future state policy on the the family.

This analysis is based on material gathered from several studies of Moscow youth (between 1992 and 1994) from which it is was possible to discern the most painful set of problems faced by young people forming their identities which, in the most direct way, impacts on their family orientations. Above all, this concerns the rapidly developing new tendencies in the consciousness of young women. 'Game tests', which formed the basis of our methodology in studying the value orientations of youth, convincingly show that gender identity is significantly less fixed among young women than young men. The girls studied (aged between 15 and 25) clearly demonstrated a tendency towards free experimentation in sex-role behaviour, in effect allowing boys only the opportunity to react. This observation, made during the course of the research, led us to seek the primary cause of changes in family orientations among youth in the value scale of girls.

The dominant innovative trait in behaviourial models of the female respondents is referred to as 'a masculinity complex'.[1] We use this concept tentatively to mean all those value motivations which logically led the girls participating in the research to choose a non-traditional behaviourial model for Russian women.

As a rule, the 'masculinity complex' is characteristic of girls with clearly 'aggressive' behaviourial strategies. Again, as a rule, such girls are relatively energetic and focused. A specially prepared psychological test used in advance of in-depth interviews showed that they are independent, active and ambitious, that they have a strong sense of competitiveness and seek leadership roles, and that they have clearly formed identities. Their personal self-characterization in the letter-essays, a complementary method employed in the research, were saturated with lexically striking expressions and impressive stylistic phrases:

I like official receptions and businesslike, well-mannered men. I adore tea roses [*chainie rozy*] and big dogs.

(Student, 18 years old)

I can handle a computer, a soldering iron, a cookery book, men and a camera ... I like sport and society gossip.

(White collar worker, 23 years old)

I am a sociable girl who makes an impression, feminine and coquettish, erudite and therefore demanding, principled and ... unpredictable.

(Student, 19 years old)

Sporty, quick on my toes, cheerful and carefree, brave and energetic.

(School pupil, 16 years old)

Independent, emancipated and difficult to predict ... I like to be the centre of attention in noisy and cheerful groups of people ... I try to change myself and all those around me.

(Freelance artist, 22 years old)

The basic postulate declared by girls of this type is the absolute prioritization of their creative self-realization in work over all other socially meaningful functions of a woman in the modern world. The ideal woman, in their opinion, is above all a working woman, moreover a woman who works with passion and total dedication:

She has an interesting job, a woman realizes herself via her profession, work brings her satistfaction, an awareness of her own significance. Colleagues and management value her. The scope of her professional activity is limited only by her inclinations, interests and desire.

(Student, 20 years old)

She has a creative nature. Life itself inspires her and then she works: she writes poems, composes music, etc.

(Telephonist, 17 years old)

She is a psychiatrist, has a private clinic, dedicating all her time to it.

(Student, 17 years old)

Today her mood is even better than usual. The joy at her own success fills her heart. She is satisfied with the day which has passed, but doubly satisfied with herself. Her most intimate wish, to which she has devoted so much energy, has come true: she was the first, the best in a beauty competition! How much interesting work lay before her!

(School pupil, 16 years old)

She definitely has something she enjoys doing. She is a science fiction writer. She writes novels, short stories, tales which are enjoyed by many. This is her main occupation for which, incidentally, she receives good money.

(School pupil, 16 years old)

She is a businesslike woman by nature, although her work may not be connected with enterpreneurship. She might be a teacher, a stewardess, an interpreter. She has just enough free time to rest but not to get bored.

(Unemployed woman, 18 years old)

Above all she is a businesslike woman. She works in a private firm, a middle-level manager. Although she might well head her own business of some kind. The most important thing is that she needs to express herself through creative work and satisfy her need for communication with other people.

(Student, 21 years old)

The great value attached by girls of this type to creative self-realization in effect subordinates all other spheres of their lives, but not unambiguously. It is the efforts expended by girls in creating their own individual image through style which are most compatible with the way of life of the businesslike woman. In contrast to Russian women of earlier generations, whose style was an unflattering severe, male-cut, grey-brown suit, hair scraped back into a bun, a set facial expression and no make-up, and an obligatory file of official documents, modern career girls attach a wholly different significance to their appearance. For them it is a means of bringing their individuality to a world of competition. Standing out brings success:

She is not necessarily beautiful, but she has charm ... she likes fashion but does not follow it blindly, preferring clothes which suit her ... She has her own favourite perfume, which is a symbol of success and a positive frame of mind for her.

(Student, 20 years old)

She carries herself like a queen. But this does not mean she is 'proud and grand' ... Any style should emphasize the dignity and independence of a woman's personality ... She may be mysterious or even risqué in appearance, but if so this should be combined with a clear demonstration of her intellectual capabilities. A woman should have a very sharp mind so that she is able to extract herself from all the uncomfortable, funny and unpleasant situations in which life might place her.

(Television journalist, 19 years old)

She considers it out of the question to shock those around her by her appearance ... The colour range and cut of her attire should 'work' in order to bring success in particular negotiations, presentations, etc ... Her dress should not overdo the 'feminine' details (this may encourage the opponent to adopt a tone of conversation which she does not want), make-up should be so light that it is virtually unnoticeable, whilst emphasizing all the good points of her appearance.

(Student, 21 years old)

It should be noted that girls of this type are not prone to using their natural feminine qualities to aid their careers. The creation of image through style is a limited part of their creative self-realization and is essentially the same kind of conscious work as the acquisition, for example, of professional skills. Coming up against the masculine mentality dominating the business world, however, forces them to seek compromises. Girls of this type on the whole demonstrate a tendency towards reinforcing their behavioural model which, in effect, means the re-evaluation of the significance of traditionally female functions in the existing system of sex-role values.

This process is in reality very complex and inevitably involves losses for both women and men. Our research showed also that the girls themselves had difficulty in recognizing the changes taking place in their consciousness. Thus, the subjects for discussion in our situational interviews (relating to domestic life) were received positively initially by our respondents. The girls responded with enthusiasm to the request to describe, for example, how they considered a woman would behave typically when she returned home from work in the evening. The description had to include the presence of a husband in her life and it was also presumed that the marriage was successful and that the married couple understood each other completely. The general picture which emerged was along these lines:

> her house does not resemble a food shop in any way. She prefers to lunch and dine in a comfortable little restaurant not far from her office. This is understandable; she does not manage to return home until late in the evening – she has so many things to do at work still! Her understanding husband, if he is not busy himself, often joins her ... Of course, she is a wonderful hostess [khoziaka] and loves to cook. Thus, when close friends are invited home, she allows herself to potter about in the kitchen rapturously and shine before the guests with the preparation of several exotic and tasty dishes.

In other words, in the ideal value positions of respondents of this type, there is virtually a programmatic masculine approach to domestic arrangements. Precisely due to this, girls do not link their expected future with that permanent function of Russian women – the daily buying and preparation of food in the family – and they do not torment themselves (as they develop the plot) with questions such as 'What will I feed my husband today?'

In general, the life-ideals of this type of girl are difficult to combine with a 'domestic life'. In the majority of answers domestic life is described very vaguely or looks so refined that it reminds one of an advertising cliché. Very characteristic in this sphere is the theme of 'home'. The vast majority of our respondents (89 per cent), in selecting their optimal living space for family life, in effect reproduce the latest (at the time of the survey) adverts from television and magazines:

> She has her own house on the Mediterranean coast, not far from Marseilles ... it has all the necessary equipment ... Despite the fact that all her free time is spent travelling to different countries, nevertheless she likes to spend the odd week at home, in domestic comfort.
>
> (Radio journalist, 22 years old)

She has her own flat in the centre of a big city, which is kept in

ideal order ... She likes to relax there sometimes with her boyfriend or husband ... But it is not in her character to be at home
constantly.

(Student, 20 years old)

Her home with all its modern equipment gives a sense of the era
in which she lives ... Her constant housemates are a cat and a
dog – two silent friends.

(School pupil, 17 years old)

Home, in the interpretation of girls of this type, is characteristi-
cally half-empty – beautiful, comfortable, but not inhabited by relatives or others close to them. Home for them is a site of personal
relaxation, and even then not for a long period. Their lives take
place primarily beyond its walls and the home thus loses its value
in itself. Domestic life as a traditional system of values in a woman's
life is not only reduced to second place, giving way to professional
career, but there is a devaluation of this system in the mentality of
young Russian women of the 'initiating type'. All this is connected
to the internal world of domestic life which to them lacks any
prospect for development.

The tough, strong woman has never been rare in Russia. However,
when society is developing in relatively stable conditions her qualities, as a rule, have been expressed within the family, manifesting
themselves in some kind of authoritarianism. The dramatic mile-
stones in Russian history (revolution, wars and grand construction
projects) often forced women of this type to the forefront of national
events. But despite this, the new roles expected of women
(temporarily) only put them on the same footing as men in the
interests of the attainment of a single, common goal. In the stabliiz-
ation which began after the ritual total cataclysm, public morality
turned its back on women's masculine potential, and returned each
sex to 'their own circles'. And the majority of women themselves
accepted this as totally natural, again becoming first and foremost
the 'protectors of the hearth' and not even seriously trying to
broaden their social horizons.

The traditional sex-role balance in Russia has persisted longer
than in many Western countries. In the opinion of Olga Voronina
(a Russian researcher studying the emergence of Russian feminism),
this was the result of the power of the totalitarian regime in the
country founded on firm patriarchal relations in all spheres of

society. And today, judging by the bitter struggle of the young Russian democracy with totalitarianism, feminist ideology, preaching in its most rational and humanistic form the principles of human community, will hardly find easy access to mass public consciousness in Russia.

Precisely because of this, in our opinion, the process of the adoption by young Russian women of a new mental paradigm will not be easy. Girls of the 'initiating type', judging by the data from our research, clearly demonstrate these difficulties and contradictions which characterize this process. Being incapable – due to their personal-psychic peculiarities – of coming to terms with the conservativeness of the traditional 'domestic life' and intuitively sensing the impossibility of breaking through this conservatism, which is less subject to renewal than any other sphere of life, girls of this type practically rule it out of their ideal system of values, trying to rationally direct their efforts to a more hopeful, from their point of view, sphere of self-realization.

These girls in the main are orientated towards achieving a prestigious position in society which, to them, means a successful professional career, material wealth and marriage to an affluent person. Their ideal hero shows leadership in all spheres of life and it is with this category of men that such girls seek relationships.

The clash between traditional female sex-role identity and a woman's conscious orientation towards professional or creative success is the basic source of conflict for this kind of woman in her relations with men. This is a conflict which takes place at a deep psychological level and is expressed in a lack of correspondence between the woman's conscious and subconscious aims. The research showed that the 'masculinity complex' which is suffered by many of these girls who challenge traditional sex-role models leads to a permanent destabilization of their own self-evaluation as women and to a sense of their own sexual inadequacy. This, in turn, as the evidence of psychologists suggests, makes housework and the care and upbringing of children particularly difficult for them. In effect, in Russian society as it is at the moment, a woman as a creative individual cannot exist simultaneously in two spheres of life – the personal and the social. Traditional feminine orientations, instilled in childhood, clash with the real situation in society, where in order to survive, the majority of women are forced to work on the same basis as men.

It should be added here that the high rate of divorce, given that children generally stay with their mothers, encourages women to direct themselves towards career success. Given the current social environment, an active, businesslike woman has significantly more chance of surviving and successfully bringing up her children. It is the harshness of the current socio-economic situation which above all determines the choice of the modern Russian woman in favour of greater and greater independence which is achieved at the cost of family harmony. This is the source of the peculiarities of Russian women which foreign researchers like to point to: authoritarianness, sharpness and hyper-control over children. As a result, values associated with the development of positive contacts with men on the domestic, familial level are often devalued.

Strictly speaking, the type of woman under discussion here is not a modern invention, but has its own history which is inextricably bound up with the historic fate of Russia itself. As is well known, pre-revolutionary Russia was a predominantly rural society, whose domestic structure was based on patriarchal relations. Men's authority in society and the family was strengthened via the system of differentiated sex-role identity, which governed all spheres of the life of the individual. The Russian patriarchal paradigm manifested itself, in a crude form, in the man (basic bread winner, representative of the family in society) and the woman (mother, defender of the hearth). The priority of her life was the internal world of the family and from this stemmed the sex-differentiated behavioural norms proscribed in rituals characteristic of any traditional culture.

However, already by the end of the nineteenth century these behavioural models gradually began to be destroyed. No small role was played in this by the phenomenon of the seasonal migration (*otkhodnichestvo*) of men in search of temporary work in cities and industrial centres. This meant that for long periods of time the real head of the family was the woman, who took on the male role. To no small extent this may be seen as the origin of the original type of independent, strong woman notorious in Russian culture.

After the 1917 revolution, but especially at the beginning of the 1930s, when the rapid switch from extensive to intensive paths of development began in Russia (expressed above all in the rapid pace of industrialization), women's labour came to be utilized as much as men's labour in all spheres of production. If one takes into account also the new gender ideology – which posited women as the basic subject of socialist construction – provoked by the sharp demographic imbalance as a result of the revolution and civil war, then it becomes clear why in the lives of Russian women work and public life became dominant. These tendencies were strengthened after the Second World War when women, generally single mothers, were obliged to simultaneously bring up their children and restore the economy destroyed by the war. The result was a female type which became characteristic for several generations of Soviet women and which is partially reproduced even today.

How do these women fare in their everyday family life? This 'masculinity complex', expressed above all in an independence in decision-taking, comes into constant conflict with traditional subordination to the husband. This tradition was reproduced in Russian cities by migrants from rural areas (generally working as *limitchiki*[2]) and hindered the development of egalitarian relations within the urban family, strengthening many patriarchal relations in the domestic sphere. The gap in value orientations between different strata of society led to conflicts in a number of spheres, not least in the sexual sphere. Such conflicts have been experienced particularly acutely by independent women striving to play an active role in sexual relations with men.

As the results of our questionnaire on the subject of 'love, sex, marriage' (conducted in December 1994) showed, these kind of women tend towards experimentation in sex. More than half of the respondents thought that some pre-marital sexual experience should be acquired by women as well as men. They also considered sexual incompatiability discovered by partners after marriage to be sufficiently important to constitute grounds for divorce. Thus, for this type of women, sex is not a side issue but has a value of its own and, on the whole, they have a democratic attitude to sexual orientations and practices. Evidence of this is revealed by responses to the survey question 'What would you think about giving homosexuals equal rights with other citizens of Russia to have their own family?'[3] The majority of girls of this type were not opposed. They substantiated their answer with the notion that, in a democratic society, people should be able to choose their own sexual preference in total freedom. Those girls characterized by an adherence to more traditional views on marriage and family relations were categorically against single-sex marriages.[4]

CONCLUSION

The democratic orientation towards marriage and the family uncovered amongst the type of young woman at the centre of the discussion here, is even more important given the continuing hidden processes of standardization of the individual in Russian society.

Society forces upon men and women alike a traditional system of sex-role behaviour manifested in a range of what are considered to be desirable qualities. Any retreat from these normative codes, strengthened in culture and in ethno-social identity, leads the individual into conflict with society on a deep psychological level of consciousness. Moreover, the reaction of the individual is determined not least by their ethno-cultural association.

The task of any society really striving towards democracy is to be able to see both men and women as individuals shaped not only by their biological sex but also by a range of socio-cultural and ethnic parameters which determine their value orientations, including those regarding family and marriage. An understanding of these differences should encourage a tolerance of the right of every such individual to be different and it is precisely this tolerance, it is argued here, which may ensure the future development of equal partnership in marriage.

NOTES

1 The research allowed the discernment of three main models of value orientation amongst young women in relation to family and marriage: 'initiating', 'sensitive', and harmonious. Only the first, and most common (being found among around 50 per cent of young women in our research), is discussed here. The second group was characteristic of about 45 per cent of those surveyed and was manifest primarily in the adherence to traditional family relations where the leadership role of men went unchallenged. The third type (around 5 per cent) of young women combined masculine and feminine qualities harmoniously and was the most successful of the types in establishing egalitarian relations with their partners.

2 Those coming from villages and small towns to the prestigious cities and working and living on the edge of the latter in the hope of being granted a resident permit.

3 One answer had to be chosen from the following:
   1 I think it is fine.
   2 Society is not ready for it.
   3 I don't care.
   4 I am against it.

4 It is worth noting here that both groups based their answers on knowledge gained from the media rather than their own or friends' experience.

8 Young people's attitudes towards sex roles and sexuality

Lynne Attwood

The first chapter in this section explored the subjects of gender, sex and sexual identity primarily from 'above'. It looked at the views of 'specialists', particularly those in the field of education, and at recent journalistic writings on apparent changes in sexual practice in the post-Soviet era. The aim of this chapter is to approach the subject from the opposite direction and consider the opinions of young people themselves.

The study was conducted in the autumn of 1994, amongst students at two teacher training institutes, the Moscow Pedagogical University (formerly the Lenin Pedagogical Institute) and the Pedagogical University of Foreign Languages in Piatigorsk, a town of some 200,000 people in the Northern Caucasus, 1,500 km from Moscow. Trainee teachers seemed a particularly appropriate focus because of the interest that education professionals have shown in the subjects of gender and sex. Much of the relevant literature has been produced by educational theorists and published in the pedagogical press, and schools have been the principal vehicle though which sex-role socialization has been conducted.[1]

The students were given a series of questions which they were asked to answer in their own time and in as much detail as possible. The study was carried out with the help of a lecturer at each of the two universities, who explained to the students the purpose of the study and passed out the written questions. The original intention had been to conduct, in addition, a series of in-depth interviews, but this proved impossible to organize in the time available. In Piatigorsk a group discussion with the students was organized during which further questions were asked, prompted by the students' written responses. This did not prove possible in Moscow, where the lecturer insisted that the students themselves had no interest in discussing the issues further. This was surprising, both because their written texts had suggested considerable interest in the subject and because the students in Piatigorsk had been very eager to follow the texts with a discussion.

Given that the majority of teachers are female, a gender imbalance in the study had been anticipated. Nevertheless, the extent of the discrepancy came as a surprise. While thirty-one Moscow students participated in the study, only four of them were male. In Piatigorsk twenty-one students took part, only five of whom were male.

The questionnaires were anonymous, the students being asked to give only their age and sex. Four students did not give their ages, but the others were all aged 19 to 21, apart from one male student in Moscow who described himself as 'over 30', and two Piatigorsk male students who were 22 and 24. In the case of the Piatigorsk students at least, military service had delayed their entry into higher education. They were not asked about their marital status, and only one (student no. 10)[2] ventured the information that she was married. Another female student had a regular boyfriend with whom she spent all her free time (35), while one male student was engaged and was already living with his fiancée (50). From the answers they gave to questions about their free-time activities, it would seem that none of the other students had steady relationships.

The students were not asked directly about their sexual behaviour or their sexual orientation. This was mainly because the project was conducted with the help of lecturers, and discussions with a number of members of the teaching profession led me to believe that the majority of students would not be happy discussing their sexuality in such a context. I was told that teachers often see themselves *in loco parentis* in relation to their students and feel compelled to notify parents of any behaviour which concerns them. Even though the students were assured that their answers were anonymous, few had access to typewriters and the numbers were sufficiently small that the lecturers concerned would have been likely to recognize their handwriting. This was confirmed by the lecturer in Piatigorsk. It was felt, then, at best, that their answers to 'intimate' questions might not be entirely truthful; they might also be incriminating.

There is, of course, no suggestion that this is a random sample. Nor is the number of students involved – fifty-two in total, only nine of whom are male – sufficiently large to allow us to make with any confidence general statements about youth attitudes. All the study claims to do is to give an indication of the attitudes of two groups of young people, one from the capital and the other from a provincial city, on gender and sexuality. However limited this aim, it is felt to be better than ignoring the voice of young people completely.

IMAGES OF THE 'FEMININE' AND THE 'MASCULINE'

The students' responses to the first question, concerning the traits they most associate with men and women, were in surprisingly close accord with the views of the 'specialists' discussed in the first chapter of this section of the book. At the top of the list of male traits was 'strength', which was mentioned by twenty-one students. Next came 'the ability to earn money and to provide for a wife and family' (nineteen students, including all but one of the boys). This was followed by 'intelligence' (fourteen), 'the role of protector' (twelve), 'courage' and/or 'bravery' (ten), and 'self-confidence' (eight). Other traits mentioned by more than one student were 'decisiveness', 'endurance', 'honesty', and 'reliability'. Five students, all female, mentioned 'kindness' as a male trait; one, however, felt that 'cruelty and arrogance' summed men up better.

At the top of the list of female traits was 'kindness' and 'beauty', mentioned by eleven students each. Others which figured prominently were 'intelligence', 'tenderness', 'maternal orientation', 'charm', 'emotionality', 'softness', 'sensitivity' and 'fragility'. Only two female students explicitly included 'weakness' in their lists, one of whom qualified this by adding: 'the ability to be weak at the same time as having inner strength' (27). 'Intelligence' was the one trait which figured prominently in both lists: while seventeen saw it as an important male trait, ten associated it with women (six of the female and one of the male students listed it as both a male and a female trait; eight female and two male students linked it exclusively with men; and two female and one male student mentioned it only in relation to women). The majority of students, male and female, saw the man as the principal breadwinner. Seven, however, all female, stressed that women should not be materially dependent on men (with one adding: 'but I'm not talking about feminism!') (4).

Most of the students echoed the view espoused so often by the pedagogical writers, that men and women had different but complementary personalities and functions. In the poetic words of one female student from Piatigorsk: 'The woman is someone light, soft, and tender like the breath of a breeze, like warm water; the man is more fundamental, a huge mighty tree with widely spread branches and many leaves' (36). Two students repeated the familiar concept that men and women are 'two halves who join together into a single, wonderful whole' (18), 'two halves of an apple' (11).

The different male and female roles in relation to the family were stressed repeatedly. A typical statement reads as follows: 'The man is the protector and breadwinner, while the woman is responsible for tending the family hearth and reproducing the human race' (15). However, a number of students thought that the distribution of functions was not entirely harmonious. Five, all female and all from Moscow, thought the female lot was harder because of the double burden of work and family obligations. As one put it: 'On the whole, men go to work and spend their free days sitting at home, while women work the whole week long and spend their free days going to the shops'(12). Another argued that 'three shifts in one day has become the usual regime of the woman'; these were paid work, domestic work, and 'remain[ing] a woman, with all the concerns about personal appearance which stem from this' (18). On the other hand, two students, one male and one female, both from Moscow, suggested that men had the heaviest burden, since the task of earning money fell more heavily on them. 'They really need to earn more than they are able', wrote the female student (5). 'A man is, unfortunately, primarily there to provide money', wrote the male student (30).

Two of the female students, both from Moscow, challenged the notion that the differences in male and female personality and behaviour were innate and inevitable, and refused to assign separate traits to men and women. One explained that: 'Everyone is first and foremost a person and an individual' (9), while the other said that: 'Being a feminist (a moderate one), I consider that the only differences which exist between men and women are connected with biological sex.' The principal biological difference, in her view, was that man's sexual needs were greater than those of the woman (10).

Asked what they considered the most important things in life for the majority of men and women, the general consensus was that for women it was the home and family, while for men it was work, career or, in three cases, 'social position'. A typical statement runs as follows:

on account of their biological peculiarities, man and woman have different functions. The woman must give birth to and bring up children, and the man helps her in every way possible by creating the best possible conditions for her. Therefore for the man it is important to be strong, faithful, honest, and the woman must be patient, caressing, and have great endurance.

(43)

One student suggested that work was also important for women, but 'most of all to earn money' (25). Another posited that 'any woman can freely choose between career and family', but added that, 'Of course it is more difficult for a woman to be self-affirming; even I (a future woman) imagine I will have a man in the role of teacher' (32).

Fifteen students, all of them female, thought that there had been some erosion in the difference between male and female functions. Some saw this as a positive development, allowing for greater personal choice. To give two examples:

We choose what is most important in our lives for ourselves, regardless of sex. For some it is work, for others the family, for a third group it is free time activities.

(21)

In contemporary society [what is most important] depends above all on the psychology of the individual. People who live in cities now occupy professional positions which would earlier have been filled only by either men or women, and have taken on the traits of the opposite sex ... In our country both sexes are sufficiently emancipated, and women can take on high posts, and men can look after the home. This is their business, their choice.

(26)

Others students expressed concern about these changes, however. One Piatigorsk student was cautiously positive about the fact that 'some of the stereotypes are changing, and men and women are able to take from life what they want', but warned that:

the main thing is not to take emancipation and feminism too far. Men and women must remain men and women. The woman must not forget that her destiny is, above all, motherhood. For the man it is being strong, being the protector.

(33)

The Piatigorsk students tended to adhere to a more idealized image of differentiated gender roles than the Moscow students. Several of the female students in Moscow expressed reservations about the traditional masculine/feminine divide, and about men's willingness and ability to pull their weight in the division of responsibilities. As we have seen, five of them considered women's lives harder than those of men. A further two expressed downright cynicism about men:

> Apart from my father I have never seen any real men (other than on cinema screens). . . . Men tend to live for themselves nowadays, whereas the majority of women live for their families.
>
> (23)

> In our country men are weak, dependent, petty-minded, inclined towards passivity. They do not respect women . . . The contemporary Russian woman is the supporter of the man and even has to protect him, he is so helpless.
>
> (16)

The male students adhered without exception to a strict, traditional gender divide. Comments include:

> A man must take care of his sweetheart and a woman must back up his deeds.
>
> (50)

> 'Man' is the foundation of the whole family, of prosperity, of the state; he is the 'purse' and the protector of the family. The woman should work only half the day and the rest of the time take care of the children, husband and home.
>
> (28)

> Man is the hunter, protector, provider. Woman is his companion in life, the keeper of the home.
>
> (31)

> Man is the emotional and physical force [in society and family]. One of the most important things for a woman is to feel that someone is taking care of her. In adult life a man will bring in the money, work a lot to support his family, while a woman will do all the housework, bring up the children, cook the food, do the shopping and so on. Maybe she will also work.
>
> (48)

The pride in manhood which comes across in these comments reaches its apotheosis in the response of one male Piatigorsk student. He begins by stating that men and women need each other, and then continues:

> some might say that lesbians can perfectly well do without men, but this is only a relative truth. Society would not have been able to progress so far without male genius. Women are capable of education, but not of the higher mental activity required by the more advanced sciences and certain forms of artistic production. They are ideally suited for the role of nurses and teachers of small children because they themselves are childish and frivolous ... The courage of a man is shown in commanding, of a woman in obeying. For men, the important traits are: courage, bravery, common sense, patience, quick wit, an ability to work hard and earn enough not to live from hand to mouth, understanding, loyalty and readiness to help. For woman, they are beauty and kindness, common sense, love of children, charity, fidelity, correctness, consideration towards other people, neatness, no smoking or heavy drinking, and no use of obscenities. One of the worst developments in present-day life is women's increasing independence.
>
> (52)

The male students who took part in this study are, as we have noted, a small minority of young men training for a profession generally seen as female, in the midst of an overwhelmingly female student body. The aggressive tone of this student's words could, perhaps, be a defensive response to a feeling of discomfort at being associated with 'women's work'. In the course of his paper he made it clear that he did not intend to enter teaching but was studying English in order to find work abroad. (This has to be good news for female pupils, who would presumably receive little encouragement from such a teacher in the development of their intellectual abilities!) However, his words are a clear reflection of the literature on gender which is discussed in the first chapter in this section and which in many ways constitutes a glorification of manhood.

IMAGES OF THE FUTURE

Asked what they expected to be doing in ten years' time, fifteen of the students chose not to answer, or made vague comments about hoping they would be happy.[3] Several explained that they had not thought about the future as yet. Given the changes Russia is undergoing and the resultant uncertainty about the coming years, such a response is hardly surprising. Thirty-six students in total, twenty-nine female and seven male, did attempt to predict the future, and there was no obvious difference here in the responses of the Moscow and the Piatigorsk students. Twenty-one of the girls thought that their lives would consist of a combination of family and work. Twelve placed the family in the primary position, explaining, for example, that:

> I will have a family, and I hope I can divide my time between bringing up the child or children and taking care of my husband and home. But at the same time I would like to work for the first half of the day.
>
> (39)

> I would like to have work I enjoy, but in a choice between family and career I would choose family.
>
> (43)

Five female students did not mention work at all, and talked only of the families they hoped to have. Nine, on the other hand, saw work as equally or, in some cases, more important than family.

> I will have a job that I love, and will spend free days with my husband and children.
>
> (5)

> I will have a good job and a family (husband and one child).
>
> (40)

> I imagine myself as a first rate specialist. If we have a child, it will have a nanny.
>
> (35)

Three did not mention family at all, and described their adult lives only in terms of work:

> I will be working in a school.
>
> (41)

> My life will be much the same as now, only with work instead of college.
>
> (23)

> I'll probably have a new circle of friends, and will be working.
>
> (25)

Of the seven male students who answered the question (two from Moscow, five from Piatigorsk), three mentioned both work and family, though placed work in the primary position:

> I'll work a lot, which means I won't have enough time to spend with my family during the week.
>
> (48)

> I will have a well-paid job as an interpreter or will be working in some firm. I will have a family, two children, a boy and girl.
>
> (50)

The remaining four mentioned only work, making comments such as:

> I'll be earning a lot of money.
>
> (49)

> I'll work hard, and relax by walking in the countryside.
>
> (51)

> I want to be living abroad: Italy, Canada, America, Australia or New Zealand.
>
> (52)

> My material situation will be better, so I'll have more possibilities and ways of spending my time.
>
> (28)

For the students involved in this study, then, the family would seem to remain primarily a female concern, although not one which all of the female students felt they were obliged to take on.

SOURCES OF SEX-ROLE STEREOTYPES AND INFORMATION ON SEX

Asked which magazines, newspapers and books they read, the majority of respondents claimed that they had no time to read anything unconnected with their courses. If they did find any spare time, ten favoured the Russian classics, eleven relaxed with a detective novel and six preferred science fiction. Six of the female students enjoyed the romantic fiction now flooding the kiosks (Mills and Boons and others of the same ilk translated into Russian).

Of the students who regularly read newspapers or periodicals, eleven read *Moskovskii Komsomolets*, and at least seven read *SPID-info*.[4] Despite the fact that these were trainee teachers, none made any reference to the pedagogical periodicals aimed at the teaching profession such as *Vospitanie Shkol'nikov* and *Sem'ia i Shkola*, which have been at the forefront of the campaign to resurrect masculinity and femininity.

Asked about their free-time activities, most of the students claimed to be working so hard at college that they had little time for leisure. Three had partners with whom they spent what free time they had – one of these was married (10), another was engaged and living with his fiancée (50) and the third was in a committed, long-term relationship (35). None had any children. Five (four female, one male) said they divided their free time between friends and parents. Two held down part-time jobs: one female student in Moscow worked at a children's hospital (27) while a male student in Piatigorsk worked for a firm improving home security by fitting locks and reinforced doors (52). One male student claimed to spend all of his free time having sex (31).

Asked where they had got their information about sex, most students referred to friends, publications such as *SPID-info* and feature films. Only two students said they had been given any information at school, and only eleven said their parents had been of any use. Seven said they had worked things out as they went along. One female student, a 21-year-old from Moscow, said she still knew 'almost nothing about sex, since this subject does not interest me yet' (23).

Information about AIDS came from much the same sources. The newspaper *SPID-info* and the American feature film *Philadelphia* were said to have been particularly useful, but several stressed that there was now no shortage of information available. Accordingly, most claimed to have a clear understanding of the illness, with only one admitting she knew very little about it (1). Curiously, when they summarized what they did know about AIDS, they invariably placed as much stress on transmission through non-sexual as through sexual means. This might be a specifically Russian response reflecting the much-publicized infections of children through the re-use of contaminated syringes in hospitals. This concern about non-sexual transmission also accounts for the otherwise surprising responses to the question about what influence AIDS had had on their own behaviour. One student wrote: 'I have become very sceptical in my attitude towards our medical authorities' (24). Another said that she was determined to avoid surgery of any kind from now on (12). Three said that they would insist that disposable syringes were used if they needed medical treatment, or would take their own (23, 25, 26). One would no longer have her hands manicured at the local hairdressers (38) and another had given up drinking water from automatic drinks machines (which do not use disposable cups in Russia), even though she knew it was supposed to be impossible to get infected in this way (5). A female student in Moscow summed up the mood:

> Now everyone, it seems to me, has become more cautious. In hospitals and clinics everyone demands disposable syringes, and rarely gets shaved or has a manicure or pedicure in a beauty salon.
> (25)

In contrast, few students mentioned any change in their sexual behaviour. Indeed, twenty-three (thirteen from Moscow, ten from Piatigorsk) stated explicitly that AIDS had not resulted in any such change. Seven of these, all female, implied that this was not necessary since they were not yet sexually active. Two, also female, said that neither they nor their friends (and, presumably, their sexual partners) were in 'high-risk' groups since they neither used drugs nor had 'immoral sex' (25, 46). One said she had only one sexual partner whom she trusted implicitly (12), while another was married and said that her husband shared her belief that fidelity was essential (26). One student pointed out that her sexual behaviour had not actually changed on account of AIDS because she had always had to take AIDS into consideration:

> like the rest of my generation, I have been brought up with this subject and know practically all there is to know about it. Therefore my behaviour has been formed in connection with this knowledge.
> (4)

Another student acknowledged a feeling of danger, but said that it was not a trait of her character to allow this to affect her behaviour (18).

Eight female students did think that AIDS had had an influence on their behaviour. Four said that they would not now consider being promiscuous while four others talked of the need to take precautions, especially in relation to 'chance sexual liaisons'. One of these said she had never had penetrative sex without protection (11), while another wrote:

> one must not forget about preventative measures, and then everything will be okay.
>
> (15)

A third summed up the situation in one word: 'condoms' (19). All but one of the male students indicated that they used condoms and/or were cautious about sexual contacts. Responses were along the lines of:

> I act sensibly (if this is what you mean).
>
> (29)

> Yes – I use condoms.
>
> (30)

> I'm afraid to have casual sexual relations, especially with someone I don't know.
>
> (48)

> I think that every person should lead a normal sexual life: they should not have casual sex and, of course, men must use condoms.
>
> (50)

One, however, was less responsible; although he did say that he had begun to think more about the risk of AIDS, he admitted that as yet it had not had any impact on his behaviour (28).

Only one student mentioned any link between AIDS and homosexuality, writing that: 'AIDS is a virus transmitted through sexual intercourse and by homosexuals' (52). The fact that the other students did not mention homosexuality in this context might be explained by the fact that the newspaper *SPID-info* is one of their main sources of information on AIDS and, as noted in the first chapter of Part II, it pays scant attention to the fact that gay men are at particular risk from AIDS. Alternatively, they may all consider themselves heterosexual (this is, at least, implied by their responses to the questions), and so have decided independently that homosexuality is simply not an issue which concerns them.

VIEWS ON SEXUALITY

The final question asked specifically about attitudes towards homosexuality. Given the lack of awareness about homosexuality in relation to the previous question, the students' responses were surprisingly sympathetic. There was no noticeable difference between the attitudes of students in Moscow and Piatigorsk. In total, twenty-eight students – twenty-five female, three male – thought homosexuality was neither an illness nor a crime, but a perfectly acceptable way of life. Some went further and urged greater tolerance towards homosexuals. A selection of these responses reads as follows:

> Society must show tolerance and an understanding attitude towards homosexuals; they are normal people, no less valuable than others.
>
> (6)

> I have a calm attitude towards homosexuality. People have the right to live as they want. But society often seems to concern itself with problems which I do not consider to be the most important. We often hold in contempt or fear those things about which we have little information, or which do not fit into our existing moral framework.
>
> (11)

> Homosexuality is not an illness! It goes without saying that it is an acceptable way of life. I see no moral problem for society.
>
> (4)

> Homosexuality exists and will never disappear.... It comes from nature, and it is impossible to blame a person for something which he cannot help. For me such a way of life would be unacceptable, but I do not judge and throw stones at those who will clearly have to spend their whole lives fearing social hostility.
>
> (15)

> Homosexuality has always existed, so I cannot understand the unhealthy interest in this type of relationship. For me it is in no way a crime, nor is it behaviour which has no right to exist, and it is certainly not an illness, although many sexpathologists connect the growth in homosexuality to the increased attention given to the problem. It is possible that this is true, and that for some

people it is a fashion rather than an essential and vital philosophy of relations with someone of the same sex. I hope that with the discontinuation of persecution and changing views on things, homosexuality will cease to be a cause of social discord.

(25)

I have a calm reaction towards homosexuality. There is no need for aggression either on the part of homosexuals or 'naturals'. These are simply attitudes which stem from the violation of the biological norm: the continuation of the human race. However, from the psychological point of view, it is enough that people feel comfortable with each other. It is an acceptable way of life. It is only a problem for society if there is any type of oppression or aggression.

(26)

It is not an illness, nor a crime. It is an acceptable way of life, although it is better not to be like this. It is a problem for society in so far as people have been brought up from the earliest age with a single understanding of interpersonal relations between men and women, and have an inadequate understanding of sexual activity.

(19)

Why not, if it is consensual and is not attended by violence... Everyone has the right to his self-expression: the main thing is not to do harm to other people.

(38)

Not all students were so tolerant, however. Eleven described homosexuality as an illness, four as a moral problem, and three as both an illness and a moral problem. All the same, even amongst these students, eight reasoned that homosexuals could not help the way they were, and so it was pointless to persecute them. In the words of one of them:

Homosexuality is an illness and a moral problem for society, since it is, after all, a violation of human nature. But I still consider that people should be able to live as they want.

(14)

Two students were still struggling to sort out their feelings.

I don't know. Perhaps it is an illness, since I cannot imagine sexual intimacy of any type other than between men and women. I have a negative attitude towards homosexuality, but perhaps this is just a way of life for people who are not like me and my friends.

(23)

I find it hard to understand. I do not in any way judge, but all the same it does not seem to me to be normal. I do not think it is an illness; perhaps it is determined by a person's chromosomal and genetic composition. It is not a crime; these people do not disturb or harm anyone else. Perhaps it is easier to live like that; you can be together with someone of your own sex, someone like you, who behaves in a similar way. This does not create a problem for society, but it is a threat to the institution of the family.

(21)

There were, however, two students, one female and one male, who were extremely hostile.

Homosexuality is a crime, first of all against God, then against your own body. Homosexuals are perverts. Of course it is a moral problem for society. We must get rid of such things. I think it's a kind of mental illness, such people have something wrong with their psyche.

(46)

I consider this to be a serious illness, and if it is not possible to cure them, they should be isolated from society.

(28)

The male students were proportionately less tolerant than the female students, though so few male students took part in the study that no real generalizations can be made. A total of eight male students answered the question, three of whom described homosexuality as an illness. One wrote:

If I am honest, deep down I hate homosexuals and those who propagandise that way of life. But I would not do anything to interfere.

(52)

Two others expressed indifference, but this was tinged with a faint hostility. For example:

I have no opinion on this at all. It is their problem.

(30)

Three expressed sympathy and tolerance.

On the whole, given the attitudes expressed by the 'specialists' in the literature looked at in the first chapter in this section, the students' attitudes towards homosexuality were more tolerant than might have been expected. However, they are people in higher education, who one might expect to take a more reasoned view. It would be interesting to compare their views with those of a cross-section of the population. The discussion on homosexuality and lesbianism in the first chapter makes it clear that members of the gay and lesbian community are still a long way from being accepted as full, legitimate members of a pluralistic society.

DIALOGUE AND CHANGE

In Piatigorsk I was able to have a personal meeting with thirty students – twenty-two female and eight male – after reading their written responses to my questions.

I started by asking the students about the traits they had assigned to men and woman, and whether they thought these were derived from nature or determined by social conditioning. At first they said unanimously that they were derived from nature, but when we began to talk about the ways in which children learn appropriate behaviour in childhood, one boy recalled that his father had always told him not to cry because this was not something boys did. A female student then said that when she was small most of her friends were boys and she had enjoyed rough and tumble activities, but her mother had not liked this and had continually told her off for not being ladylike. I asked about the *Trud* (labour) class at school, and they responded with laughter. It turned out that in all of the schools they had been to, girls and boys had been divided into separate groups for this class. The boys had been taught carpentry, how to drive, how electricity works, and so on, while the girls learned how to cook and sew.

I asked if they thought equality between the sexes had ever been achieved in the Soviet Union. All of them said it had been. I asked what equality actually meant, and they explained that women were able to do the same work as men and get the same pay for it. I then asked what happened when they came home from work; if the husband and wife did the same job outside the home but the woman did all the shopping, cooking and child-care, was that equality? They agreed it was not. One male student said that men now did a lot of housework and child-care, but was met with cynical laughter. Six of the eight male students said they were able to cook, but one explained that this was because they lived in a student hostel and had no option.

I asked the students to compare the relationships they had had with both of their parents. At first the general consensus was that there had been little difference between them. However, after considering the question for a while, most agreed that they had spent far less time with their fathers than their mothers because their fathers had been so involved in their work. In all but four cases their mothers had also worked, but the students said that work had not been the main thing in their mothers' lives. One female student said that she had always felt that her mother was there for her, but this was far from the case with her father. One male student said that now he thought about it he realised he hardly knew his father, and that he would like a closer relationship with his own children. Five of the eight boys agreed that they would like to be closer to their own children than they had been with their fathers. Asked how they would achieve this, they said that they would spend more time with them, go for walks with them, try to develop a deeper emotional relationship.

Several of the students had written that women must have children, that this was an essential aspect of being a woman. I asked what they meant by this. Most said it was simply natural for women to have children. One female student said that children gave meaning to a woman's life. Another said that she wanted to leave something behind her in the world. All of them saw children as more central to a woman's life than to a man's. None, however, accepted that it was a woman's social duty to have children.

With one exception, a female student who was not yet sure, all of the students wanted a child or children of their own. Asked if they had any preference about the sex of the child, fifteen (a mixture of boys and girls) said they would rather have a boy, seven (six girls and one boy) said they wanted a girl and the remainder (eight students) had no preference.

I reminded them that many had listed 'financial support of the family' as an important male attribute, but the statistics showed that more than a third of marriages ended in divorce. If men were the family's main financial support, did this not put women in a very vulnerable position? The female students agreed that this was something they should consider and most said they would like to ensure that they were financially independent. This did not mean that they would have to earn as much as their husbands, but they should have enough to survive on if the marriage broke up. However, one said facetiously that if her marriage broke up she would simply find another man to support her. The male students all insisted that they would be exemplary fathers and continue to provide for their children after a divorce.

What emerged from this study, therefore, is that these two groups of young people retain a high level of acceptance of traditional ideas on gender traits and behaviour, and continue to see male and female differences as 'natural'. When asked to think about specific points more closely, however, many of them did begin to reconsider certain of their views, although some essentialist ideas about male and female difference remained unshakeable. This was particularly the case concerning the differential importance of children for men and women. Although most of the male students in Piatigorsk said they wanted to be more involved in their children's lives than their fathers had been, the consensus still appears to be that children are primarily a female concern, and that for men the main thing is to earn money.

The old Soviet notion that women's equality means nothing more than participation in the work-force is generally accepted by these students, though the Piatigorsk students, when prompted, did acknowledge that women were perhaps not really equal if they had to do all the work at home in addition to their paid work.

Asked about their attitudes towards homosexuality, most students showed a relatively high degree of tolerance. All the same, when explaining their views on gender difference and the family they remained unwaveringly heterosexist. The assumption was that 'normal' people were heterosexual, lived in couples and had children. Unless specifically asked to do so, they did not consider the possibility that homosexual relations could be seen as an acceptable alternative way of life. Homosexuals remained for them 'other', not a legitimate part of a pluralist society. Even for those who did not consider homosexuality a crime or an illness, it was still an abnormality. It could be argued that it will continue to be seen as such until a less rigid understanding of male and female roles becomes widespread.

The meeting with the Piatigorsk students revealed, however, that the students were willing to rethink their views when presented with new ideas. The development of an increasingly diverse media means that access to a greater variety of views is increasing, while feminist literature has also begun to appear in Russia, though in small print runs and confined largely to specialist libraries. If exposure to alternative viewpoints and lifestyles continues to improve, we might expect rather different responses to the questions posed in this study from the next generation of young adults.

APPENDIX 1

Table 8.1 Information about respondents

Number	Sex	Age	Place of study	Number	Sex	Age	Place of study
1	F	N/K	MPU	27	F	21	MPU
2	F	N/K	MPU	28	M	20	MPU
3	F	19	MPU	29	M	20	MPU
4	F	19	MPU	30	M	20	MPU
5	F	19	MPU	31	M	30+	MPU
6	F	19	MPU	32	F	N/K	PPU
7	F	19	MPU	33	F	N/K	PPU
8	F	20	MPU	34	F	19	PPU
9	F	20	MPU	35	F	19	PPU
10	F	20	MPU	36	F	19	PPU
11	F	20	MPU	37	F	19	PPU
12	F	20	MPU	38	F	19	PPU
13	F	20	MPU	39	F	19	PPU
14	F	20	MPU	40	F	19	PPU
15	F	20	MPU	41	F	19	PPU
16	F	20	MPU	42	F	19	PPU
17	F	20	MPU	43	F	19	PPU
18	F	20	MPU	44	F	19	PPU
19	F	20	MPU	45	F	20	PPU
20	F	21	MPU	46	F	20	PPU
21	F	21	MPU	47	F	20	PPU
22	F	21	MPU	48	M	19	PPU
23	F	21	MPU	49	M	19	PPU
24	F	21	MPU	50	M	19	PPU
25	F	21	MPU	51	M	22	PPU
26	F	21	MPU	52	M	24	PPU

Key
MPU – Moscow Pedagogical University
PPU – Piatigorsk Pedagogical University
N/K – Not known

NOTES

1 It should be acknowledged that teachers' pay and conditions are such that many trainee teachers will choose not to go into the profession after graduation if they can use the skills they have acquired to find more lucrative work. Since the students who took part in this study were all training to be language teachers – Spanish in the case of the Moscow

students, English in the case of the Piatigorsk students – at least some are likely to try to get better paid work as translators, interpreters, tour guides, etc.

2 Hereafter students will be referred to by number only. A full list of respondents is included as the Appendix to this chapter.

3 This confirms the reluctance to answer questions about future profession and family status noted among school-leavers by Elena Dmitrieva in Chapter 5 of this volume.

4 The uncertainty is due to the fact that several students who did not list it amongst their reading preferences later said they had got much of their information about AIDS from this source.

9 Beliefs about reproductive health
Young Russian women talking

Anne Murcott and Annie Feltham

INTRODUCTION

At first sight, beliefs about women's health in Russia hinted at a distinctive picture. To keep well, a young woman advised:

> pour cold water on yourself every day, on the street, standing with bare feet on the ground ... [You] ask nature to give you good health and you pour[ed] cold water over yourself every day.

Changes in the weather, explained the acupuncturist employed at a modern health clinic, cause menstrual irregularities. 'My friend has had two abortions', said another young woman, as if recounting just another ordinary fact of life; 'she is now seventeen ... and she got over it easily.'

Though beliefs such as these might distinguish Russia from other industrialized societies, this chapter presents material to suggest they are consistent with a great many others found elsewhere. Young Russian women's judgements of their general health, the measures described for taking care of themselves and their views about managing their sexual health bear strong similarities to those reported in the English language literature for the 'West' – similarities that outweigh the differences conjured by the instances cited above.

Before moving on to discuss those similarities, this introductory section sets out the background to the study of young women's reproductive health beliefs on which this chapter is based.[1] The body of the chapter then divides into two sections, covering young women's beliefs about health in general and about reproductive health in particular. It concludes with a brief report of women's aspirations for their future and prevailing images of gender in contemporary Russia.

The broad context of the study centres on the high rate of induced abortions officially reported for Russia. The abortion rate is such that some commentators regard it as probably the highest world-wide, pointing to estimates that annually at least one in ten women of reproductive age has an abortion (Popov, Visser and Ketting 1993), with approximately two abortions to every live birth. Policy discussions are currently geared to exploring options for shifting the balance away from abortion and towards the prevention of unwanted pregnancy.

Against this broad background of policy concern, a number of further considerations informed the study. To begin with, it is well established that beliefs and behaviour about, knowledge of, and priorities for health commonly do not correspond with prevailing medical advice about self- and home-care, the prevention of disease and the promotion of health. On this basis, it is argued that policies devoted to providing health services and to improving the public health generally are likely to be less successful if they fail to take account of people's beliefs about their own health, however much those beliefs are at odds with professional advice (cf., Stimson 1974). Put another way, approaches to policies and the provision of services need to be 'bottom-up' as well as 'top-down'. If this is the case for health policies generally, then it is especially so in the sexual and reproductive health arena, given its potential delicacy and sensitivity on so many different fronts.

The investigation of lay health beliefs, including those concerned with sexual and reproductive health, has been well established in the English language literature for three decades and more (e.g. Davison, Davey-Smith & Frankel 1991; d'Houtaud and Field 1987; Wellings, Field and Whitaker 1994; Stoltzman 1986; Williams 1983; Zborowski, 1952; Zola, 1973).

Although a good proportion of this research relies on quantitative methods, there is a strong commitment to the value of qualitative methods, especially ethnographic interviewing, derived from social anthropology and sociology as particularly suitable for uncovering the nuances and complexities of beliefs about health and illness.

Since work of this kind was, as far as is known, wholly absent for Russia, the study from which the material presented here is drawn was designed as a small-scale feasibility project. One of its feasibility elements[2] turned on the scope for adopting qualitative research methods, other than long-term participant observation, in the con-temporary Russian context. On the face of it, data collected amongst a general population less familiar with researchers seeking indi-viduals' own opinions obviously may differ markedly from those collected amongst people accustomed to the practice. In any case, there are good reasons to suppose that those with some kind of position of responsibility, including researchers, may not be trusted. In the event, though there was virtually no opportunity to explore the matter thoroughly, this supposition was tentatively supported in one instance during the fieldwork. A young woman explained that she knew of the contraceptive pill, but was wary of side-effects, even though she had heard a radio programme reassuring listeners that these were minimal. She doubted the programme's truthfulness. Commenting on her disbelief, a health-worker observed:

> People have a lot of doubts. For so many years people were deceived. And they have been deceived up to the present day, so there will be no real confidence.

Moreover, in a social context in which power was controlled within a centralized and strongly hierarchical political system, individuals as a whole and young people in particular, were likely to be unused to having their views canvassed. At the same time, a possible – and, for many, a desirable – consequence of talking directly with young women further constrained by a youth culture which is strongly gendered, is to empower them by demonstrating that they can have a voice on matters that concern them.

The study itself was carried out in September 1993, in St Petersburg and Samara, responding in each city to health authority and health professional staff who expressed a desire for support in developing policies and services for women's health, and who, in turn, facilitated research access.[3]

Augmented by opportunistic observation and interviewing with health-workers (midwives, gynaecologists, etc.) and staff of women's centres, a total of thirty-five unstructured, ethnographic audio-taped interviews of approximately half an hour each, were conducted with sixty-three women, singly and in groups.[4] Approximately half the women were interviewed when they attended a health facility, largely but not exclusively as out-patients, such as a family planning clinic, drop-in women's health centre or a specially dedicated young person's health clinic. The remainder (in almost equal numbers) were either pupils interviewed at their schools or students and others post-school, who were interviewed at times and places of mutual convenience. The majority were aged between 16 and 22, with all the school pupils aged between 14 and 16, as were eleven of those attending a health facility.

By way of rounding off this introduction, three comments on the status of the material to be presented must be made. What follows is derived from only part of the data collected in the interviews with the young women, and it is presented as a composite account.[5] Thus, as is the intention in this style of work, it is the range and variety of phenomena that is displayed. Second, it should be noted that documentation of health beliefs cannot be treated as report of actual behaviour. Moreover, any assumption that beliefs and attitudes might predict behaviour must be treated with circumspection. Last, given that the project was set up as a feasibility study, overall, the material presented represents what in other circumstances would be a well-developed but still preliminary research statement to be used as a basis for more extensive and detailed investigation.

HEALTH IN GENERAL, REPRODUCTIVE HEALTH IN PARTICULAR

Divided into two parts, this section begins with women talking about various aspects of health – what it means, the remedies they use if unwell – both for themselves and for women generally. The second part concentrates on their views of reproductive health.

General health

Most of the women did not consider themselves healthy. They volunteered different types of account. The first invokes beliefs that poor health could be explained by factors peculiar to events overtaking a particular individual, e.g., aching legs and bronchitis believed to be caused by 'deposits of salt' or lingering damage held to result from sports injuries. A second type relies on explanations that are more general and are external to individuals. Some women talked, for instance, of the adverse effects of the weather and of changes of temperature between, for example, school (where the heating was powerful) and home (where 'there's hardly any heating').[6] Others referred to having poor food or not eating properly, to air pollution in the centre of the city, to what was considered an incorrect lifestyle or stress induced by work and study. A third set of beliefs attributed poor health to a person's inherited constitution leading to a generalized vulnerability, an inborn condition that meant having 'quite weak health by nature'.

Even for those who did think of themselves as healthy, the idea of health was neither agreed nor unitary. Thus, though describing themselves as healthy, they conveyed an image of health as a state from which departures may from time to time occur – e.g. I'm "generally" a healthy person; 'as a rule I'm healthy'.[7] Similarly, not being healthy was seen as something people could grow out of:

> before the age of 5 I had some problems with my health like, I think, all children

or was akin to 'growing pains':

> I . . . get heart problems . . . but now it doesn't hurt at all. . . . the reason why? I just don't know. They say that it is just a transitional age, that your body is growing and it's because of that.

Such variants on the notion of health accord readily with those reported among women (e.g. Pill and Stott 1982, Blaxter 1983, Pill and Stott 1985) and both men and women (Pollock 1988, Blaxter 1990) in the UK and elsewhere (e.g. Punamäki and Kokko 1995).[8] In other ways, however, the images of health presented included hints that could possibly be peculiar to contemporary Russia:

> I think it's generally very difficult to be healthy . . . just at the moment . . . our life is quite difficult.

> I think that now everything's unhealthy – the weather, food products, everything is poisoned now, everything is poisoned, literally. So that means that everybody, if you take anybody, they'd not be able to say that they were completely healthy and I don't think that I'm going to get ill, and that I'll (just die) from old age.

And one woman went so far as to declare that:

> Though you don't feel any physical pain . . . there are probably no healthy people now.

These assessments could either/both imply a generalized, society-wide explanation for individual poor health – uncertain times cause uncertain health – or stand as a metaphor – uncertain health and uncertain times represent one another. Very recently, however, work reporting beliefs about health among British adolescents (both males and females) provides striking parallels. In addition to a similar tendency to define health as the absence of disease and to emphasize aspects of lifestyles (including poor diet), environmental problems such as pollution and traffic also figured prominently (Brannen *et al.* 1994). Though the British study's design and methods make exact comparison impossible, it is further noteworthy that among the items young Britons reported as among the three most worrying things about the future, unemployment, destruction of the environment and nuclear war were most frequently listed after the death of themselves or of a close relative. Evidence such as this, then, serves as an important 'corrective' to interpretations treating the Russian data as distinctive in time and place.

As to their general health, women talked about taking care of it from two angles: measures taken when unwell and those pursued in order to stay healthy. The former included considering seeking a medical consultation[9] and self-medication, using either commercially available or home-prepared remedies.[10] As is commonly found worldwide, by and large these appeared not to be mutually exclusive alternatives. Instead, either or both were adopted depending on an individual's own assessment of the circumstances. As one woman in Samara observed 'everyone has their own ways'.

Of particular interest are the measures believed to protect, sustain or promote health. Though various types of measure were mentioned, the data provide clear evidence of a general belief that, in principle, it was within an individual's capacity to take some steps to maintain good health. Thus, a suitable diet, refraining from smoking, consuming only a little alcohol, taking regular exercise but also assuring adequate rest, were all readily mentioned.[11] Taking a holiday out of the city at least once a year, visiting a health resort, trips to the forest, the benefits of fresh air and the use of herbal infusions – described as a traditional Russian method of preserving health – were also believed to be important to maintain good health. And significant emphasis was laid on sport for people of all ages, though it was also noted that work left insufficient time to participate.

Once in each city pouring cold water over oneself was described as a means of avoiding ill health. A psychology student in St Petersburg thought of herself as naturally having weak health and combined the cold water treatment with a weekly, twenty-four hour fast. The technique was evidently familiar to a group of five 16–25 year olds in Samara, one of whom volunteered the fuller description already quoted at the beginning of the chapter: a special system devised by Porfirii Ivanov to toughen yourself, bare feet on the ground even in the snow. The method has twelve guiding principles to follow, rules 'like those in the Bible, you were not to steal, nor wish evil on your nearest and dearest, those sorts of things'. Since, however, they were agreed that it was too demanding, it is unlikely any of these women followed the method themselves.

Other measures were described, with some anxiety, over which a single individual had little control. Along with the need for fresh air – and passing reference to high levels of air pollution in the city – clean water was also noted as important to preserve good health. For instance, a group of women in Samara[12] were concerned about the quality of the water supply. They explained that the water was heavily chlorinated and they were especially worried by a recent incident when:

> not long ago they found bacteria from a corpse ... in the reservoir ... it had come from the cemetery.

Talking about the general state of women's health inevitably entailed reference to obstetric/gynaecological matters. These, unsurprisingly, were on the minds of four women with a history of obstetric difficulties, hospitalized – though ambulant – during pregnancy. When asked what are the main issues for women's health, their agreed response was 'bringing babies to term'. The discussion continued by enlarging on their previous experiences: one, for instance, had had a termination, another a miscarriage. Then, as if remembering to explain to foreigners:

> Women in this country sometimes do very heavy work, and lift things.

Echoing these points, a 20-year-old at a health facility in Samara said:

> They can take care of their health, not get too cold, women shouldn't carry too heavy loads ... protecting yourself from pregnancy, from diseases.

Protection from the cold and damp was a recurrent theme; insufficient heating indoors, the direction of the wind and 'frequent changes in the weather mean a lot of colds, and chest problems'.

Some women took the view that women were more vulnerable than men; men's bodies are more adaptable, men are stronger.[13] Two nursing students were eloquent about differences between men's and women's health, and argued that the hardships of current circumstances bore especially on women:

> Now at the present time, the problem that's arising is that society ... generally at the moment in this country there is such an upheaval. It's very hard for us to live at the moment. There are a lot of stresses, you could say, most of which fall particularly on women. If family life was easier, with fewer stresses, women would be a lot healthier.

The main effects, they claimed are those related to premature ageing (including heart diseases) and those which are psychological – 'shaking up' the nervous system.

> It's very hard, particularly now, to get hold of money, to get hold of groceries. It tells on her health. The times we are living in are such that you don't know what tomorrow will bring. Maybe there'll be a coup, a change of government, that all of course tells on people's health.

Although men also suffer – with worrying about their responsibilities as head of the family – they 'are somehow a bit more relaxed about these changes'. Women were thought to be 'more sensitive to what's going on'.

Reproductive health

Over and over again, women reported what became a familiar series of sources from which they themselves received, or one could acquire, information about reproductive matters. These sources were both informal – especially women's own mothers,[14] but occasionally an elder sister or other female relative or female friends – and formal – lessons at school, talks by nurses or psychologists visiting schools and consultations at clinics or with gynaecologists. In addition, women referred to books, television and radio, magazines and newspapers. This range is illustrated in the following extracts from interviews with respectively, a 14-year-old schoolgirl, two nursing students interviewed separately, and a 22-year-old student:

> When I had my first period, my mother explained everything. Then I read a bit about it in books . . . [and] there are those sorts of conversations [at school with other girls] . . . Most of it, of course, I found out from books . . . at home we have books about it.

> When we were just about to leave school, probably in the ninth class . . . a psychologist came in to see us and in front of the whole school, read a lecture. It was all about sex and contraception and those things . . . Then my mother told me . . . When I was about 16.

> The first information I received was when I was at summer camp. I was then about 11 or 12. The conversations were only with the

girls. We'd sit around the table . . . a huge range of very interesting questions came up.

When I went into the first class there were children from all sorts of different families and they told me that babies aren't found under cabbages nor brought by storks, but are born, and after a while I asked my mother and she told me the general outlines of what happened. So I knew before a lot of other children know, that men and women have relations, sexual relations. My mother always said that this had to be based on love and then children are born.

Not all sources, however, were either generally available or equally highly regarded: friends may get things wrong; nothing was provided in school; the information in general circulation amongst young people was unreliable. Mothers themselves might be ignorant, out of date or out of touch with what women thought their generation needed to know. Nor was the provision of information always well timed: one woman, wholly unprepared by anyone at the time, described how alarmed she was by her first period. Embarrassment was always a risk, no matter what the source of information and, as a number of women remarked, it was not widely acceptable to talk 'aloud' about 'such things' – until now.

Change is under way, in that information has recently become more readily available, with more books and greater media coverage. But it is very recent; reflecting thoughtfully on her own experience a few years before, an 18-year-old trainee *fel'dsher*[15] observed that:

this was a time when it was only just beginning, the books and radio programmes. It was not morally [acceptable]. In a nutshell, it wasn't the Soviet way.

Overall, like their counterparts in the West, the schoolgirls and a number of the older women interviewed at health facilities were keen to have information about reproductive health. It should be accurate, up to date, at the stage women needed it (e.g., before periods start, only after they had a boyfriend and were contemplating a sexual relationship), and was best provided, many thought, in the family context by the mother.

Focusing more closely on knowledge and beliefs about contraception,[16] women across the whole group of interviews, routinely talked about condoms, the pill and the coil. Caps, the rhythm method, withdrawal and (presumably spermicidal) pessaries also received mention. Instances of lay rather than medically advised techniques were only occasional. For example, doubt was expressed by a woman who described her own mother's use, recognized by others in the group, of lemon or tablets made from household soap and by a 22-year-old student who had come across the idea that:

> after having sex you need to only wash yourself, and, maybe, well, I've heard that you must take a Pepsi and wash yourself with Pepsi.

When expressing a preference for one or other method, women's opinions were, in the main, firm and decided. Just one or two thought there were dangers, concerned about complications or the difficulty of deciding which types best suited which women. Though firm and decided, there was, however, no unanimity. On the one hand, the pill was considered 'the best . . . the most convenient' and the most effective at '90 per cent', but on the other it was also thought to be 'strong' with an unknown adverse influence on hormonal development or risking weight gain. Contraceptive pills of Soviet manufacture were, however, considered of inferior quality and not trusted. The coil was thought by one woman preferable to condoms, to be met with a rejoinder from another in the group who worried that there 'are a lot of health problems with the coil . . . [and] it doesn't suit some people'. Others believed the coil to be carcinogenic and one knew women who had used it 'and some have got pregnant even'. Even though some considered the poor quality of condoms to make them suspect – 'they sometimes just burst' – others preferred them.

Knowledge about, and choice of contraception has, however, to be set against the background of availability – described most fully by the women in their twenties, a number of whom were either married or had a regular partner. While it seemed that contraceptives had become more readily available in recent years,[17] with condoms widely sold in kiosks and chemists, the pill was far harder to come by – you had to have contacts, they are sold in the streets – and price continues to be a consideration, with one or two hinting at a black market. Overall, women presented a picture of persisting difficulty of access.

The younger women we interviewed had little to say about availability. The schoolgirls had (or admitted to) little or no direct experience of established contraceptive use; and the teenagers attending the health facilities included those who had had unprotected sex. Among the latter were found the very few among whom the acceptability of contraception could not be assumed and, moreover, who said so. For example, a pregnant 15-year-old in St Petersburg explained that none of her friends used contraception. Nor did a sexually active 17-year-old in Samara; when gently pressed a little further, she declared that if she became pregnant she would manage, though it would not be easy, since her mother would help with the baby. A 16-year-old faced the difficulty of her partner's refusal to use anything at all, talked of wanting to be fitted with a 'permanent coil'.[18]

Some men's refusal to consider contraception was mirrored in a number of interviews. Many were believed to dislike condoms (partly because of reduced sensitivity), were said just 'to forget', or were suspected of only pretending to have made sure they had acquired them in readiness. There were, however, strong hints of more than simply dislike of one method as opposed to another, conveying rather an idea of a more general difference in women's and men's attitude to contraception. A 14-year-old schoolgirl in St Petersburg articulated a view that was perhaps surprisingly fully thought through for someone of her age:

> generally boys of our age and a bit older are not, it seems to me, interested ... [they] think that taking precautions is a problem and concern for the girls ... well I don't think it's right, because if the girl gets pregnant it will be his problem and it'll be his child too. So boys should pay more attention to this, because girls of our age can't [take] the pill. The only method that's available at this age is the condom. But of course the boys [don't like them].

Though the rates are particularly high, clinically induced abortion was a topic that spontaneously arose in the interviews less frequently than other aspects of reproductive health; as a student explained 'we're used to keeping quiet about this subject'. Being well aware of the high rates did not translate into women's automatically regarding abortion as desirable. Rather, they displayed a possibly resigned and certainly sympathetic pragmatic acceptance of it. Sure 'it could be harmful', said a 14-year-old schoolgirl in St Petersburg, but she still saw nothing wrong in it. Two older women in Samara considered it risky in certain circumstances. One had heard from her mother:

> 'if you have an abortion before your first pregnancy it could be that you can't have children at all'.

The other agreed:

I know, a friend of my mother tried to have a second pregnancy, but she'd had an abortion after her little girl, and how ever many times she got pregnant, she'd miscarry in the third month.

Only in some women's view was having an abortion bound to be 'a blow' or risked being unduly upsetting. More considered it inadvisable when women were still young. In any case, there were circumstances that made it essential, in the event of rape, for instance, if the woman's health was threatened or a child was likely to be disabled: 'Why should he suffer, a tiny baby?' None the less, a strongly expressed view of its immorality did at times come through: 'I don't understand, you kill a living thing. I couldn't', said one. 'It's very frightening . . . you know you shouldn't kill', explained another. Though not specifically asked about, occasional reference was made to self-induced abortion. For example, a woman in Samara told of a friend of a friend who has had three terminations and

induced other abortions herself . . . four or five times (lifting heavy weights, doing things to herself).

Infusions of bay leaves seemed to have quite wide currency as an abortifacient, with references being made to this preparation in interviews in both cities. For instance, the mother of a 16-year-old (who had not informed her about contraception) had told her she should control herself but, if not, then she should drink bay leaf tea.

Views varied, but overall the material provides a picture of more or less reluctant acceptance in the face of too few alternatives.[19] Women's pragmatism turned on the material circumstances of life in general. Housing, they (and those we consulted) explained, was in extremely short supply, with multiple, and three-generational, occupancy being common. Incomes, and indeed employment, had recently become uncertain and prices were now increasingly deregulated.

I think it's bad that there are so many abortions, but the situation in the country is such that it's not possible to have many children. It's impossible to provide them with the bare essentials, that is, schooling, clothes and even good food, So young people at the moment are deciding not to have children, because it is very hard. There are just very few families who have everything they need and it is really very hard.

CONCLUSION: GENDER AND IMAGES OF CONTEMPORARY RUSSIA

Talking with women about their health was set in the broader context of hearing about their aspirations for the future, on which they enlarged quite readily. For virtually all of them, adulthood meant both a career or job *and* marriage (ideally) followed by parenthood in equal measures. Now and again the discussion turned to the desirability of paid employment among mothers of quite young children, with one or two believing it preferable that a woman devote herself full time to the children, home and husband. Most, however, appeared either to assume employment was an economic imperative to be positively welcomed or simply regarded as unexceptional.

Co-existing with this anticipation of employment and/or a career was a powerfully expressed expectation of marriage and motherhood. It is striking how commonly women prefaced their talk of wanting to get married and have children with 'of course'. Indeed, an image of the future for the unmarried majority not only meant marriage and children but already included a decision as to the number, sex and birth order of sons/daughters. A recurrent motif was the idea that female/female and male/male relationships – whether across generations or between non-kin – were closer, warmer and more mutually supportive than female/male relationships. Thus, women would express a preference for a daughter, value a good relationship between themselves and their own mothers and believe mothers to be more likely than fathers to be responsible for girls' health and sex education.

Though the recommended age varied between 16 and 20, those women who spoke of it believed that girls should not embark on sexual activity prematurely. Some schoolgirls even talked in terms of the age they themselves planned to begin having sex. Disapproval was expressed of girls having casual sex or multiple partners from the age of 13 or 14[20] – a judgement that could be qualified as they reflected on the dangers of inadequate sex education. They also referred to more diffuse public disapproval of girls who were known to be sexually active or became pregnant even at an age nearer their own idea of what was acceptable – disapproval which was believed to be harsher for girls than for boys of an equivalent age.[21]

This double standard in sexual behaviour was of a piece with the overall impression of a prevailing gender ideology[22] (cf. Watson 1993b). In asides and passing remarks, women conveyed an image of segregated gender roles, coupled with an attribution of distinctive psychologies for men and women.[23] While women were ordinarily expected to be employed, they were also ordinarily expected to undertake the care of children and take responsibility for the domestic sphere, as well as doing the associated household work these responsibilities involve. This extended to women's being responsible for – and taking pride in – keeping her husband clean and neatly turned out. Challenge to the prevailing gender ideology was rarely expressed and, when it was, the very fact of the challenge was described as unusual.[24]

Hardly surprisingly, for these women 'life is different now', as one of them put it. They expressed a mixture of optimism, as well as uncertainty, if not pessimism. After all, it was well-recognized that a new climate of opinion allowed the more open provision of sex education. And one or two confidently greeted it as an advance on older ways. A most enthusiastic reception for the current social changes was provided by two aspiring history teachers in Samara. Their generation, they reckoned, would be able to adapt more easily than their elders to the welcome opportunity of being able to express their own opinions; 'we are the children of perestroika'.

At the same time, women were also acutely conscious of possibly worsening degrees of economic hardship, particularly with reference to aspirations for family size. Fear of rape was also evident,[25] along with a newly heightened anxiety about perceived increases in public drunkenness, shootings and street crime. Some schoolgirls (of whom one or two talked of being subjected to newly imposed parental restrictions on going out) had become more cautious in travelling about the city alone or in the evenings.

In conclusion, the overall picture provided by these sixty or so young women about their health is very much more like that prevailing in the West than first impressions might suggest. While care must be taken to recall that this picture derives from a preliminary small-scale study and more extensive investigation is desirable, it can, however, be regarded as suggestive. The effectiveness of health policy thinking could be enhanced were it to revolve around three features: the receptiveness of young women to reproductive health education; women's dual consciousness of termination of pregnancy as a method of fertility control in terms of morality and pragmatism; and the reputed reluctance of young men to take responsibility for and to use contraception. And, as anywhere, appreciating and harnessing women's own views holds out the promise of supporting improved sexual health.

NOTES

1 The support of the Overseas Development Administration is gratefully acknowledged.

2 The other was devoted to examining the various options for collecting data that either during fieldwork and analysis or thereafter would have to be translated. For details, see Feltham, Murcott and South (1994).

3 The co-operation of those concerned and especially the women themselves – all of whom necessarily remain anonymous – is gratefully acknowledged.

4 Both authors were present at almost all the interviews. Permission to audio-tape record was sought on each occasion. AF conducted the thirty-two in Russian; two in English and one interpreted by a student were conducted by AM who also undertook the analysis and writing up of the data. Julia South undertook the translation and verbatim transcription of all audio-taped material; her sensitivity to the topic in hand, knowledge of Russian affairs and willingness to undertake more work than was originally envisaged is very gratefully acknowledged.

5 Differences between each city were relatively small. Limitations of space preclude presenting detailed analyses of the variations in (a) the reaction to being asked to talk and (b) the substance of their responses between women interviewed in schools compared with health facilities.

6 These references may have been prompted by the conditions during the period of fieldwork. The day-time temperature was only a little above freezing level but few interiors (with the exception of the schools in both cities and a young person's hostel in Samara) were heated at all, with operating theatre lists in one clinic in St Petersburg being cancelled on account of the cold. The hot water supply in St Petersburg at the time appeared uncertain and it was reported that for the previous four months, the whole city of Samara had been without hot water.

7 They could, however, on the same grounds just as readily deny that they thought of themselves as healthy, as did one 16-year-old year old schoolgirl in saying 'sometimes I have a cold'.

8 For a recent review covering research in the United States and parts of Europe see Radley (1994).

9 Both satisfaction (e.g. praise by a mother of one of the women attending a health facility for the obstetric care she herself had received) and dissatisfaction (e.g. facilities were judged as outdated or of inferior quality, complaints of inappropriate treatment) with medical care was expressed.

10 Home remedies mentioned included: taking herbal infusions (e.g. camomile tea); using garlic, onion or honey; massage; and a procedure that translates as 'cupping', which appears to refer to a technique whereby a vacuum is created within a glass placed on the skin in which a small taper is briefly burned.

11 Care of sexual health was little mentioned in this context – for example two nursing students included avoidance of casual sexual contact – but the topic was more fully discussed in other parts of the interviews.

12 None of those who happened to be interviewed in St Petersburg mentioned clean water, even though giardia in the city's supply means its whole population has to boil all drinking water.

13 Their view does not accord with the evidence. Since 1989 mortality rates in Russia have risen sharply and, as a UNICEF report (1994) demonstrates, it is men in the 29–59 age range who have been dying in unprecedented numbers. Both this recent evidence and the women's views need to be set in the context of the general finding for the West of the 'paradox' that premature mortality is greater among men than women, but that the reverse is reported for morbidity (cf., Waldron 1983)

14 By and large it appeared taken for granted that of their parents it would be their mother, not father, from whom they received their information. In one instance, a woman explained that she 'talked with my mother, but never with my father' – which accords with evidence for the UK (cf., George and Murcott 1992). Another, however, said that it was her father who 'began to explain things to us. How girls develop into girls', and who later advised them to read books about it all – adding that her mother did not get on as well with her and her older sister as did her father.

15 The *fel'dsher* has traditionally often been the mainstay of out-patient care in the countryside. In the absence of a permanently available doctor, the *fel'dsher* is something like a cross between a paramedic and a health visitor. She, and the overwhelming majority are women, has the approximate equivalent of an advance nursing qualification.

16 The approach adopted in the interviews assumed, first, the desirability of controlling fertility, family spacing and completed size, and second, the acceptability of the use of some medically advised contraception in preference to termination, infanticide or abandonment. No special enquiry was made about the practice of abandoning children, but health workers in St Petersburg referred to the phenomenon. The views of any women who dissented from these assumptions – with one or two exceptions – are thereby not apparent in the data.

17 There was no opportunity to make any independent check on either availability or price

18 This, however, brought her up against some disagreement amongst healthworkers at the clinic where she was interviewed as to the suitability of this method – and its cost – at her age.

19 See Lopez' (1987) analysis of the way historical events, medical presumptions of ethnic women's inability to take responsibility for their own contraception and economic deprivation combined to produce an apparently automatic acceptance of sterilization amongst Puerto Rican women.

20 Echoing the anxieties voiced by a number of health workers that a greater laxity now prevailed.

21 As one schoolgirl put it, 'the man is not considered guilty, the woman is always guilty'.

22 See Paiva (1993) for parallels in what she calls the 'predominant sexual culture' which contains self-contradictory dimensions of Brazilian teenagers.

23 Cf., of the 1970s,

> those aspects of Soviet development that have tended to promote the equality of women have been substantially offset not merely by the persistence of traditional values but by economic and political priorities and *by patterns of authority that have sustained and reinforced the differentiation of male and female roles.*
>
> (Lapidus 1978: 235; emphasis added)

24 Only one woman said she did not want to get married – not wanting to be dependent on a husband. She did, however, want children – 'as many as possible' and would 'count on her own initiative' to manage as a single parent. Two days later we asked three schoolgirls their opinion of a woman who claimed she did not want to marry. Though they had met girls who did not want children, they found not wanting to marry very unusual – every girl must have a husband or friend who lives with her. They cast around for reasons – maybe she was unable to find a good man – and decided it promised to be very hard for her.

25 Staff at a women's centre observed that, of every hundred cases of rape that came to the attention of a rape crisis centre in St Petersburg, only one woman had reported the incident to the police. In their view, the police were unsympathetic and inclined to assume that women were either 'asking for it' or did not really mean 'no'.

10 Sexual violence towards women

Tat'iana Zabelina

INTRODUCTION: THE CONCEPT OF 'VIOLENCE' IN THE SOVIET UNION

In the Soviet period violence against the individual, including sexual violence, was not discussed openly. It was not directly forbidden to talk about sexual violence, but it was nevertheless subject to a kind of taboo. This meant that there was virtually no research done on the subject: no public opinion surveys conducted, no statistics published and what analytical material did exist was stamped 'for official use only' and left to languish in the Ministry of Internal Affairs. The media observed a virtual total silence on the subject; since, apparently, there was no social basis for wide-scale violence in the USSR. Individual cases, which nevertheless came out, were explained away as the actions of sex maniacs or common criminals. In the most detailed of the Great Soviet Encyclopedia (Volume 41, 1939), violence was described as 'premeditated actions (blows, beatings, etc.) incurring physical pain', that is, it was reduced to its definition in Soviet criminal law which makes no mention of sexual, moral or psychological violence. However, special attention was devoted to violence which 'occurs in conjunction with politically motivated crimes (counter-revolutionary crimes against the administrative regime and violent resistance to Soviet power)' as well as 'the use of violence aimed at destroying collective farms and forcing farmers to leave it'. No amnesty applied to people convicted of such violence in accordance with the 1932 law on the protection of socialist property. This law was notorious for its wide interpretation and, after 1935, children from the age of 12 were subject to punishment under it (*Bol'shaia Sovetskaia Entsiklopediia* 1939: 256).

Marxism–Leninism interpreted violence above all as the weapon of class rule in an antagonistic society and as the most important condition for a revolutionary change of the basis of society. In particular, the revolutionary role of violence in establishing the rule of the working class was emphasized. In the Soviet Encyclopedic Dictionary of 1980, of which millions of copies were published and which can be found in virtually every library (state or personal), the entry on violence does not mention actions against the individual at all. Instead, mention is made only of violence in class and inter-state relations (*Sovetskii Entsiklopedicheskii Slovar'* 1980: 873). Thus, it would appear that, with time, violence against the individual became more rather than less ideologized, producing several gener-ations of Soviet people unaccustomed to thinking about violence as a violation of the rights of the individual and unable to see the problem of violence towards children and women. Not even peres-troika pushed these questions to the top of the public agenda and it was only in the 1990s that a breakthrough was finally made. Glasnost gradually illuminated more and more dismal periods of the Soviet past and present and eventually even penetrated those hidden corners of the Russian home where violence lurked. It became clear that Russia was no exception; there, like everywhere else in the world, human rights are violated and children and women are subjected to physical, psychological and sexual violence.[1] Nowhere can women and children feel completely safe and they are among the innocent victims of inter-ethnic conflicts, terrorist acts and clashes between criminal gangs.

VIOLENCE, SEXUAL VIOLENCE AND GENDER IMAGES IN POST-SOVIET RUSSIA

One victim of gang rape articulates clearly what worries many women in Russia today:

> Now when I'm out in the city, I look at the men around me and think – he would be capable of doing what they did. And he would, and he would. If only a convenient opportunity arose. Sometimes I think, and where do we go from here? What will happen if life becomes even harder and authority even weaker? There will be nowhere to hide from these 'animals', we won't be safe even in our own homes.
>
> (Surkov 1994: 3)

The lack of trust in the authorities expressed by this woman is reinforced by the lack of respect for women evident in the state-ments made by state officials on opportunities for women in the labour market, management and political bodies as the transition to market relations begins. The media also shapes public opinion in a misogynistic way. Even overt sexual discrimination is hushed up and many journalists and publishers choose to interpret press freedom – the most important victory of perestroika – as total freedom from any kind of self-regulation. As a result, society is bombarded with certain stereotypical images of women: the 'natural predestination of women', women's 'victim status' and women's partial blame for the violence inflicted on them. Women are blamed for aggravating many social and demographic 'problems' (divorce, the movement towards smaller families, the fall in the birth rate, the rise in juvenile crime, prostitution, the spread of AIDS, HIV and sexually transmitted diseases and even for the increase in unemployment and the depreciation in the health of the nation). The commercialization of women's sexuality is particularly obvious in television advertising.

In the face of this onslaught, the majority of the population, and even specialists on women's rights, have had no means of defence, since they have been denied access to the texts in Russian of the United Nations' Convention on the elimination of all forms of discrimination towards women as well as the draft 'Declaration on the Elimination of all Forms of Violence Towards Women' presented to the United Nations by Canada. Even after the declaration has been approved in Russia – and hopefully it will be ratified, given that Russia was one of the first to ratify the Convention on the prohibition of all forms of discrimination against women – the majority of women in Russia nevertheless may not find out about the existence of this document or about their rights unless the attitude of society, the state and the media towards the problem of the violation of human rights and the discrimination and violence against women changes.

The dominant stereotype of women as second-class citizens is encouraged by the fact that they are seen primarily as sexual objects whose role is simply to please men, both at home and at work. Whether intentionally or not, even some women's publications, which claim to express and defend the interests of the female population, promote the ideology of a 'woman's place'. The journals *Mir Zhenshchiny*, *Krest'ianka* and *Rabotnitsa* and the newspapers *Delovaia Zhenshchina*, *Mir Zhenshchiny* and *Sudarushka*, for example, all devote space to fashion competitions, the lives of film stars, the art and secret of eternal youth, whether one should marry for 'looks' or 'security', the orthodox religion, horoscopes, fortune-telling and fashion. Of course, they also carry stories about business

women and their successes or about individual, selfless women from
provincial backwaters, but more typical is the following quote
from the journal *Delovaia Zhenshchina* citing the popular singer
and symbol of eternal youth, Edita P'ekha:

> Not for nothing is there a proverb which says that 'the woman is
> the neck and the man is the head'. Everyone has their role in
> life. So let the weaker sex fulfil the role of the neck, given them
> by nature, with brilliance and wit.
>
> (*Delovaia Zhenshchina*, 1993, no. 2).

The rubric 'Devichnik' ('Hen party') in the newspaper *Komsomol'-*
skaia Pravda also calls upon girls to oblige their men thus:

> Advice no. 22: Don't argue with him or with others in front of
> him. Keep quiet!
>
> (*Komsomol'skaia Pravda*, 21 October 1993)

Such statements surely can encourage neither a sense of dignity, a
belief in one's own strengths nor self-respect.

At the same time, domestic violence and sexual harassment at
work and in educational and reformatory institutions is only
extremely rarely the subject of debate or publications. Instead, popular journals revel in exposing women's violence towards men. Two
popular and widely read publications carried articles with the same
title 'Men Killers' in which they 'raise' the subject of women who
have murdered their husbands and/or cohabitants, in the worst traditions of the gutter press (*Argumenty i Fakty*, no. 15, 1994; *Novii
Vzgliad*, 1993, no. 24). The article in *Novii Vzgliad* was accompanied
by a huge collage of a vamp with a sword and the severed head of
the victim in her hands. Although the articles note that women are
often driven to murder by years of torture at the hands of their
husbands, nevertheless, the way in which the material is presented,
the headline and the form the article takes convinces readers of the
opposite; all evil begins with women, who are cruel and terrifying.

The dominant attitude in the media reflects that of the average
uninformed person; such violations of individual rights are accepted
as the norm. Moreover, this conspiracy of silence turns such violence
into the personal tragedy of each victim, hides it from the public
eye and drives abuse into the underground of impunity.

SEXUAL VIOLENCE TOWARDS WOMEN IN THE EYES OF THE LAW

The crude form of market relations which currently exist in post-Soviet Russia brutalize inter-personal relations and facilitate criminal activity. According to figures published by the State Committee for Statistics, in 1993 3.5 times more organized crimes were registered in Russia than in 1992, and the increase in the number of crimes against the individual is particularly noticeable (Savichev and Sargin 1994). The number of registered rapes is also rising: in 1990 there were 12,000 registered rapes and in 1993, 15,500. The clear-up rate for rapes meanwhile is worsening (down by 11.6 per cent over 1992) ('Proekt. Doklad o vypolnenii v Rossiiskoi Federatsii konventsii o likvidatsii vsekh form diskriminatsii v otnoshchenii zhenshchin' 1994: 23).

In their statements, publications and arguments, however, representatives of law enforcement agencies, the courts and even academia continue to refer to the 'provocative behaviour' of the victim herself. During an international seminar on the contemporary family (1992), for example, one participant, a philosopher, declared that '70 per cent of rapes are associated with the frivolous or provocative actions of the victim'. Included in the definition of 'provocative acts' for this academic were, 'careless walks in the evening, agreeing to meet unknown people in secluded places, drinking alcohol and even listening to music together' (Semashchko 1992: 130). This is a useful justification of his actions for the rapist: 'We had a drink together, listened to music, well and . . . I just couldn't stop myself, m'lord!' Lawyers also refer to 'fake resistance', which once again 'hints' to the rapist, 'explain to the court that you thought the woman was resisting only out of coquetry, that she was playing hard to get'.

The police inquiry – if the victim goes to the police – and the judicial investigation often traumatize the victim since the psychological aspects of rape are not taken into account; those who have suffered violence need the help of a specially trained psychologist and often experience distrust of all men, including those in police uniform. The victims themselves say that the police sometimes 'dissuade' them from registering the rape, and if the case does go to prosecution then the woman is forced to recount what happened six or seven times, to various 'bosses' (Samuseva 1994). According to legal expert Margarita Kachaeva, 80 per cent of girl victims of rape attempt suicide in the period immediately after the crime or during the process of police and judicial investigation (Kachaeva 1994).

A professional psychological report on rape victims is far from always conducted, even though in 1988 a special set of guidelines was produced for the use of investigators, judges and expert psychologists. One of the authors of these guidelines, psychologist Liudmila Konysheva, studied and analysed 337 criminal cases of rape against juveniles, the sentences of almost 300 men convicted of rape and ninety psychologists' reports on the victims (of which she personally participated in twenty). Her research showed that in many cases where the 'behaviour of the victim' was judged to have 'facilitated' the crime, in fact the victims were simply helpless, since the girls were too young to understand what was being demanded of them, what was happening to them or were simply paralysed by shock and fear such that they were incapable of running away, screaming or even moving (Konysheva 1988: 5).

Judicial institutions often apply a double standard in their approach to the rapist (a man) and the victim (a woman) in that they are prepared to recognize the possibility that the criminal did not really understand what the woman wanted and thought that she was responding to his sexual solicitations. However, women and girls, even juveniles, are treated differently; very rarely do judges consider the fact that a girl, often a child, may not have realized what was happening to her, may not have had the skills, first, to recognize a violent situation (especially if the rapist was a relative or acquaintance) or, second, to resist that violence.

Konysheva's research also confirmed that the kind of rape experienced by juveniles is dependent upon their age. For girls up to 12 years of age the most likely kind of rape is that by a single known adult, but as victims get older (15–17 years) so the danger of being raped by peers, including by a group of acquaintances, increases (Konysheva 1988: 14). Indeed, 13 per cent of rapes take place on dates, and not infrequently girls themselves help in the rape of a friend, viewing the rape as either 'revenge' or as part of the rituals of the youth gang. According to the well-known criminologist Dr G. Min'kovskii (1992), girls take part in about one in ten of all rape-related crimes. The process of court investigations into such cases has revealed gaps in current legislation, since the Russian criminal code does not cover the participation of women in such crimes. This is not the only legislative improvement needed; the concept of 'criminal violence' *per se* as yet has no recognition in Russian legislation and there are no strictly determined criteria of responsibility for various forms of violence.

The Moscow legal expert Dr Anatolii D'iachenko, speaking in

October 1993 at the conference 'Women, Youth, Violence' noted the growth in recent years of particularly violent crimes, of the kind where violence is inflicted for several hours and is accompanied by the deliberate humiliation of the victim, a desire to inflict particular suffering and barbarous means of suppressing their resistance. This is particularly typical of gang rapes by teenagers. According to D'iachenko (1994) three-quarters of rapes are accompanied by such acute suffering; in 80 per cent of cases physical violence is inflicted on the victim and in 60 per cent of cases they are threatened with death. Half of all rapes are accompanied by physical injuries to the victim, a quarter lead to their defloration. D'iachenko's findings on the age of victims is particularly alarming; 37 per cent are juveniles. Moreover, during the time he worked as an investigator he came across cases of the rape of not only 7–10-year-old children but also of babies not more than 3–4 months of age (Zabelina 1994: 27).

D'iachenko also notes the problem of the low rate of reporting of rape by victims and confirmed that only a small proportion of victims (around one in five) turn to law enforcement agencies for help (some experts suggest that as few as 3 per cent do so) (ibid.: 27). According to Russian law, a case is prosecuted only if the victim makes a complaint. D'iachenko's observations suggest that women do not go to the police for the following reasons:

- sheer fear;
- the possibility of revenge by relatives and friends of the rapist;
- concern for their children;
- shame;
- the lack of desire to recount what had happened to them;
- a lack of belief that the perpetrator will be found and punished;
- concern for their reputation (especially for victims living in rural areas).

D'iachenko emphasizes the need to study international experience in helping victims, to train police officers to deal with rape and to revise legislation. He considers it essential to introduce legislation which will protect women from coercive sexual contact (involuntary but non-violent) including that occurring at the workplace. In his opinion, it is also essential to introduce punishment for the sexual trade in people (including the kidnapping and capture and sale of women and children) and for encouraging people into prostitution.

Although the encouragement of minors into prostitution is punishable already under criminal legislation in Russia, it goes virtually uncontrolled by state bodies. In the draft report on the implementation in the Russian Federation of the 'Convention on the Abolition of all Forms of Discrimination Against Women' (1994) it is recognized that there is no special department dealing with prostitution and that the encouragement of minors is generally uncovered only after the occurrence of a criminal breach of the law. The absence of statistics in this area is also noted as well as the fact that this 'prevents the state from both evaluating the extent of the phenomenon and controlling it' ('Proekt. Doklad o vypolnenii v Rossiiskoi Federatsii konventsii o likvidatsii vsekh form diskriminatsii v otnoshchenii zhenshchin' 1994: 22). Despite the lack of precise statistics, expert evaluations suggest that about 70 per cent of prostitutes begin their trade at the age of 14–15 and that the encouragement into the sex business of minors, girls from rural areas or provincial towns and of mentally retarded young people is a growing tendency. Moreover, these young people are often tricked or coerced into prostitution.

According to Russia's Deputy Minister of Internal Affairs, Aleksandr Kulikov, the country is currently unable to fully fulfil the demands of paragraph 34 of the 'Convention on the Rights of the Child', which obliges the state to take measures to prevent 'the encouragement or coercion of a child into any illegal sexual activity, the exploitative use of children in prostitution or any other illegal sexual practice and the exploitative use of children in pornography' (Budartseva 1994). The rapid growth of venereal disease and abortions among juveniles is also causing concern among police personnel, medics and psychologists. Whereas in Moscow in 1989–90 1,582 girls under 18 terminated pregnancies, in 1991–2 this number had more than doubled (ibid.). The number of cases of young mothers abandoning their babies is also increasing; babies often conceived as a result of rape. Fearing publicity, lack of understanding or the anger of relatives, some young women are driven to killing their newborn babies.

VICTIMS OF SEXUAL AND DOMESTIC VIOLENCE: THE FIRST STEPS TOWARDS SUPPORT

The psychologist Natal'ia Gaidarenko, one of the first people in Russia to begin to help rape victims, notes in an interview with a popular Moscow newspaper:

Rape leads to severe psychological shock which is detrimental to women. To overcome this, the understanding and sympathy of those close to you is very important.

(Savel'ev 1994: 3)

However, of those who turned to Gaidarenko few had received such understanding; of 107 young women only nine had told their parents about what had happened. As a result, two had been shunned by the family, one had been beaten and in only six cases had girls found support. One of the victims, not finding anyone she could trust, had related her story to the dog (ibid.).

The study of the psychology of both victims and perpetrators of violence shows that the roots of many crimes must be sought in the family and, given the general level of stress, moral disorientation and material difficulty in which people live, in many families violence has become commonplace. Some suggest that patriarchal traditions (about which it is currently very fashionable to talk) predispose the head of the family to maintaining 'order' in the family by any means. As a result, in 1993 alone 56,400 women received serious injuries at the hands of their husbands and 14,500 died ('Proekt. Doklad o vypolnenii v Rossiiskoi Federatsii konventsii o likvidatsii vsekh Form diskriminatsii v otnoshchenii zhenshchin' 1994: 23). Among the victims of domestic violence there are many young women. Particularly noticeable are the wives of 'new Russians' who, as they take their first steps in business, vent their frustration at their failures and stresses on their wives. Cases of rape within marriage are also frequent (as is clear from those using the help-lines and from the evaluation of experts), but since such crimes are virtually never registered by the police and are not considered worthy of publicity, judicial investigations are not initiated and statistics not gathered. Driven into hiding within the family, this problem may develop into an even bigger one – impunity pushes the rapist or domestic hooligan to murder. According to legal experts, up to 40 per cent of all registered murders occur among relatives; moreover, for every one murder of a husband by his wife, seven wives are murdered by their husbands (Dodolev 1993). Specialists emphasize that, in the majority of cases, women resort to murder only in self-defence or when they are driven to this by uncontrollable drunkenness or battering by their husbands or maltreatment of their children.

Supporting women who have suffered domestic or sexual violence is not always easy, however. Experts note that Russian women, regardless of their social status, subconsciously accept 'suffering' as the cross they must bear, for it is evidence of their own guilt; when there is conflict within the family, women blame themselves for being bad wives, or for not being attractive enough to their husbands.[2] The years of Soviet power have also left their mark on Russian women's attitudes towards violence. Many people genuinely believed that the state and the collective could defend and help them. Now that the Soviet state has collapsed, the role of the collective is very small and many women have completely lost their direction. They do not know to whom they can turn for help if they are abused (in the family, at work or even on the street). The trade union and party committees, work collective and women's councils of the Soviet era are no longer active. As a result Russian women, now more than ever, 'keep it all inside' and 'retreat into their shells'.

Above all, however, women are forced to tolerate violence simply because they have no escape; they have nowhere to go, no money to rent accommodation and provide for their children and nowhere to turn to for support or understanding. In the West women in such circumstances might approach support groups or crisis centres, or use help-lines. In Russia, however, millions of women suffer in silence. This is not only due to distinct cultural stereotypes or a peculiarly Russian mentality; they simply have no one to tell. Nobody is interested in them and they know that more likely than not nobody will help them. Even those who turned to priests have encountered little sympathy; one woman was told, 'Look for the cause in yourself. Your life is not working out because of your sins.'[3]

State bodies and the women's parliamentary fraction are only just beginning to take the first initiatives with regard to women who have suffered violence, by gathering information and participating in conferences and discussions. Local administrative bodies in a number of cases are helping to set up centres of social and psychological help for victims of sexual and domestic violence. A shelter for women and their children has been set up under the Ministry of Social Protection of the republic of Buriatiia,[4] for example, while in the Western Siberian city of Tiumen' a hostel for women who have been subjected to domestic violence is already in existence. In Samara oblast' (in the Volga region) a crisis centre for young women is running and in Saratov oblast' by 1993 three state shelters were receiving both adults and children ('Proekt. Doklad o vypolnenii v Rossiiskoi Federatsii konventsii o likvidatsii vsekh form diskriminatsii v otnoshchenii zhenshchin' 1994: 23–4). In many cities telephone help-lines are in operation often financed from the budgets of the regional authorities. In Moscow the Ministry of Health has set up such a help-line to help prevent suicide and the Moscow city authorities are financing a help-line for children and teenagers in addition to other 'youth' and 'children's' lines already operating. Several similar projects are being developed in St Petersburg and Ekaterinburg (formerly Sverdlovsk).

The widespread and socially dangerous nature of domestic violence received indirect recognition in the decision by the parliamentary fraction, 'Women of Russia', to initiate a new law on domestic violence in December 1994. Of course, how progressive this law is can only be judged after its text has been released, and how effective it is only after it has been put into practice. However, the very fact that such a law is being worked on will help draw the attention of the public to the problem of family (domestic) violence.

In the meantime, a significant proportion of the burden of supporting the victims of sexual or domestic violence is borne by public and charity organizations which are funded only via donations, often from foreign funds and organizations. With the help of the Austrian charity organization 'CARITAS' a crisis centre for battered women has been operating in Moscow since 1993. It provides telephone and face-to-face counselling with victims and is working towards setting up a shelter. It is aiming to rent a seven-room flat for this purpose and to pay for the services of the police to protect it. Marina Pisklakova, who runs the crisis centre, notes that they receive more than 150 telephone calls per month, and if they are able to publish any information giving the number of the help-line or to talk on the radio or on a television programme, then the telephone really becomes a 'hotline', ringing constantly. The need for it is very great. In her public talks, which are treated no less importantly than the counselling sessions with the victims, the emphasis is placed on explaining to women and men that violence should not be tolerated, that those who beat and rape fear publicity and thus the apparent impunity and indifference of society plays right into their hands. The aim is to convince women who have suffered from violence that it is not normal behaviour. The message is: you are strong, you will find a way out, try to protect yourself. Women are advised to demand that the police register their complaints, to demand proof from the medical services they turn to of the beatings and injuries received and to inform their neighbours and friends of their husbands' behaviour. Such advice is particularly important for young, inexperienced women and, amongst those who turn to the crisis centre, there are many who are no more than 18 years old.

There are also many young women who turn for support to the 'Sisters', a Moscow-based, independent, charity centre for victims of sexual violence (the author is one of the founders and a member of the administration of this centre, which was registered in March 1994). From April 1994 a help-line has been in operation and by December 1994 the ten young female counsellors had answered more than 1,500 calls. Analysing records of the calls taken between April and November 1994, the executive director of the centre, Natal'ia Gaidarenko, found that about one-third were emergency ('crisis') calls and that about half of the attackers had been acquaintances or relatives of the rape victim. The help of the 'Sisters' is anonymous and free. The counsellors not only provide psychological support but also offer advice on which establishment to turn to for those who need medical help, where to go to register an incident and, if a victim decides to prosecute a case, what her judicial rights are. Unfortunately, the centre exists on donations from the Women's Global Fund and other organizations, and its financial means are severely limited. State bodies have so far shown no interest in the activity of the 'Sisters'. As a result of the lack of money to rent a building, the centre as yet cannot conduct face-to-face counselling with the victims of violence. However, a number of Moscow academic and teaching institutions have generously allowed the centre to use their buildings free of charge and several training sessions for counsellors, self-defence classes and an international conference 'Violence Towards Women' (July 1994), in which about 100 people took part, have been held. Workers and activists of the centre have translated much foreign literature on violence, teaching manuals and pamphlets and participated in the collation of the first guide for those trying to organize centres to help victims of sexual violence in Russia (published in May 1995). The centre is conducting a sociological survey on violence and help set up the first refuges for women suffering from such violence. Many of the centre's activists are involved in publicizing the work of the centre and educating the general public about the problem of violence towards women via the press, radio, television, seminars and conferences, meetings with students, medics, social workers, parliamentary representatives and public and state officials. In all of their work the 'Sisters' try to implement the basic principles of the centre, which are best summed up by the slogan of the 'Sisters' – 'We are building a society free of violence' (see Appendix 1).

The emergence of the first crisis centres and help-lines for women has revealed a need for the exchange of information, experience and mutual support. Large-scale projects have emerged which have required the efforts of several organizations and large groups of activists. In 1994 the idea of establishing an Association of Russian Crisis Centres for Women was discussed in existing crisis services and in October of that year an initiative group representing women's organizations of various regions of Russia and existing crisis centres ('Sisters', 'The Women's Crisis Centre' (both Moscow), the 'St Petersburg Crisis Centre', the Centre 'Anima' from Ekaterinburg and others) decided to create an association which will act as a network and will try to unite efforts to fight violence. The most pressing task of this association is to conduct a national survey on violence which will be partially funded by the Global Fund for Women.

VIOLENCE AGAINST WOMEN, INTER-ETHNIC AND MILITARY CONFLICT: THE 'TABOO' LIVES ON

Women suffer enormously as a result of inter-ethnic and military conflict, although this subject is one of the remaining taboos in the Russian press. The Russian mass media failed to inform the population about the mass violence against women in the former Yugoslavia, during the Karabakh conflict and the Armenian pogroms in Sumgait, and in the course of the Georgian–Abkhazian conflict. Now there is absolutely no information about violence against women, in Chechnia although, according to the Constitution, this territory is part of the Russian Federation. Thus, violence towards women is still being hushed up and only a few non-governmental organizations are speaking out to defend women in areas of military conflict. An example of one such initiative is the joint appeal made by the St Petersburg Centre for Gender Problems, participants of the Moscow 'Art against Violence' action, and several participants (including the author) of the Conference 'Women and Development: Rights, Reality and Prospects' held in December 1994. The text of the address distributed by the St Petersburg Centre for Gender Problems is included as Appendix 2.

CONCLUSIONS

Given the paucity of serious sociological data on violence in Russia (especially on domestic violence, on sexual harassment and violence against disabled women, women prisoners, women refugees and migrants and women in war zones), any strict academic comparison between the peculiarities of violence in the West and in Russia would be premature. However, the evidence of experts allows us to make some preliminary remarks about the specifics of violence in Russia.

Forty per cent of all murders take place as a result of domestic conflicts, most often under the influence of alcohol. A new form of violence has also appeared in the form of the murder of elderly women in order to acquire their housing.

Not only wives but other female members of the family suffer from violence in Russia (the mothers of either the husband or the wife, grandmothers, aunts, etc.), since as a result of the housing shortage two or three generations live together in the same flat or house. Currently 43 per cent of newlyweds live in a room in the flat of their parents and 6.5 per cent live in the same room as their parents (*Sbornik: Molodezh Rossii: Tendentsii, Perspektivy*, 1993: 26).

The level of violence in wealthy families is very high, especially among the 'new rich', where husbands, having become businessmen and joined the 'high life' are embarrassed by their 'simple' wives who have been with them through their difficult transition from poverty to unexpected prosperity and thus remember them as hungry students or when they were still selling things in street kiosks. 'New Russians' want to appear in society accompanied by bohemian women who, in their opinion, are better suited to their new lifestyles. There are many cases when husbands do not return home for several days, beat their wives, deprive them of money, subject them to moral and psychological pressure and humiliate them in front of the children. Often such husbands try to 'buy' the favour of the children with presents, money or holidays, hoping to make them their allies in the 'domestic war'. Such tactics cause double suffering for the woman in her role as both wife and as mother.

Attitudes of society, the police and judicial organs towards victims of domestic and sexual violence also differ between Russia and the West. If a woman goes to the police with a complaint against her husband – especially if it concerns rape within marriage – and if she has no clear physical injuries, then often the police do not want to involve themselves in investigating the case, claiming they do not want to 'interfere in family life'. They sometimes even laugh at the victim (this was reported by many women phoning the Moscow help-line). Although on paper the law protects every woman citizen from violence, in fact the law often does not work and is not implemented. The low level of legal education and knowledge in Russia means that women do not know their own rights nor the obligations of the police and thus fail to insist that their complaint is taken up and investigated.

Thus, in contrast to the West, women extremely rarely take their complaints to court, fearing revenge or the judgemental attitude of society. The West has benefited from twenty-five years of work by social and state organizations aimed at destroying the old view that 'a women is always guilty' in any violence suffered, or that she has 'provoked the man by her behaviour'. In Russia, on the other hand, these old views have proven very durable both among the population at large and among police, investigators, judges and lawyers. Women also fail to pursue their complaints, since the state often simply cannot cope with the volume of crime and the women often think it is a waste of time to follow up a reported crime.

Without a national-level investigation into the nature of violence (as conducted, for example, in Canada) it is impossible to create a full picture of the specifics of violence in Russia. Whether in the West or East, however, violence towards women is a manifestation of historically formed sexual discrimination and at the same time one of the social mechanisms which continues to force women to occupy an unequal position in relation to men. Violence against women takes many forms: sexual, moral, political, psychological and national/ethnic. In every manifestation, however, it constitutes a violation of the basic rights and freedoms of the individual.

APPENDIX 1: THE PRINCIPLES OF THE WORK OF THE CENTRE 'SISTERS'

The 'Sisters' centre was set up in Moscow in 1993 by a group of women who realized that people who have experienced violence need support and it works to the following principles:

- We recognize that sexual violence is mainly experienced by women and children.
- We are convinced that all women and children have the right to live in safety and without fear and that this includes within their own homes.
- We consider women's rights to be human rights and rape to be a crime against the individual. We love women, and are for them; this does not mean we are anti-men, but anti-violence in any shape or form.
- Our mission is to create an atmosphere free from all forms of violence and humiliation; an atmosphere in which the victim is not

blamed for rape, incest or any other form of violence experienced. Nobody wants to be raped, nobody deserves to be raped. The victim never provokes rape.

- We work collectively in an atmosphere of trust and confidentiality. Workers at the centre reject racism, sexism, homophobia or any other prejudice affecting women.
- The 'Sisters' are obliged to accept all people who have suffered violence and to value, not condemn them. This also applies to women who work with victims.
- The 'Sisters' help ALL those who have experienced rape or sexual violence, especially those who find it difficult to find help elsewhere and those who society chooses to ignore, i.e., lesbians, women and children with HIV or AIDS, prostitutes, women alcoholics and drug addicts. The help is free and anonymous.
- For us everybody is equal, regardless of age, sex, social position, nationality, background, belief or sexual preference.
- We help people think and decide for themselves and defend the right to choose as a universal right. We want all human relations to be based on equality and respect.
- The 'Sisters' are in solidarity with all women and children and try to encourage positive change in people's views and in society in general.
- We recognize all the possible forms of violence against women and children including verbal, emotional, physical, economic, sexual and spiritual. We want victims to rediscover their dignity and their strength and to begin to take control of their own lives again.
- We are certain that the process of healing and re-finding one's inner strength takes place through education, information and support from the socio-political system which so often influences, sometimes even controls, our lives.
- The aims of the centre 'Sisters' are: to raise the consciousness of society; to teach people to see the roots and sources of violence against women; to develop a strategy to end violence and to create a network of refuges and help-lines.
- We are building a world free from violence.

APPENDIX 2: APPEAL AGAINST VIOLENCE TOWARDS WOMEN IN CHECHNIA

Today, when our government, our parliamentary representatives and the mass media have exhausted us with their talk about events in

Chechnia, it is about time to turn our attention to the specific position of women in the region.

The Chechens and the Ingush are representatives of traditional cultures with a growing fundamentalist tendency. In the last two to three years the region has been experiencing a localized war. The Russian-speaking population has largely left. The majority of the male population is armed and belongs to some opposition grouping. Traditional and strict behaviourial codes prevent free and equal relations between the sexes. Women are expected to be wholly dependent on male family members: their fathers, brothers and husbands. And if previously the latter had to ensure their defence and protection, now (just as with their care of the elderly), these traditions have been abandoned and forgotten. As a result, a huge number of women in Chechnia and Ingushetiia are being subjected to the constant danger of being raped. Our informants (whose names are not revealed for reasons of security) inform us of the following facts:

- In August of this year at a bus stop in Groznii a young woman was shot. Some men had got out of a car, approached her and suggested that she go with them 'to have fun' [*razvlekat'sia*]. She told them to go and 'have fun' with their sisters, for which she was shot in the head on the spot and in front of several witnesses.
- Suggestions of this kind are relatively widespread and women on their own or in pairs can simply be dragged into a car, driven out of town and group-raped before being abandoned there or returned to the place from which they were taken.
- Male relatives in such situations not only fail to defend their women but may even kill or punish them for their 'shameful' behaviour.
- A similar case took place, also in the summer, with a woman whom it had been rumoured had a lover (she was unmarried). Her brothers forced her to get her stuff together, drove her to the forest, ordered her to dig a grave, killed and buried her. When they returned home they threw her things at her mother accusing her of having brought up a 'prostitute'.

Since virginity is fundamental to this culture but there are far too many cases of rape, incest and sexual coercion, our informants tell us that operations to restore virginity cost $1,000. Often women who have been coerced choose other ways of having intercourse, but this does not spare them further and constant violations, which means that they have to do this as a consequence.

All this information comes from reliable sources; from witnesses and victims of violence. They are not isolated cases – it is a mass phenomenon! However, neither in the mass media nor in state organs is this subject being raised. Throughout the world the mass rape of women on the territory of military actions in the former Yugoslavia are well known. The whole world press has reported this, except for the Russian press. In our country, obviously, nobody is concerned with these women's problems.

We will pass judgement on the political and economic games of male politics. Here we are appealing to women for their solidarity. It is time to turn our attention to the situation of women in war-torn Chechnia. It is time to act, in order to change that situation!

Petersburg Centre for Gender Problems

December 1994

NOTES

1 Of course men suffer violence too, but this phenomenon requires separate sociological research and is not discussed here. In Russia men do suffer rape, but not on the scale that women do; the majority of cases of rape investigated take place in prisons and army units. A prisoner who is raped is referred to as a *'petukh'* (rooster) and the violence meted out known as *'opushchenie'* (putting down) which suggests similar motifs of humiliation and hierarchy of power as are found in the rape of women.
2 Of course, it must be remembered here that although Russians constitute the vast majority of citizens of the Russian Federation, nevertheless there are more than a hundred ethnic groups in the country whose mentalities vary greatly. Even among ethnic Russians, rural and urban women have very different notions of suffering.
3 This information was provided by a help-line counsellor.
4 Buriatiia is one of the constituent members of the Russian Federation.

Part III

Gender, identity and cultural practice

11 'Youth culture' in contemporary Russia

Gender, consumption and identity

Hilary Pilkington

One of the major achievements of youth cultural studies in the last decade must be its success in removing itself from the academic arena. The concepts of 'youth subculture' and even 'youth culture' in general now appear part of a past discourse in which vertical divisions of dominance and resistance (sub- and counter-culture), fixed subjectivities ('youth'), single reading positions and unidirectional action reigned supreme. In the 1990s it is the 'discursively produced subject' which defines the research agenda whose contours consist of horizontal relations, multiple incursions, grey areas, incorporations and spaces, and disparate and diverse identities. This is more than rhetoric; developments in macro social theory have had a significant impact on the study of youth cultural practice at the micro level. It is no longer possible to talk of a single 'youth culture' which facilitates socialization into a fixed social space during a 'difficult' period of life, thereby securing social stability (functionalist approach) nor of various 'subcultures' which resist this fixation into subordinate positions of 'working-class', 'black' or 'female' youth articulating their resistance through ritual or style (neo-Marxist and Gramscian-based resistance theories) (Pilkington 1994a: 8–43).

Discontent with the notion of 'youth culture' in particular, however, should not lead us to neglect the cultural sphere in general; the significance of the latter in studying society is increasingly recognized, reflecting as it does general shifts in social activity and its study away from production and towards leisure and consumption (Reimer 1995: 120). The postmodern agenda, therefore, does not just sweep away past certainties but opens up new avenues for exploration. With relation to youth there are two central pillars of this agenda: youth's positioning in discourse (produced by ever-changing media, academia and state and social agencies); and youthful negotiations of this positioning – the creation and reworking of identities.

Thus 'youth culture' is used by the present author to signify:

- texts, cultural products and artefacts, and media forms (music, film, video, computer games) which shape youth styles and position young people as subjects;
- practices of consumption (shopping, watching, listening, eating), leisure activities, style creation, music and dance, media use, language;
- and the interaction between the above, which is precisely where youthful subjectivities are created and recreated.

The first of these provides the focus for this chapter, the second and third are considered in Chapter 13 via an empirical study of the contemporary Moscow youth scene.

GENDER AND YOUTHFUL SUBJECTIVITIES

Gender has been a key parameter of youth discourse and of youth cultural strategies and identities. If, in crude terms, post-war Western industrialized societies have been characterized by a 'have fun while you're young' ethos, then young women have been posited primarily as passive *consumers* of fashion commodities manipulated by male desire or as moral and sexual deviants in a male subcultural environment. Even what Griffin describes as the 'radical' discourse on youth (Griffin 1993) largely ignored the issue of gender, and indeed the presence of young women themselves, in its model of dominant culture and resistant subculture premised on a class-based reading of white, male youth cultural practices.

Thus, it was feminist interventions into the debate on youth culture and subculture which first led to the reassessment of women's object status by focusing not on the manipulation and control by the producers of cultural commodities but on the *use* of those products by their consumers. In her study of female consumer culture in post-war Germany, for example, Erica Carter argued that the almost universal adoption by young women of nylon stockings was evidence neither of 'girls' blind submission to the dictates of the market, nor . . . female capitulation to fetishistic "male" fantasy' (Carter 1984: 208). On the contrary, the wearing of stockings was used by young women to articulate certain positions; an aspiration to freedom, democracy and the *American* way of life or an expression of luxury, excess and resistance to parental moderation (since they were designed not to last) (ibid.: 208–12). Research on subcultural lifestyles was also subjected to such interventions. The earliest focused on the alternative spaces of female youth culture, such as Angela McRobbie and Jenny Garber's (1976) study of 'teeny-bopper' and 'bedroom culture', which pointed to the importance of close female friend relationships and fantasy romances with pop stars in the cultural experience of young women. Later studies have tended rather to look at the spaces created by young women for themselves *within* male-dominated subcultural environments, such as Anne Campbell's study of women in New York gangs and Lesley Roman's discussion of class and gender divisions within the American punk subculture (Campbell 1984; Roman 1988). The concept of 'fandom' has also received more attention; Lisa Lewis, for example, points to a type of fan (the 'wannabees') who use idols less for playing out fantasy romances than for their own identity construction. By imitating the style and dress of female stars they articulate their desire for (male) success and power while affirming female culture (Ganetz 1995: 90).

The 'grey area' between cultural consumption and production is a central theme in the study of young people's cultural practice in the 1990s and is rooted in real changes in society which have blurred the distinction between the two (McRobbie 1994: 159–63, 177–85). Even the most apparently straightforward manifestations of consumption (shopping sprees) might be interpreted as more than purely economic activity. Ganetz, for example, marks out the 'fitting room' as an important space for girls away from social and parental control in which not only clothes may be discussed (if rarely bought) but advice and compliments passed, and the self confirmed (since shopping is only done with a person who shares the same taste) (Ganetz 1995: 85–6). Indeed, this may not be an exclusively feminine practice; as Ganetz notes, boys are increasingly decorating their bodies as well, whilst consumption research suggests there is a general increase in leisure activities taking place in the home (a traditional site of 'feminine' youth cultural practice) (ibid.: 78, 89).

The 'first wave' of feminist interventions into the debate on youth culture might be seen as focusing primarily, although not exclusively, on the structures binding, limiting and controlling young women. At the most general level Barbara Hudson talked of the deeply rooted conflict between the discourses of femininity and adolescence (Hudson 1984). Central to this conflict for Hudson is female sexuality, which may be used by girls to resist some of the binds placed on them (sexualizing their image accelerates their passage out of girlhood) but which is difficult to align with accepted feminine norms: 'the teenage girl has to tread a narrow line between "getting too serious too soon", and being regarded as promiscuous by her elders and as a "slag" by her peers' (ibid.: 40–7). On the basis of her ethnographic study of sexuality and adolescent girls Sue Lees has shown how the cultural label of 'slut' or 'slag' works among young people as a wider 'general mechanism of control of girls' sexuality' (Lees 1986: 139). A second theme is the importance of the differentiation between the 'public' and the 'private'. Mica Nava's consideration of the gendered nature of youth provision (first published in 1984) uncovered a structural marginalization of girls by the youth service. This, she argued, was because whereas boys were assumed to require controlling 'on the street', the primary site of the control of girls was the home (Nava 1992: 71–93).

In the 1990s, in contrast, increasing consideration has been given, often by the same authors, to the unfixedness and diversity of femininities and the process of their creation. Angela McRobbie, for example, considers: the changing representations of femininity in girls' magazines; the simultaneous hypersexuality but sexual protection articulated through rave style; the feminine creativity in producing and reworking retro styles (the rag market); and the 'calls and responses' of ragga girls to the sexism of the music makers (McRobbie 1994: 163–7, 169–70, 146–53, 183–4). Mica Nava, in contrast, turns her attention to what she terms the 'radical potential of consumption' via its use in fantasy, identity, meaning and protest (Nava 1992: 195). Ganetz quite simply notes that the relationship between women and the market is one of mutual use; while the market uses women (creating new fashions to follow), women also use the market for creating their own unique style (Ganetz 1995: 72–3).

These writings are not only suggestive of wider trends in cultural sociology emphasizing difference, diversity and subjectivity but, grounded as they are in everyday experience of that 'difference', they are frequently leading the process of theorizing from below. Of course, gender is only one social structure which positions the youthful subject and shapes her/his experience and cultural practice and it should not be prioritized over other structures. However, the very process of the discursive production of the subject reveals the deep-rooted nature of the connections between youth, gender, consumption and identity formation, and it is these connections which will form the basis of the discussion of 'youth culture' in late Soviet and post-Soviet Russian below.

YOUTH AND CONSUMPTION IN THE SOVIET CONTEXT: THE DEVELOPMENT OF 'RATIONAL NEEDS'

Although the terms 'youth culture' and 'subculture' have been absent in Soviet writing on Russian youth except in relation to rejections of the appropriateness of such terms (Pilkington 1994a: 71–8), nevertheless the relationship between identity formation, leisure, consumption, music and style among youth have been discussed at length and this chapter seeks to trace the parameters of the discourse which has emerged, focusing on its gendered nature.

In pre-revolutionary Russian village culture, it was girls who were the key movers in youth cultural practice; traditionally they were responsible for organizing the *posidelki* (working bees or evening gatherings of young people) which followed village seasonal work patterns and were based around women's domestic work (Worobec 1991: 130–1). However, they were also essentially evening parties accompanied by accordion music, singing, drinking, dancing and the playing of intimate games essential to pre-marriage courtship (ibid.: 131; Gromyko 1986: 161). This system of youth self-regulation of sexual relations, however, suffered from the same 'double standard' for young men and women described by Sue Lees in contemporary British society (see above), since it demanded of a young woman:

> a constant balancing act between the necessity of preserving her dignity and chastity . . . and mastering an unfettered manner of communication with boys . . . The danger of overstepping the 'limits' was high since caresses, hugs, kisses, nights spent together etc. were all within the norms of the game.
>
> (Bernshtam 1991: 252)

Those who were unskilled or did not join in the game[1] were despised by both the male and female youth communities and might be teased, given offensive nicknames or even excluded from the youth community and thus threatened with becoming 'old maids' (ibid.). As Bernshtam notes, the folklore surrounding the transition to maturity in Russian traditional culture reveals that adolescent youth were seen to have 'wild' (immature, unbalanced) psychic qualities which demanded the isolation of the group during its leisure and entertainment. Yet this clearly clashed with the virtue and maidenly honour required of an unmarried girl, and the censure of girls when they overstepped the thin line they were required to tread was harsh indeed (ibid.; Worobec 1991: 138–9).

The youth cultural practices embedded in village tradition were viewed as backward by the post-revolutionary regime and were criticized and fought against well into the Soviet period. Other than this, however, young women appeared to attract no particular attention. Their needs were not viewed as special, simply dual; being both young and female, young women were considered doubly politically backward, naive and vulnerable. The backwardness associated with young women's cultural practice is manifested in descriptions of their tendency to 'gossip', 'fortune-tell' and generally be 'frivolous' (Plesko *et al.* 1936). However, such women are also seen as needing protection. In a rare discussion of the way of life among young women in a small textile town in the 1930s, young men are criticized for behaving 'improperly' at house parties (the urban equivalent of the *posidelki*) and for getting women pregnant and then abandoning them to the shame of the community (ibid.: 16–21). The solution found was to involve young people in meaningful activity in their spare time; one successful initiative is described in which hooligan lads from the next village were persuaded to play football instead of getting drunk and being riotous (ibid.: 74–5). There is also criticism of the tendency of *Komsomol*[2] groups in provincial towns to content themselves with providing sewing and knitting circles and meetings with gynaecologists to fill girls' leisure time when the latter's horizons should be being broadened (by introducing them to knowledge of Stakhanovism and record-breaking) (ibid.: 34).

It was in the post-Second World War period, however, that the debate about teenage leisure and consumption became a serious matter of concern in the Soviet Union. This reflected general improvements in the standard of living, the introduction of a shorter working week and day and the widening of access to education which, together, created a society of work plus leisure (in the towns at least) rather than of work alone. Although there had always been a concern that young people should be spending their leisure time productively, it had previously been associated with the legacy of the pre-revolutionary order (the culture of the textile village described above, for example, was stained, according to the authors, only by its capitalist past) (ibid.: 5). In the post-war period, however, the fear of the growth of passive cultural consumption was associated with a 'Westernization' or 'bourgeoisification' of youth in the context of the opening up to the West which characterized Soviet society in the 1950s and 1960s. This was linked to the popularity of

Western radio channels, primarily the BBC and Voice of America, which broadcast into the Soviet Union and were accused of being the transporters of alien styles and youth cultures to Soviet youth, whose political naivety led them to 'imitate' them.

Just as in the West, therefore, a post-war 'teenage consumer' debate is evident in the Soviet Union. In contrast to the polarized Western debate, whose parameters might be marked by Mark Abrams' positive notion of the youthful consumer on the one hand, and Richard Hoggart's Americanized, mindless, milk-bar haunter on the other (Abrams 1959; Hoggart 1957: 248), the Soviet debate was characterized by a unanimity about the ideological dangers of the Soviet teenage consumer. These were twofold. First, young people tended to 'consume' rather than 'create' their own entertainment;[3] but second, the content of that which they were passively consuming was perceived as fundamentally opposed to, and subversive of, the socialist personality (*lichnost'*). Consumption was not an evil in itself; indeed, the consumption of spiritual and leisure artefacts (cinema, concerts, theatre and fashion) was considered a normal part of responsible 'free time' activity (and reflected the much-propagandized rapid rise in the material well-being, level of education and culture of young people). 'Consumption', however, was sharply contrasted to 'consumerism', which represented the disharmony of material and spiritual demands and which turned people into the slaves of 'things'. The development of 'rational needs' was the way in which consumption in socialist society was differentiated from the 'consumerist psychology' alien to socialism. Rational needs were not those based on narcissistic pleasure principles which allied self-gratification with particular commodity forms (Cohen 1986: 43–5), but had a much more social context. They were those which: ensured the conditions for life activity of the individual (*lichnost'*), facilitated the all-round and harmonious development of the individual and did not contradict the demands of society but facilitated its progress (Kozlov and Lisovskii 1986: 92–107). This interpretation of the role of consumption persisted as long as the Soviet Union itself; describing consumerism as the 'cause of the dehumanization of the life of the younger generation', Lavskii, Naidenko and Semenchenko, writing in 1991, argued that rather than simply improve the production of goods for young people, what was needed was to educate them with skills of 'rational consumption' (Lavskii, Naidenko and Semenchenko 1991: 12).

GENDER, CONSUMPTION AND 'IRRATIONAL NEEDS': 1985–91

The post-war period saw a new problem for the Soviet state; the increasing visibility of youth cultural groups who openly expressed the heretical prioritization of style over content. Beginning with the *stiliagi*,[4] a host of subcultural styles were evident in Soviet society throughout the 1950s, 1960s and 1970s (*stiliagi*, *bitniki*, *shtatniki*, *bogemy*, hippies, football fans and punks). In the early 1980s and especially from 1986, however, there was an explosion of such obvious manifestations of alternative cultural lifestyles and it was their existence and activities which dominated discussion of youth cultural practice in the late Soviet period.

The cultural practice of young people in the perestroika period was read above all politically and a struggle was waged to 'win back' and 'channel' youthful energies into the party-led programme for the revitalization of Soviet society. This politicization of the debate on the '*neformaly*' (informals) meant that the youth cultural world was portrayed as almost exclusively male. Where gender issues were raised they were done so within the confines of the sex-role socialization debate and focused on the difficulties faced by young men in developing a positive sense of masculinity given the general 'feminization of the youth sphere' (Borisov 1991: 247). This, it was argued, produced subcultural strategies which provided space for the expression of characteristics associated with being a 'real man' (strength, courage and decisiveness) which were stifled in other spheres of life (family, school) (ibid.; Aleshina and Volovich 1991: 77).[5]

There is, therefore, virtually a complete absence of writing on young women's cultural practice. An exception is Tat'iana Shchepanskaia's gendered study of the *sistema*,[6] which suggested that although young women participated actively in the hippy culture, they were effectively shut out of the symbolic system of the group (Shchepanskaia 1991). Elsewhere, in the author's own study of youth culture in Moscow, it is argued that girls were able to carve out strategies for themselves and produce and transform cultural meanings on the youth scene, although the domination of masculine codes meant that the space in which they did this was circumscribed and subject to renegotiation beyond their control (Pilkington 1993; Pilkington 1996).

Despite the apparent absence of women on the youth cultural scene, gender remains a key parameter of the debate for commentators on the late Soviet period. It does so, it will be argued below, in as much as the discourse on youth in the perestroika period positions young women as either irrational consumers or the objects of (male) consumption themselves.[7]

Music: its uses and abuses

By the mid-1980s many *Komsomol* activists (responsible for the moral and ideological development of Soviet youth) were themselves children of the rock and roll era and thus largely accepted that they were unlikely to succeed in eliminating rock music from youthful activities – the most they could do was channel its use in the least harmful way. The targets of this campaign were young men – since, from its emergence, the rock community (of both producers and consumers) was defined as male[8] – and its focus was, thus, rock music's gradual erosion of masculine characteristics, especially *rationality*. Rock, it was claimed: had been primarily designed 'to help destroy rationality' and people's ability to appreciate real culture by inculcating blind consumerism (Chistiakov and Sanachev 1988); encouraged social passivity through a process of gradual 'stupefaction' (*effekt oglupleniia*) (Sarkitov 1987: 94); ruined the brain (Bekhtereva 1988) and encouraged spiritual primitiveness (Bondarev, Belov and Rasputin 1988: 6). The consumption of rock music was seen to threaten male rationality since it induced states where body ruled mind (emotion, dancing, *jouissant* pleasure, etc). Practical attempts to combat the negative effects of rock music therefore also focused on the need to make it more mind-ful. Attempts to do this focused on re-siting the consumption of rock in controllable spaces where vulgarity and tastelessness in the practice of music-listening would be prevented (Filinov 1986) and exposing the commercialism or anti-Soviet nature of what they listened to thus enabling them to adopt a rational position towards the music (Avilov 1987; Vasilov, Kupriianov and Cherniak 1986).

Young women's music use was viewed as inherently irrational, however. Girls were not music listeners but *'fanatki'* (female fans), who were generally viewed as 'hysterical girls' (Alekseeva and Iur'eva 1990). The 'two fan types' to be found in Western discussions of fandom – the 'obsessed individual' and the 'hysterical crowd' (Jenson 1992: 9) – are also located in Soviet literature and, given Jenson's explanation of the origins of the fan discourse as lying in a critique of modern society's material wealth but spiritual poverty (ibid.: 14), this is not surprising.[9] In the Soviet media, these 'types' are clearly gendered, however: the male fan (*fanat*) is a plural phenomenon taking the form of either football fans who act in a crowd, are aggressive and sometimes violent, or hard rock fans (*metallisty* or *rokery*) whose frenzied crowd behaviour defines them; while the feminine form (*fanatka*) is a singular concept and denotes, as a rule, a young woman in love with a male rock star whose behaviour is portrayed as morally degenerate and egoistic. 'Moral degeneration' includes anything from smoking, having a 'dirty' or 'scruffy' appearance, talking in slang, or swearing, graffitiing walls, fighting over souvenirs, drinking, spitting on local children and playing loud music (ibid; Letter 1989). 'Egoism' indicates the effect the behaviour of the fans have on the object of fandom; they make abusive and threatening phone calls to their heroes, rob their flats, limit their freedom by mobbing them and even threaten journalists (Shavyrin 1989).

The most extreme form of fandom is that in which the personality of the fan can only be expressed through her relationship with the star. This state, it is claimed, often leads young women to actively pursue their heroes; they hang around major concert complexes and are prepared to spend the night with anyone if, as a result, they can get hold of the telephone number of their hero. But even if the girl achieves her aim (of sleeping with her hero) she is unable to gain that which she is seeking – attention and value in the eyes of others through her relationship with the star. The star soon forgets she exists and the girl ends up being passed from one to member of the group to another and thus remains the object of male sexual consumption (ibid.). This impression of the rock community as confining women to the kitchen whilst treating them primarily as 'sex' objects is confirmed by Easton based on his observation of the Moscow scene (Easton 1989: 72).[10]

It would appear, therefore, that there is a strict gender divide in the binary discourse on fandom in the Soviet Union; while male fans dissipate masculine aggression in a 'pack' or 'crowd' context via fandom, female fans are pathological individuals whose behaviour symbolizes the 'fall' of society and culture in the modern age.

Style, dress and consumption

Consumption in dress and lifestyle is also portrayed as explicable, if not laudable, amongst young men whereas girls' consumption is seen as frivolous and fundamentally reproachable (comparable even to treason). Young men's desire for material goods and an extravagant lifestyle are seen as being satisfied by recourse to second economy dealing or petty crime; indeed, young men often fall into crime (stealing cars and video films) precisely in order to impress girls and satisfy the latter's materialistic demands (Babich 1990). Young women's consumption, on the other hand, is not only of specific goods, but of the 'high life' associated with the 'underground' world of black-marketeering, foreign goods and, especially, prostitution.

The key connection which is made, at various levels of explicitness, is that between girls' frivolous attitude towards their maidenly honour and their desire to consume. Girl members of the 'highlife' group the *mazhory*,[11] claims Fain, sold their bodies (became the girlfriends of the lads) in order to finance the expensive lifestyle of the group.[12] The means by which they gained the material prerequisites for entrance into the group, however, also ensured their ultimate exclusion, since these girls were looked down upon by the male *mazhory*, who sought 'steady relationships' outside the group in order to avoid sexually transmitted disease (Fain 1990: 27).

It is not only women's deviancy which is sexualized, however, but their leisure activity *per se*. In 1985 a debate developed in the youth newspaper *Moskovskii Komsomolets* on the lifestyles of young women which revealed that the majority of readers interpreted what girls saw themselves as a 'normal way of life' (going out, going to the cinemas, etc.) as being a meaningless way of spending their time.[13] Although the sexual element here was not as explicit as it was to be made later under the spotlight of glasnost, it was nevertheless clear that girls were being criticized for their 'flirtatiousness' and 'frivolous' attitude to their honour.

By the end of the 1980s one could talk of a general cultural stereotype whereby young women were seen to be exchanging access to their bodies for material goods. It had become an accepted truth that, as one male letter writer put it, professional prostitution was only the extreme of a general tendency – much worse was the fact that tens of millions of girls were involved in hidden prostitution, refusing to get to know men once they found out the size of their pay packets (El 1990). And by the early 1990s this had been internalized by young women themselves who, just like their pre-revolutionary counterparts, now must forge their identities in the narrow space between the men with whom they play sexual games (in the post-Soviet period these are so-called 'sponsors') and those for whom they must remain 'pure' enough to secure a 'successful' marriage.

The consumption of girls

The final way in which girls are positioned in the youth, leisure and consumption debate concerns their 'common use' by men in territorial gangs which are portrayed as male groups with an 'exclusively consumerist' attitude to them (Orlov 1991).

The phenomenon of organized territorially based gangs is particularly associated with the provincial Russian cities situated along the Volga and there is ample evidence to suggest a real problem of the sexual abuse of girls by and in such gangs (Kashelkin 1990: 235). Girls' only choice, it is suggested, is that of whether to become the 'property' of one of the lads, or end up a 'common girl' (*obshchaia devushka*): 'Girls are now treated like a live good which can be taken, transferred from hand to hand and even sold' (Eremin 1991).[14]

Girls were not only victims, however. In a 1989 study of gangs meeting in basements, parks and courtyards in three districts of Leningrad, 30 per cent of the 345 young people interviewed were girls (Kofyrin 1991: 83). Girls were found to have their own gangs and to engage in exactly the same activities as the lads: fighting, having fun, drinking, taking drugs, extorting money and petty thieving (Gromov and Kuzin 1990: 26). Although there is very little discussion of girls' active participation in such groups, what there is indicates two 'types' of behaviour.

The first suggests the deceiving or manipulative sexual role of the girl in the group. Thus, girls might willingly spend the night with a lad and then demand money from him in order not to cry rape; one such story described a 'basement Emannuelle' who had the entire local population of 15–20-year-old lads in one outlying district of Moscow living in fear of her reporting them to the police for having sex with a minor (Medvedkin 1991). The second behaviourial type is the 'frustrated consumer' a type premised on the practice known as *obut'* (attacks by gangs on individuals during which their clothes or attributes are stolen). In relation to girls this practice is explained thus: for girls the only way to stand out is to look beautiful; this requires consumer goods; since they cannot afford to buy these, they steal them. In the final instance, however, the means disrupt the end-goal, since the way in which they achieve the feminine ideal is seen to destroy all femininity; the girls are described as 'very aggressive, cynical to the point of insolence' (Ivanova 1990). Thus, while the discourse of deviance and delinquency is universal, as Barbara Hudson (1984) indicates, expressions of 'adolescent rebellion' among girls are seen not only as disruptive of public order but of the natural order of society *per se*; girls engaging in youth cultural activities are, in the words of two commentators, '*mutanty ponevole*' (unwilling mutants) – the product of the lack of gender-specific education in the family and at school (Sukhareva and Kuindzhi 1992).

'YOUTH CULTURE' IN POST-SOVIET RUSSIA: MARGINALIZED MEN AND TREACHEROUS WOMEN

The paradigm change in the youth debate as a whole is not coincident with the formal dissolution of the Soviet Union but can be traced back to 1990. It was then that the dominant image of youth as constructors of the bright (communist) future was replaced by that of young people as a lost generation with neither past nor future (Pilkington 1994a: 193). Young people began to be viewed as socially marginalized victims of 'the Soviet system' which had exploited their youthfulness whilst failing to protect their social and economic interests. With the advent of rapid marketization and its increasingly obvious negative social effects, this paradigm has been strengthened in the post-1991 period. The new themes of marginalization, delinquency and 'selling oneself for a quick buck' also serve to reinforce specific gender themes of the past. Although young women are no longer simply absent from the discussion – as they had been in the glasnost era debate on the *neformaly*[15] – nevertheless, the normal subject of discourse remains male.

The market, marginalization and male pride

The 'marginalization' discourse is rooted in the discussion of the underprivileged position of youth in the new Russia which has suggested that not leisure (or pleasure) but 'material welfare' is the most important issue for youth today (Levitskaia, Orlik and Potapova 1991). Economic marginalization, it is argued, is expressed among young people in aggression, juvenile crime and a poorly developed level of cultural interests (manifested in their resort to alcohol) (ibid.). This has been facilitated by 'the deep spiritual crisis in society' and the failure of traditional socializing institutions (primarily the family and educational institutions) (Plotnikov 1991). The broad social base for what is referred to as a new group of 'youth-marginals' is generally seen to be young people who are neither working nor studying and thus are deprived of even those tenuous links with society which young people generally enjoyed (Alekseenkov, Baranov and Nevar 1993: 6). However, all young people are considered potential marginals, since even those who do work live on the bare minimum and are often forced to turn to petty trade in order to survive, and are thereby gradually de-skilled and de-professionalized (ibid.).[16]

There are three key social threats posed by the marginalization of youth discussed in academic literature and the press: the emergence of aggressive subcultures, the drift into criminal culture, and general cultural and moral degeneration.

Aggressive subcultures

Although it is increasingly recognized that youth culture may play an 'integrating' role (in that it facilitates self-assertion and expression within a peer group), young people who remain 'outsiders' (primarily those neither working nor studying) are seen to develop distinct behaviourial patterns which reinforce their marginality. These centre on exaggerated masculinity, crudeness, aggression and belligerence (Plotnikov 1991: 15). The advent of the market (in its particularly crude form) is seen to have facilitated the emergence of a range of new youth subcultures which are often aggressively oriented towards each other (Alekseenkov, Baranov and Nevar 1993: 6). For some the Moscow youth scene consists of no more than multiple layers of young lumpens: lumpen-intellectuals (student-traders); lumpen-elite (investing hard currency abroad or in Moscow bars); the hidden unemployed in factories and vocational technical colleges (PTU); and semi-criminal traders (who will eventually drift into mafia structures) (ibid.).

There has also been speculation about the attraction of thousands of such 'lumpen teenagers' into the ranks of the neo-fascist forces. The Right Radical Party (*Pravo-radikal'naia partiia*), whose goal it is to 'preserve the gene bank of Russians', according to Chelnokov, uses the popularity of well-known right-wing rock stars (such as Pauk from the band *Korroziia Metalla*) to attract into its ranks a wide stratum of young 'apolitical marginals' (Chelnokov 1993a). Certainly, there is evidence of neo-fascism emerging among young people (Chelnokov 1994a; Chelnokov 1994b;), and racist and exclusivist orientations are commonly found among those to whom young people look.[17] Chelnokov is suggesting, however, that the radical right is particularly recruiting to its cause subcultural groups (specifically punks and *rokery*[18]) who hang out in the new, more commercially orientated clubs and discos. It is the latter, he says, who are 'the new outsiders of the former Country of Soviets' (Chelnokov 1993b: 1).

After closer encounters with these young people themselves, however, Chelnokov argues that in many cases youth cultural groups are manipulated into neo-fascist actions and share few of the ideological convictions of the politicized organizers. This conclusion is reached after the journalist himself was detained by special Ministry of the Interior troops along with other rock fans who had rioted after a band, rumoured to be playing at a certain venue, did not appear and it emerged that what was actually being held was a festival organized by extreme right-wing groups. Talking to the *rokery* it became clear to the journalist that they had not known who the organizers of the festival were and that their apparently fascist *symbolica* were not consciously imbued with neo-fascist meanings (Chelnokov 1993b).

If Chelnokov's retreat from his ideological interpretation is well grounded – which it surely is – then this only acts to reinforce the wider interpretation of youth cultural activity as a site for the expression of masculinity. Aleshina and Volovich, for example, argue that subcultural (or as they term it 'deviant') activity is essentially masculine; the majority of members of informal associations of teenagers are boys, and masculinity is emphasized in appearance (leather and metal), basic values (cult of risk, strength) and leisure practice (fights, strength sports, motorbike races, etc.). Youth cultural activity is thus interpreted as providing a supplementary channel for the acquisition of a male sex-role necessitated by the feminization of institutions of mainstream society (school and the family) and thus the deprivation of young men of opportunities to express and develop their own masculinity (Aleshina and Volovich 1991: 77).

Drift into crime

The market and marginalization of youth it brings, however, is seen, above all, to encourage young people to drift into criminal subcultures (Alekseenkov, Baranov and Nevar 1993). The most marginalized of groups are those (often very young) children who end up on the street, often referred to as modern-day *besprizorniki*[19] – unloved and uncared for (Osheverova 1994). This modernness is symbolized by the more complete alienation of the children involved (not even the traditional 'school of thieves' exists to support them today) and by the fact that they spend the money 'earned' not on the bare necessities of life but on Mars, Snickers, expensive cigarettes and fashionable clothes (Mikhailov 1994).

Thus, the drift into crime is not always related to abject poverty but may be a result of new values brought by market culture. This may encourage young people even from affluent families to prioritize earning money (selling food or drink on the street, washing cars or windscreens at junctions, reselling petrol, delivering newspapers)[20] over successfully completing their education. Since territory is all-important in this kind of crude capitalism, these young people quickly become involved in protection and racketeering circles. Those teenagers unable to find such work tend to drift into more 'traditional' forms of extortion such as demanding money from fellow pupils (*kachat' den'gi*). However, this can get out of hand: in Kostroma in 1993 a 14-year-old kidnapped an 8-year-old boy, killed him and then extorted 300,000 roubles from his parents, while in Krasnodar a 17-year-old demanded 40 million roubles for a kidnapped and murdered child (Chelnokov 1993c; Osheverova 1994).

Apart from 'rapid social stratification' creating as it does new needs, a second reason is cited for the rapid growth in juvenile crime; the closure of (or exorbitant charges for) youth leisure facilities. A survey of youth attitudes and leisure behaviour in Ufa (capital of Bashkortostan) concluded that young people's leisure needs were far from being met and accused the local authorities of providing 'fertile ground' for the development of criminal activity, drug abuse and drunkenness through their policy of allowing co-operators and private business to buy out youth leisure facilities for their own profit (Gareev and Dorozhkin 1993: 125). The direct connection made between 'kids on the street' and the rise in juvenile crime is spelled out in attempts to control youth crime in Ul'ianovsk which focus on measures to attract teenagers away from the street such as the creation of the association of teenage clubs under the main administration of education and the formation of the fund *Gruppa* (Group) to struggle against youth gangs (Gordeeva 1994). Young men thrown out onto the street in the provincial cities are seen as being in particular danger of drifting into existing territorial gang structures which themselves are becoming increasingly connected to formal criminal structures (Alekseev 1994; Fedorov 1994).[21] As is spelled out by Egorova, it is very difficult to prevent kids meeting in uncontrolled spaces (traditionally in Russia in basements of blocks of flats). The fine for such illegal gatherings is only one-tenth of the minimum wage (1,400 roubles) and while elite youth might be able to spend thousands of roubles on tickets for concerts, ordinary young people had nowhere to go (Egorova 1994).

Particularly noticeable is a new, and familiar to Western readers, debate about crime committed by very young children.[22] The police are most concerned about the under 14 age group since they are exempt from criminal responsibility; police statistics suggest that the growth of crime among children is ten times faster than that of adults (Osheverova 1994; Repin 1994). Part of the problem lies with the exploitation of legal loopholes by the adult criminal community which is increasingly using minors to fence stolen goods and sell drugs or weapons, knowing that until they are 14 they are not liable to criminal punishment (in the first half of 1993, 3.5 times as many juveniles were arrested for selling drugs as in the same period in 1992 and almost four times as many were arrested for extortion) (Chelnokov 1993c).

However, the problem is largely seen as a social one. One important factor cited is the vicious circle whereby exclusion from school for delinquency leads to further delinquency; in Novosibirsk, in the last two years, more than 13,000 children in classes 5–9 were excluded from school and not taken in by any institution (Repin 1994). This reflects the fact that since schools were relieved of responsibility for what have traditionally been known in Soviet society as 'difficult teenagers' (in accordance with the education law passed in 1993) the police has been the only agency dealing with these children (Osheverova 1994).[23] The need for additional institutions to intervene to end this vicious circle has been recognized and was reflected in the presidential decree 'On the prevention of the neglect of and crime among juveniles, and the protection of their rights' which set out to reorganize work with 'difficult teenagers' following the collapse of previously existing institutions. The document, amongst other things, suggests: the creation of special institutions for teenagers in need of social rehabilitation; the reorganization of reception-distribution centres into centres of temporary isolation for juvenile criminals; and the establishment of treatment institutions under the auspices of the Ministry of Education (Chelnokov 1993d). However, even though the social origins of juvenile criminality are recognized, infrastructural weaknesses mean that often brutally 'effective' (in the short term) policies are relied on; in the words of a police representative in Ul'ianovsk their aim is simply to 'decapitate' the gangs (Egorova and Zimina 1994).

Moral degeneration

In the discussion of market, marginality and juvenile crime, young women are not generally an issue at all. One article even openly suggests that the problem has been turned into a male one by society's tendency to cater better for young women's leisure than young men's. This report, from the city of Nizhnii Novgorod, contrasts the story of a group of 10–12-year-old lads who sleep rough in the city's railway station and drink and gamble their money away on slot machines, with the situation of girls in the city who may enrol at a youth club attached to a small enterprise where they can learn choreography, languages, business and even computing (Baklanova 1993).[24]

The national survey on teenage culture reveals why girls are not seen as a 'problem':

- girls are less likely to spend their time on the streets – whereas 60 per cent of male teenagers said they spent their time meeting and hanging round with friends, only 54 per cent of girls did so;
- girls were more likely to go to controlled spaces to enjoy leisure – they went to discos and cafés, watched television at home, did domestic things or spent time with their parents;
- girls showed lower rates of approval of the use of violence in settling problems (19 per cent of boys as opposed to 7 per cent of girls approved), of drinking (7 per cent of boys, 5 per cent of girls approved), of underage sex (18 per cent of boys, 6 per cent of girls approved) and of drug use (2 per cent of boys, 1 per cent of girls approved).

(Goskomstat RF 1992: 33, 126)

Where girls are discussed in terms of juvenile crime, a familiar sexualization of their behaviour is evident. Osheverova, for example, notes that girls seeking to earn money in the new 'market' environment turn increasingly to the 'oldest profession' and in particular to a new means of extortion: having served a rich client and received money from him, the young 'woman of easy virtue' blackmails the client; if she doesn't get more money she threatens to report the client for having sex with a minor. A 14-year-old, it is reported, earned 3 million roubles this way (Osheverova 1994). This attitude to sex (as business rather than as sacred) feeds into a general concern about the 'moral relativism' felt to have gripped teenagers. Plotnikov, for example, notes a significant decline in the belief in marriage and a growth in extra-marital birth rate, especially among 16–17-year-olds (Plotnikov 1991: 16).

However, there is some discussion of young women and criminal lifestyles. It is noted, for example, that around 35,000 girls in all are registered with police organs; a significant proportion of whom have been drawn into the porn business (Chelnokov 1993d). A mere 3.7 per cent of the current prison population is female and younger women (18–24-year-olds) do time mainly for 'narcotics' (39 per cent) and 'hooliganism' (40 per cent) (Kraminova 1993). However, of particular interest in the media is female sexual crime; a feature on women in prison profiled those convicted of picking up foreign men and then stealing their wallets as well as those girls used by men to earn money (Musina 1992). Also sensationalized are women who are violent, murdering either their husbands or their children (Kharitonenkov 1992).[25]

Sex, 'sponsors' and selling the nation

> Have we any right to close our eyes to the fact that in pursuit of the latest foreign 'rags', these girls are selling not just themselves but us – our pride, our name and our honour?
>
> (Konovalov and Serdiukov 1984: 8)

The connection made between girls' sexual purity and the national pride of the country is not new and the post-Soviet debate has some very familiar themes but also a few new twists.

At the most benign, although perhaps most pernicious, level the common-sense notion that today's young women choose their marriage partners for their wallets rather than for love is persistently reaffirmed. Old themes include the girl from the provinces who comes to study in Moscow with the single aim of marrying a Muscovite in order to obtain a residence permit (Bogdanova 1993). But, in the post-Soviet world, if a girl fails there are other possibilities; rich businessmen who will provide a flat in return for being 'visited' five nights a week, for example. Whichever path they choose, however, the reader is left in no doubt what the judgement of such women should be; 'today, thousands of girls calmly and calculatingly sell themselves' is the author's conclusion (ibid.). Other *limitchitsy*,[26] are not so successful and fall prey to the owners of striptease schools or erotic theatres, where girls are expected to offer additional services (Rezanov and Khoroshilova 1992).

Another type of modern girl is the girl who thinks that she is naturally entitled to a 'beautiful life'. This, it is suggested, is a product of the 'easy money' and rich acquaintances which can now be made by girls through beauty competitions and modelling. Such girls appear content to live off the 'sponsorship' of men and thereby escape the difficulties of 'post-Soviet reality' suffered by others. But, the commentator adds, this kind of life will leave a woman without the strength of character needed if, in the future, she wants a family and children (Bogdanova 1993).

Once again, young people appear as a symbol of the times and the future. The fear of a vulgar, unenjoyable life has created a new breed of young people – rich, cynical boys[27] and beautiful, calculating girls – who symbolize the material vulnerability, moral confusion, cultural imperialism of the West and degradation of the Russian nation which define the cultural contours of the post-Soviet environment (ibid.).[28]

A second traditional theme is the woman seeking a foreign husband in order to escape the banality of everyday life in Russia. In the post-*interdevochka* era, however, the revelation that large numbers of women (who have had no choice but to carry on living with their former husbands in the same flat for years after divorce) dream of finding a foreign husband and leaving (Shashkova 1994), are tempered by warnings that such marriages do not always bring the happiness they promise. One woman, it was reported, returned to Russia after marrying an Englishman who taught her English politeness by hitting her every time she forgot to say 'thank you', while a woman who married a Canadian was subsequently abandoned (with her two dependent daughters) by him (ibid.).

The debate on prostitution continues in the post-Soviet press and reflects new general concerns already referred to: the attraction of ever younger children into illegal activities and the increasingly organized nature of crime. In Moscow alone it is estimated by the juvenile crime department that there are at least 1,000 girls under the age of 18 working as prostitutes. Meeting resistance and violence from older prostitutes they now often have their own (16–17-year-old, male and female) pimps who pick up runaway girls at railway stations and bring them into the business by demanding they 'pay back' the help given them. Girls who refuse or who try to run away are punished; some have their heads shaved or burned with a cigarette, while others have a wineglass smashed inside them. Other children become prostitutes after being abducted or being 'sold' by their parents. The market in pornographic films involving all ages of girls has also been growing (Karmaza 1992). Other articles stress the money being made out of prostitution by pimps and racketeers surrounding the girls. These are often so called 'high-class firms' who market a distinct product to a clientele of rich businessmen (Aslamova 1992). Moscow police estimate there are about 173 such firms in Moscow, twelve of which they have managed to bust (Mikhailovich 1993). In Samara it is estimated there are a dozen such firms (Lebedev 1994). These types of organizations pay the girls only 30 per cent of what they earn (Mikhailovich 1993). Some girls do resist, however. An article in *Ogonek* discusses the case of a child prostitute who set herself up working from a trailer park used by foreign lorry drivers in Moscow and had a number of girls working for her. Since such girls avoid financial exploitation by men, they cannot be portrayed as victims. On the contrary, it is suggested that they lack sentimentality (never remember school, home, relatives) and are united by their agreement on one thing only – that men are animals and the 'enemy' (Editorial 1993: 35).

Given that the current transition to a capitalist mode of production abandons any notion of a third way or alternative path for Russia and relegates her to just another 'developing' society, the moral degeneration of women is linked to another key theme of the post-Soviet press, 'national humiliation'. One article referred to the 'export of live goods' (Russian girls) from Russia in a 'white slave trade' operating under the cover of marriage bureaux and intermediary organizations offering girls highly paid work abroad or the possibility of finding a foreign husband or becoming a model (Analiticheskaia sluzhba 'KP' 1993). It is not only the general impression of Russian girls which might humiliate the country, however, but a clear concern that it is to 'developing' not 'developed' countries which the girls are being exported (ibid). This is reinforced in other reports focusing on Russian prostitutes working in Turkey (Kulik 1994) and China (Tikhonova 1993a).

Thus, although sex is back as a subject for discussion in the daily and weekly press, it is generally associated with the selling of sex and thus the devaluation of marriage. Women no longer seek knights in shining armour but 'sponsors' who, in return for sexual favours, will support them materially (ibid.). This common-sense notion of girls' attitudes to their bodies reinforces the image of the manipulative sexually active woman as opposed to the 'victimized' sexually passive young woman, both evident in the perestroika press. One article in a local Livny (Orel region) newspaper illustrates this clearly; countering rumours that there was a Rostov type 'sex maniac' at loose in the area who attacked women, it recounts the 'truth' about two recent incidents, clearly putting the blame on the 'frivolity' of the girls involved. The first incident involved four (drunken) young men who had come into the town from a nearby village and had met two girls on the high street. 'Somehow', it is noted, 'one of the girls ended up in their car', but she turned out to be 'stubborn' and made such a racket in the car that the lads had to throw her out 'saying goodbye with a few generally harmless punches'. The second case was of a 14-year-old girl who went missing after going out to get bread. The police were alerted and a region-wide search begun. However, it turned out that the girl had simply decided to go off to relatives in the countryside without telling anybody; the journalist's recommendation is that she too should be given a few 'harmless smacks on a soft place!' (Poliakov 1994). The open sanctioning of male sexual predatoriness (and violence) and the blaming of women for 'frivolity' is clear.

On the rare occasion when the lives of young female prostitutes themselves are discussed, responsibility is also placed at the door of the girls (even though their male 'partners' are significantly older). Girls are accused of having an irresponsible attitude to their health (90 per cent do not make their clients use condoms for example) and of 'competing' with each other over who has had gonorrhea the most times (Karmaza 1992). For other commentators, they are simply sexually deviant:

> These 'nymphos' are deprived of all sense of shame … [they] show their breasts, take off their pants in unknown company, perform any 'concert' in front of others – it is as simple as drinking water for them. They have not yet grown up enough to feel a sense of shame.
>
> (Editorial 1993)

Once again it is clear that overt sexuality manifested by girls is not a forgivable sign of adolescent rebellion but disruptive of the feminine essence – shame, modesty and chastity.

CONCLUSION

Young women had a dual symbolic importance in Soviet society. As young people they symbolized the 'bright future' to which Soviet society was surely progressing (anchored in the discourse of the 'constructors of communism') whilst, as women, girls were responsible for both the physical reproduction of society and its spiritual and moral health. In the early Soviet period it was suggested that young women might stray from their tasks in both spheres as a result of their natural political backwardness or tendency towards 'frivolity', but they were not accorded any particular ideological significance. In the late Soviet period 'consumer desire' came to symbolize the lack of seriousness of youth to the construction task of youth and, in the case of girls, the consolidation of their natural frivolity (*legkomyslie*) in consumerism meant that their consumption often exceeded the limits of 'rational needs'. A sexual connotation was also attached to both frivolous behaviour in particular but 'going out' (*guliat'*)[29] in general in the case of girls. In this way, as in the West, the discourse of adolescence ('have fun while you're young') clashed with that of femininity.

Consuming behaviour also reinforced images of women as calculating, scheming and manipulative. Whilst for young men an over-narcissistic attitude might endanger rationality (by giving way to sensual pleasure), this was portrayed as the result of 'being led astray' either by girls or by the army of Western technologies trained on seducing the good Soviet patriot. In contrast, female 'irrational needs' were portrayed as personal deviancy or a product of the 'false emancipation' of women, the failure of Soviet society to correctly socialize its women. The result was that girls were seen not to consume 'rationally' but were consumed by their consumption. Their egos became dissolved into the stars they worshipped, or their bodies were consumed by men in order to fuel their voracious desire for the 'high life'. Moreover, this narcissism disrupted true femininity based on self-sacrifice and, since this essence of womanhood constituted the basis of the moral order of society, it threatened the very future of society.

In the post-Soviet period youth has ceased to be an object of overt political struggle and youth culture as a thing in itself has become difficult to separate out from other aspects of youth experience. However, it remains important to recognize youth practice outside of work, school and family as well as the significance of horizontal links and references to a wider (global) youth world via cultural artifacts and media. In the post-1991 period Russia has been opened to a whole host of new media and sites of cultural production which position young people and help shape their identities. These include Western images transferred by film, satellite and cable television, fashion, magazines, advertising, pornography, beauty shows, quiz shows, etc., and the impact of the information explosion deserves separate and much more detailed attention. From an analysis of the current debate,[30] it would appear that in the post-1991 period although sexuality and gender identity has appeared as a live issue, this has not necessarily had a progressive tone. Indeed, given the framing of the youth and consumption debate in a post-Soviet remasculinization of society, new femininities and masculinities have been high on the agenda of the new discourse but the result has been very different from the positive 'discursive explosion around what constitutes femininity' pinpointed in the West by McRobbie (McRobbie 1994: 158).

The market is seen to have generated a group of youth marginals in post-Soviet society who are, primarily, young men pushed out of the (public, male) spheres of education and employment. This exclusion (by 'the fathers') has forced them to seek alternative sites for their display of masculine characteristics and thus resulted in the emergence of aggressive subcultures on the streets of cities which often lead them into a life of crime. The market has also priced young people out of leisure facilities and this encourages street gang activity. Where young women appear at all, they are seen to have adapted to the market via a culture of manipulation and survival; they seek male 'sponsors' and thus create a uniquely female sphere of competition between each other for wealthy men. Displaced, they seek to reposition themselves in the new society *via* men.

Although there are some radical images disrupting standard discourse,[31] new femininities remain defined by the demographic discourse which calls for young women to identify primarily as 'future mothers', while masculinities are negotiated in the context of the crisis over conscription into military service and the perceived need to restore national pride. The press and academic debate on 'youth culture' in post-Soviet Russia thus fails to reflect the fluidity of contemporary Russian culture and the myriad ways in which young people strive to form workable identities – including gender identities – to negotiate their way in society. It is the concrete manifestations of such identities which are the subject of the remaining chapters of the book.

NOTES

1 'Game' (*igra*) is used by Bernshtam to describe the form of youth cultural practice in general.
2 The *Komsomol* was the communist youth organization whose first congress was held in August 1918.
3 This was a problem because it disrupted the dialectic of the 'construction of communism' by breaking the link between active physical involvement and ideological engagement.

4 Fans of rock and roll who emerged in the 1950s.

5 For a more detailed discussion of Soviet ideology on sexual difference see Chapter 5 of this volume.

6 The *sistema* is the name often given to the hippy culture deriving from the 'system' (network) developed among them which allowed people to find accommodation and support among fellow members across the former Soviet Union. For many, including Shchepanskaia, it is a wider network including a number of youth cultural styles other than hippies.

7 For a fuller discussion of the perestroika discourse on gender and youth and the strategies employed by young women in this period on the youth scene, see Pilkington 1996.

8 Soviet sociological research suggested that whereas 58 per cent of male respondents said they listened to rock (the figure was the same for Western and for Soviet rock) only 24 per cent of girls said they listened to Soviet rock and just 3 per cent to Western rock. The girls, it seemed, preferred both Soviet and Western 'popular music' (*estrada*) – 65 per cent listened to the former and 69 per cent to the latter (Kataev 1986: 107). This general trend was confirmed by the national survey of teenage (12–16-year-olds) lifestyles at the end of the perestroika period, which found that while 66.6 per cent of girls listened to *estrada*, only 14.1 per cent listened to rock music, while for boys 31.3 per cent listened to rock music and only 44.8 per cent to *estrada* (Goskomstat RF 1992: 151).

9 Jenson argues that:

Each fan type mobilizes related assumptions about modern individuals: the obsessed loner invokes the image of the alienated, atomized 'mass man'; the frenzied crowd member invokes the image of the vulnerable, irrational victim of mass persuasion. These assumptions – about alienation, atomization, vulnerability and irrationality – are central aspects of twentieth century beliefs about modernity.

(Jenson 1992: 14)

10 Men, he goes on to say, are rarely faithful to their wives or girlfriends. 'What is surprising is the number of women who take the same attitude [*sic*]' (Easton 1989: 72).

11 For a fuller exploration of the *mazhory*, see Pilkington 1994a: 248–51.

12 This theme is also present in the film by Shchekochikhin, *My Name is Harlequin*, although here the right to the girl is challenged by a good but 'simple' lad from a normal street gang.

13 See *Moskovskii Komsomolets* 29 March 1985: 2 and *Moskovskii Komsomolets* 19 June 1985.

14 It is worth noting that the same term – *snimat'* – is used by gang members for stealing objects and picking up girls.

15 Apparently, informal youth groups are no more: 82.5 per cent of youth (12–16-year-olds) surveyed for the government study of the way of life of children and teenagers in 1992 said they were not a member of any youth informal association (Goskomstat RF 1992: 166).

16 These are positions put forward by three members of the permanent youth affairs commission of the Moscow city council in 1993.

17 An interview with the popular band Two Aeroplanes, for example,

revealed racist, heterosexist and Russian supremacist views, parcelled in crude humour (Polupanov 1994).

18 Bikers and heavy rock fans. See Chapter 13 of this book for a more detailed discussion of the Moscow *rokery*.

19 Homeless children who roamed the country.

20 One group of 10-year-olds in Samara were particularly enterprising; they sold condoms outside discos (Osheverova 1994).

21 For a more detailed discussion of this process see Chapter 12 of this volume.

22 The majority of crimes committed by children (70 per cent) are thefts and robberies, but nevertheless in 1993 children under 14 committed more than 200 murders (Repin 1994).

23 Osheverova clearly posits the problem as a social not legal one and apportions blame above all to the micro-social sphere: a third of juvenile criminals are from poor families, half are from single-parent families. She recounts a particularly tragic story from Samara which has all the elements of a Soviet moral tale: the hero is a lad of 12 whose father (and presumably role model) abandoned the family when he was 1 and whose mother remarried but died soon afterwards. The children lived at first with their stepfather and his new wife but from the age of 7 they were moved into a boarding school. At 12 the lad ran away, taking his sister with him (who had 'been whoring around with men for two years already' after her stepfather had raped her at 12). Failing to find work, the lad started doing over flats (*chistit' kvartiry*), then pick-pocketing at stations (Osheverova 1994: 5).

24 They also received lectures from a beautician which is said to have had both a positive physical and psychological effect (Baklanova 1993).

25 One story told of a mother (married and divorced twice already although only 26) who killed her own 5-year-old child, because, in the journalist's opinion, she simply got in the way of her lifestyle (Kharitonenkov 1992). For a discussion of the portrayal of women who murder their husbands see Chapter 10 of this volume.

26 Those living and working on the edges of prestigious cities to which access is restricted in the hope of eventually being rewarded with a residence permit for the city.

27 Young men are not completely absolved of responsibility; it is noted that they are often reluctant to get married and risk losing their freedom, since 'bad past experiences' with women mean they do not trust them.

28 There are exceptions, such as the story recounted of a 20-year-old woman who is homeless (her mother is an alcoholic, her father a sailor who does not want to help) but who does not follow the 'obvious' route of marrying someone for their flat because she still believes in love (Tikhonova 1993b). The struggle to provide for herself and the disastrous relationships she involves herself in, however, provide no positive motivation to take this independent line to other young women!

29 This word has an immediate sexual connotation in Russian since it is also the verb used to mean 'having an affair' or 'being unfaithful'.

30 For the sake of comparability with the analysis of the pre-1991 period, only the press and academic literature has been discussed here.

31 Attention is paid in the press to the 'exotic' including successful business-

women. Among young people, at least in Moscow, meanwhile, Kseniia Strish and Sade (radio and television presenters who stretch and challenge gender norms) are extremely popular.

12 Young women in provincial gang culture

A case study of Ul'ianovsk

Elena Omel'chenko

Youth gangs[1] are currently an issue of great concern in Russia. Although the emergence of gangs is characteristic of all cities in which the construction of new housing estates and districts has outstripped the development of cultural infrastructure, in Russia the situation is intensified by the difficult socio-political context. This might be described as widespread alienation and a general break-down in social relations and communication. In such circumstances existing social tension may be significantly aggravated by a 'third force', especially if that force is associated with the criminal world. Thus, given the current deterioration in relations, not only with the former republics of the USSR but also with the autonomous republics within Russia, teenage gangs might act as 'internal detonators' of more serious conflict. If their activities become controlled by the mafia, or if the gangs become incorporated into corrupt structures, they might succeed in provoking conflict effectively even in the 'safest' of regions of the country.

> It would not be that difficult for us to turn safe Ul'ianovsk into a 'hot spot'. If necessary, within a week a struggle could be started between, for example, Tatars and Russians. This is not hard to organise; robberies, murders if necessary, are arranged and those you want drawn into the conflict are framed. It is quiet here because, as yet, that is how it suits everyone.
>
> (Gang member, Ul'ianovsk 1994)[2]

Of course, much of this is bragging, but there is probably also some truth in it; the gangs are not only 'cleaners',[3] but may constitute part of a socially dangerous 'fifth column'.

The importance of the gang problem in Russia is related also to the increasingly obvious fusion of the gangs with mafia structures and their growing links with the criminal world. The latter has been facilitated by the contact maintained with those serving prison sentences (by gang practice of assisting relatives and sending parcels to imprisoned members) and by their return to the gangs after release.

THE 'KAZAN' PHENOMENON' AND ITS IMPACT ON THE DISCUSSION OF YOUTH GANGS

Ul'ianovsk is a particularly interesting location for the study of gangs since it reproduces the so-called 'Kazan' phenomenon' whilst retaining some specifics of its own. The so-called Kazan' phenomenon received intense media attention in the perestroika period and the sensationalization of the issues has been twofold:

- First, although the media attention meant that research began to be conducted on the gang phenomenon, it also exaggerated the problem itself, encouraging other young people to follow the 'trend'.
- Second, once the 'sensation' died down, interest quickly faded. Consequently, less than five years later the reverse process is already underway; there is now very little attention and interest in studying provincial youth gangs.

This original interest has left a literature behind it, but publications, both in the press and in specialist journals, have tended to describe gangs from a purely criminological angle or to employ a narrow interpretation of deviation theory in their studies. A typical example here is an edited collection, *Sbornik: Problemy Bor'by s Deviantnim Povedeniem* (1989) (*Problems of the Struggle Against Deviant Behaviour*). The title speaks for itself. The majority of works in this area have been written by lawyers, medics and specialists in psychiatry and have focused on the study of drug addicts, alcoholics and teenagers with sexual deviations (see Arshavskii and Vilks 1990; Kofyrin 1991; Lelekov and Prokhorov 1994). Where Western sources are drawn on, the partial, and often superficial, survey of literature means analysis does not go beyond the employment of Durkheim's theory of anomie to explain the emergence of deviance in the youth sphere (see, for example, Vasil'ev 1994: 124–31). Particularly when deviant behaviour is considered in tandem with women's problems, the approach taken is almost always that of 'pathology' (see for example Nekrasov 1991;[4] or Sviadoshch 1991). It should also be noted that neither those working in the area of gender issues nor those studying gangs have as yet directly touched questions of the place and role of teenage girls in such gangs (see for example: Gilinskii 1989: 20–2; Gilinskii 1990: 30–6), whilst the poor access to Western literature means that any work that does exist on teenage girls in gangs has been unavailable hitherto in Russia.

Apart from filling an information gap left by the collapse of interest in gangs, therefore, the research upon which this chapter is based attempted to consider the importance of gender relations in Russian youth gangs. The present study is also a rare attempt to gain an insight into the gangs from inside, approaching the issue without preconceived notions of 'the normal' and 'the deviant', in the hope of understanding the values of gang members and the nature of their interactions with each other. This is rendered still more important given the fact that during the course of the research the author was made painfully aware that other institutions (police, school and technical college administrations, teachers and psychologists) were not addressing the question of teenagers in gangs. Although the material gathered cannot hope to exhaust the question of the position and role of young women in the gangs, nevertheless, it is hoped that even raising the question will provoke further interest.

PROVINCIAL YOUTH GANGS: DETERMINING THE OBJECT OF STUDY

Gangs are a unique form of association of teenagers who are drawn together in order to defend territory (spheres of influence) which may, or may not coincide with place of residence. Thus youth gangs may be classified in the following way:

According to the object of defence

This may be a place of common residence and the object defended may be:

- a block of flats or, if it is a new district, a 'mega-block';
- a whole district – as a rule this is characteristic for districts of the traditional, 'sleeper' or dormitory kind[5] – or even a village, urban settelement or small town.

Alternatively, defence could be determined by the nature of the enemy and thus the source of danger might be:

- another gang, in which case the group's own territory or the territory of several groups, if the enemy is a common one, is defended;
- the police, in which case a territory or sphere of influence is defended, and, as a rule, the interests of all groups are united;
- criminal elements, in which case it is privileges and rights to 'supervise' or 'graze' one's own territories which are defended.

According to members' age

Groups of very young children (9–12 years old) are known as '*soplivie*' (babies) or '*melkie*' (small-fry). Those a little older (11–13 years old) are called '*zelenie*' (greens) while the norm are those aged between 11 and 16 who are known as '*krutie*' (toughs) or '*normal'-nie*' (sound lads). '*Stariki*' or '*superstariki*' (old-timers) are terms used for those who have already outgrown the gang but either by habit or for special reasons continue to meet and 'work' together.

According to members' sex

Gangs may be exclusively male (as are the majority of gangs). At a fairly primitive level such gangs facilitate male adolescent 'socialization'. Such gangs inculcate in their members certain language norms, manners and a 'code of masculine honour'. The basis of these rules and laws is the criminal 'system' and prison 'code' which is transferred back and adapted to 'civilian' life. Gangs may be exclusively female, although there are very few such groups. There is some evidence that one of the all-girl gangs in Ul'ianovsk – the 'White Bows' – continues to operate but its members have no influence on the division of the city into spheres. Male gang members, however, like to refer to them or cite them as evidence of the vitality of the gang phenomenon. Gangs may be mixed, having both male and female members, but as a rule there are more lads than girls. The division of roles within such groups is discussed below.

According to the aggressiveness of the gangs

Gangs may be oriented:

- 'defensively', i.e. be relatively peace-loving, only ensuring that their own borders are not penetrated and never attacking first;
- 'aggressively', i.e. seeking constantly to expand and to extend their sphere of influence;

- 'indeterminately', i.e., not having a single position but, depending on the situation, acting defensively or aggressively.

Statistical data, collating operations carried out by the police in the city of Ul'ianovsk, suggest that although the gang phenomenon in Ul'ianovsk is being brought under some degree of control, it nevertheless remains an important and disturbing element of life in the city. In 1991 there were forty-two youth gangs in Ul'ianovsk, in 1992, thirty-three and in 1993, sixteen. In 1993 six young people died in inter-gang fighting and 759 juveniles were summoned for participation in gangs. A study of the composition of these gangs reveals a general tendency towards a reduction in the number of gang members but a worrying rise in the number neither working nor studying (see Table 12.1).

Table 12.1 Change in gang membership, 1991–3

	1991	*1992*	*1993*
Gang members in total	3,000–5,000	1,739	1,588
Juveniles[6]	2,500+	1,277	1,222
Adults[7]	500+	462	366
School pupils	—	452	311
SPTU[8] students	—	425	242
Students of other educational establishments	—	139	120
Those neither working nor studying	—	363	725
Working	—	360	231
Girls	87	44	7
Leaders	97	80	62

After the completion of the first study (1991) significant changes, both in the territorial distribution of the gangs and in the nature of their interactions with each other, the mafia and the criminal world were noted. This led to a second study which was conducted over a period of six months (from the end of 1993 to the beginning of 1994) and included ten interviews with members of the gangs: leaders and 'lieutenants', girls and 'attached' members. Members of gangs currently held in juvenile colonies (in Dmitrovgrad) were also interviewed. However, on this occasion, no survey of all gang members was possible (due to their greater secrecy and fear of publicity and our own concerns for the personal safety of the researchers). In addition, about a dozen interviews were conducted with experts working in various relevant organizations including the police juvenile affairs department, security services, education departments, drug abuse and psycho-nuerological services, mothers and children's services, psychologists and doctors.

BECOMING A GANG MEMBER: IS THERE A CHOICE?

Both studies showed that adolescents find themselves drawn into gangs at critical periods in their lives. At particular risk of being drawn into gang culture are young people whose families have very low levels of income and education or who suffer the extreme material and social circumstances of single-parent families in Russia. Many also have experienced domestic violence, drug abuse and alcoholism in the home. The self-development of young people in Russia is also inhibited by: subordination by parents, teachers and fellow school pupils; the lack of virtually any socio-cultural infrastructure in the 'sleeper districts' of Russian cities; sexual frustration and the lack of opportunity for expending physical energy; and the difficulty in developing self-esteem in a society which is itself in a state of extreme social and moral instability. Moreover, this instability, resulting from the sudden and brutal reorientation towards commerce, provides little motivation for success within existing hierarchies, whilst organized gangs and mafia structures provide protection and security and also offer a hierarchy and discipline.

However, this does not mean that it is inevitable that all young people from 'risk groups' will enter gang life. Many young people are simply forced into gang activity due to the strong influence of the gang in the district where the young person lives or goes to school. Only the central schools (Schools no. 1, 2 and 3) are considered to be completely free from gang influence. In districts where the influence of the gang authorities is particularly great, all children around the age of 11–12 must pay off a 'debt' imposed on them and are obliged to attend gatherings (*sbor*). If they refuse to pay or to attend the *sbor* they may be shunned, beaten up or humiliated in some other way. The pressure is so great that often the only way to escape the gang is to move to a new district, school or even city. Sometimes, not only money is extorted but the children are forced to steal, are intimidated and persecuted. Often the strength of the group is imaginary; it breeds fear. In fact, intervention by parents, teachers or police could end the intimidation, but either young people are afraid to report their experiences or parents think it is easier to pay off the gang rather than resist it. In some gangs, young people are accepted only after they have proved themselves by beating up or humiliating somebody or stealing something. This kind of ritual acts as a demonstration of strength, and those who fail to gain acceptance in this way are disgraced and treated as outcasts; they are beaten and humiliated by members of the gang. Entrance to the gang also requires a payment.

The gang is financed primarily by extortion; in every school in the gang's sphere of influence there is an 'accountant' who is responsible for the collection of money. If people resist payment this individual can call on the 'fighters' to assist him. The amount extorted varies; from 1,000 to 10,000 roubles.[9] In working-class districts money is collected after the factory pay-day. Ostensibly this money is collected to pay for funerals of gang members killed in fights, to support gang members in prison and to help their parents or 'wives'. However, there also exist a great number of fictitious groups who use the fear of real gangs to collect 'taxes' which line their own pockets.

THE CHANGING NATURE OF YOUTH GANG ACTIVITY IN UL'IANOVSK

Since the height of the moral panic about provincial youth gangs which, not surprisingly, coincided with the disintegration of the Soviet Union and the move to market relations (1990–2), the principles of association of such gangs have undergone significant change. Some of the groups remain more or less intact but, despite the fact that many of them have retained their original names (based on the district in which their members live), their territorial base is no longer the primary explanatory factor. Today the 'territorial principle' of association has been replaced by 'spheres of influence', above all markets, car parks, petrol stations, commercial stores and restaurants, and the gangs are mainly used by organized criminals to distract the police from more serious criminal activities or as a cheap 'mob' (see Figure 12.1). Each sphere of influence has its own 'boss' who is generally well-informed about all mob activity. Provocations take place but any action must be sanctioned by an 'authority'. Thus, if earlier gang fights were conducted in order to protect the gang's own district from intruders, now they are purely used to distract attention and act as a cover for more serious activities taking place elsewhere. However, the gangs remain of mixed nationality and there are no known cases of disagreements or fights on ethnic grounds.

Within the gangs new forms of relations are also emerging. In particular, they have begun to adopt practices from criminal culture

Development of gangs

PAST	────────────→	PRESENT

Independent

Dependent on mafia

- groups named after district e.g. '*Tsentr*' '*Peski*'

- names remain unchanged

- defend the district where members live

- defend 'spheres of influence'

- based in own district

- based at:
  - car parks
  - petrol stations
  - commercial shops
  - restaurants
  - sites of black market activity

- easy to find gathering place

- impossible to find gathering place

- non-formal youth association (reflection of Pioneer or *Komsomol* organizations)

- learn from penal institutions: underground, hierarchical, strict discipline, observation of rules of security

- more or less open structure

- semi-closed structure

- group leader and members are same age (14–17)

- group leaders are adults (aged 20–25 or older)

- no ideology

- some kind of ideology

- minimal pressure on children living in the district

- maximum pressure with financial extortion

Figure 12.1 Changes in the basis of association among gangs

which they learn from their time in prison. Such practices include: a system of seniority; an underground existence; strict rules of security; permanent combat readiness; and strict disciplinary codes. This means that, if earlier it was reasonably easy to locate a gang's gathering place, now it is virtually impossible. This is also a result of the success of the police in locating the former gathering places and keeping them under control and is facilitated by the increasing levels of equipment of the gangs. The gangs currently have at their disposal forty-four cars (registered legally in one name but used collectively), twenty-two walkie-talkies and a whole range of weapons.

The centres of concentration of the gangs have remained the same – schools, technical colleges, sports schools and sports centres. These centres are gradually becoming the main suppliers of racketeers, gang-fighters and boss-men. The importance of sheer physical strength and fighting skills (including martial arts, karate and judo) has increased. On the other hand, in contrast to the earlier gangs, some kind of group ideology and gang principles now exist. This is because the boss-men have brought their own values and opinions to the gangs. These boss-men are adults (21–24 years of age) who often have served time in prison, have a higher cultural level than the ordinary gang members and are generally involved in commercial activities.

YOUTH GANGS AND ORGANIZED CRIME

The youth gang is not simply a subordinate element of the mafia, it is an organization in itself (see Figure 12.2). Unlike in the major Russian cities such as Moscow and St Petersburg, there is no clear division between 'national' mafias (Chechens, Georgians, Azerbaijanis). Rather, there is an extremely limited number of mafia groups based on districts of the city (Zavolzhskaia, Zasviazhskaia, Kiniakovskaia). The strongest structures are in the northern part of the city (where they are known as the 'Wolves') while the weakest are in the newer districts where the structures are only just forming. The mafia uses youth gangs as a cheap and safe means of intimidation – the gangs are the most mobile units of the mafia and quickly react to their call. From 50 to 200 fighters can be called up within several minutes by phone or by walkie-talkie. However, the youth gangs retain an open organization and are well known to the local police and to some extent controlled by them. The number of youth gangs is gradually decreasing (see above) and their prestige

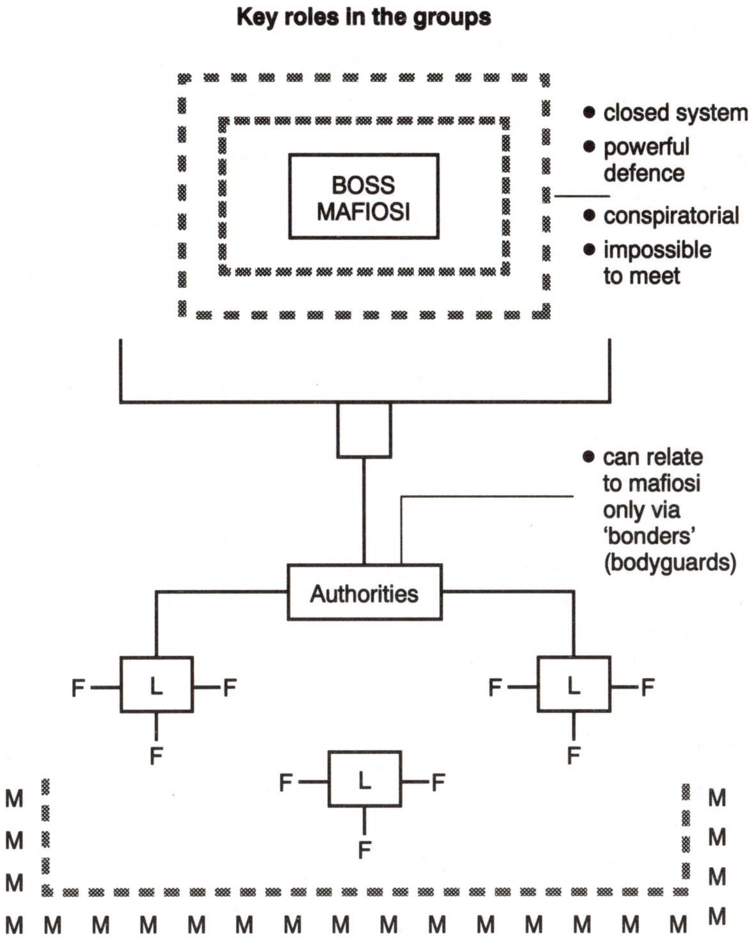

Key roles in the groups

Figure showing nested dotted boxes containing **BOSS MAFIOSI**, with annotations:
- closed system
- powerful defence
- conspiratorial
- impossible to meet

Below connected to **Authorities** box, with annotation:
- can relate to mafiosi only via 'bonders' (bodyguards)

Authorities connects to three **L** boxes (each with F — L — F and F below), and rows of **M** members.

Key
L 'Lieutenants' ('right-hand men') These people can:
   • grant licences
   • communicate with the police
F Fighters (runners or casual workers)
M Members
There are also casual members of the gangs.

Figure 12.2 Relationship between youth gangs and the mafia

is waning but, if necessary, they can still gather almost instantaneously.

The mafia has a closed system of organization based on secrecy and conspiracy. The boss-men are closely connected with the mafia and never appear in the gang openly but always via their 'right hand men' ('lieutenants') who usually have a criminal record. It is these bosses and right-hand men who are considered the most dangerous elements of the gangs and, as such, are the focus of attention for the Committee for Combating Organized Crime. Those who have served time in prison are given responsibility for keeping guard of banks and other important commercial structures. They are valued members of the gang and are often given a BMW or Mercedes on release from prison; this rewards the recipient and simultaneously buys future loyalty and dependence. Each commercial store is assigned its own *'muzhik'* ('bloke') who is paid by the mafia and used in future activities. These people are often the link between the gangs and the mafia.

The 'fighters' are generally drawn from sports schools and sections and may be highly rated members of the gang or simply younger 'toughs' who can be summoned by the right-hand men and ordered to do a particular job (such as stealing a car) for a small fee. Anybody committing a theft or other mob activity must obtain permission from the lieutenant, who is in direct contact with the mafia. Those undertaking such activities without permission (licence) are punished. The lieutenant is a middle man; he has authority, gives orders and ensures that leading mafia men can remain in the shadows. The police know the lieutenants in each district and may approach them for information about a particular crime. Often the lieutenants will hand over the guilty person, since it may be in their own interest; a prison sentence makes a young person even more dependent on the structure.

Thus, although, as yet, there is no total fusion between youth gangs and mafia structures, there is a growing tendency for youth gangs to learn and apply the methods and techniques of the mafia.

GIRLS IN UL'IANOVSK GANGS

As a rule both boys and girls are drawn into the gang in the same way – via extortion (non-payment of 'debts'), intimidation or drugs. During the period of the first study of gangs (1991), there were two purely female gangs: the 'White Bows' (*'Belie bantiki'*) and the 'Cats' (*'Koshki'*). Their main reported activities were attacks on students from the military communications college (who are seen as 'good boys' and therefore not 'real men', and who are popular with 'normal girls'). These lads were intimidated and sexually assaulted. The girl gangs were known for particular brutality and unmotivated criminal acts. They wore bows in their hair,[10] wide trousers (signifying an anti-Moscow, anti-elite style) and gaudy make-up (the most visible and tangible manifestation of femininity). Organizationally, the female gangs were smaller (between fifteen and twenty members) and had fewer levels of hierarchy; there was a single leader feared by all.

By 1993, however, there were no purely female gangs in Ul'ianovsk and the discussion below focuses on the participation of young women in mixed gangs. Particular attention is paid to girls' positions within the gang, relations to male members, relations with other young women in and outside the gang, dress styles and behavioural patterns. It is suggested that, in general, girls' positions mirror those of male members (see Figure 12.3). This classification is not fixed, however; the roles played by young women in the gangs are mobile and constantly changing.

Analysing the position of young women in mixed gangs one might say that the first classifying factor is *age*. The oldest women in the gang are the 'wives'[11] who, like the authoritative members of the gang may be over 18 (usually up to about 22). 'Prestigious girls' are between 15 and 18 (although they are sometimes older). Fighters are usually 16–17 and never older than 17. All other girls are generally very young – from 12–13 up to 15. The immaturity of the younger girls befits their marginal roles in the group; such roles are best fulfilled by those with low resistance, weak will and non-adult status. Marriage is usually the point at which girls leave the gangs, although some may move out in order to practise 'street' prostitution or to start up their 'own business'. However, even after they have left the group girls may sometimes, 'for old time's sake', help the gang by warning of a danger or pulling in somebody.

Just as for male gang members, the higher the status of female members, the more likely they are to be connected to the mafia. Thus, 'wives' and 'prestigious girls' straddle gang and, mafia life and, since they do not participate in fights directly (except when they pull in somebody or distract attention from real fights), their position is essentially marginal. For the 'ordinary' girls in the gang they are out of reach but they do not have sufficient status to enter the mafia. As a result they generally only communicate with each other and with 'their lads' (the male members of the same status).

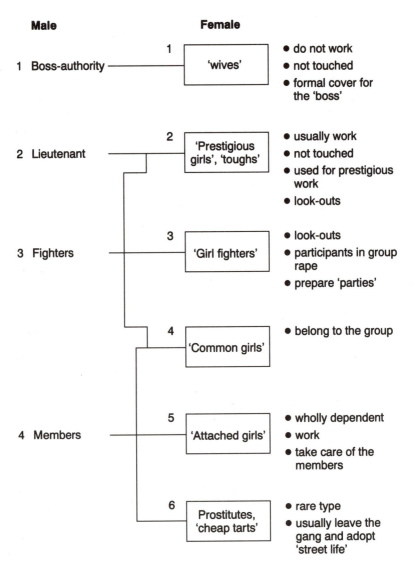

Figure 12.3 A typology of girls in youth gangs

All girls connected with the gangs (or mafia) in Ul'ianovsk share a certain dress style. This might be described as a *gopnik*[12] style and is distinguished by its conservatism. In contrast to other youth cultural styles it is not influenced by avant-garde fashion nor marked by the importance of '*fenechki*', which imbue artefacts with an individuality or personal meaning and, in other youth cultural groups, may be given as presents to one another.[13] On the contrary, what distinguishes *gopnik* style is the absolute reproduction of those objects of style having symbolic significance for group members. This conservatism is a product not simply of provincial but also of village mentality. This does not mean girls literally dress the same way as those living in rural areas but that, like girls moving to the city from villages or the suburbs, they try to merge into the crowd, not to stand out. Above all, it is important to dress like everybody else and to observe srictly the fashion norms prevailing in your own crowd.

What are the key elements of this style?

- Expensive clothes (relative to status) made of synthetic and glittery materials and in loud, unnatural colours. Alternatively, a combination of black and white is very popular, for example, white tights and leggings worn with black high-heeled shoes;
- a lot of jewellery (depending on status this would be either fake pearls, gold or silver or (modest) precious stones);
- high-heeled shoes in bright colours;
- permed and dyed hair.

Dress style and behaviourial patterns also differ according to status and role in the gang, however.

The leaders (bosses) of gangs have 'wives' who are not to be touched by other men. 'Wives' generally have secondary or secondary specialist education but a fairly narrow sphere of interests. They usually have no children (since children are an open invitation for blackmail) and, if they do, then they are usually left with their mothers in the village or another town. 'Wives' attend gatherings and parties where business is done and may be used as a formal (although rather primitive) cover for bosses to assume an apparently respectable way of life and provide alibis to the police for their 'husbands' when required to do so. The wife's role is to be at her husband's side during the conducting of negotiations and to entertain the guests when necessary. 'Wives' dress very expensively (although often very tastelessly); dressing poorly would immediately cast a shadow on their husbands' power and status. This 'dressing up' is partially necessitated by the role wives play at parties and meetings which require them to be 'dressed for the occasion'. However, it also has a symbolic importance. In Russian provincial culture expensive clothes are protected and worn only on 'holidays'; these girls are thus dressing as if it were a 'holiday' every day. 'Dressing up' involves wearing either very short or, very long dresses, often off-the-shoulder or with cut away backs; high heels; large, dangly gold earrings; a lot of expensive rings; thick gold necklaces or chains with pendants; and gold bracelets. Brightly painted nails, fluffy, dyed (often peroxide blonde) hair, heavily applied make-up and expensive French perfume are also fashionable.

There are exceptions to this style; one 'wife' interviewed, who had a degree in history and appeared intelligent and well-read, had tried to retain her 'intellectual image'. This was not always easy (she had to prevent her husband buying her tasteless presents) and she did not have close friendships with the other 'wives', whom she considered rather stupid. However, the authority of her husband meant she was not picked on for her failure to follow fashion norms and she herself did not antagonize relations with the other girls, knowing that virtually everything talked about among the girls was 'passed on' to husbands (passing on conversations was in fact a key function of the 'wives' in the gang). The stresses of the role (in particular, having to provide an alibi for her husband) had made her think about leaving the gang:

> I have got to the point of wanting to leave. But I don't know how to do it. My 'husband' loves me in his own way and says that he won't let me go that easily.

However, the lifestyle had its advantages, such as enough 'pocket money' to take a holiday abroad every year, and in a second interview this young woman appeared much more satisfied with her life; her husband's latest present to her had been a Mercedes. In fact, in general women of this status were completely satisfied with their roles and many rationalized their behaviour. One 19-year-old girl explained her life thus:

> I think that it is the most dignified way of earning money for women. Firstly, you do not have to sleep with 'them'. Secondly, others don't touch you. And, thirdly, that is what these men are there for; to earn money and in this f****** country, in this s**** which is my life, this is the only way.

Girls who really loved their husbands were rare and viewed as 'romantic fools'. However, the commercial relations which form the basis of the 'marriage' are not all one way; when required to do so the girls fulfil their obligations to provide alibis to the letter.

The girls of right-hand men ('lieutenants') are known as 'prestigious girls' or 'toughs' (*krutie*) and are not touched by other men either. They carry out prestigious jobs (such as picking up 'fat cats', stopping cars needed for specific purposes) or act as look-outs during raids or burglaries. Prestigious girls are usually younger than the 'wives' and their dress style is concomitantly poorer and even less tasteful. They are less inclined towards dresses and more towards brightly coloured or white leggings with a short, brightly coloured skirt sometimes over the top and a very loud blouse or sweater. They also wear a lot of jewellery, paint their nails and wear high heels.

As a rule they 'work' together (in a small group) and get on fairly well, although relations remain quite business like. Outside the gang they rarely retain friends, and their peers fear and envy them. They generally have secondary or secondary specialist education (sometimes they are still at school) and try to forge some kind of career for themselves (often working in commercial shops or booths as sales girls, as hairdressers or in small, semi-legal, private firms). Above all, however, they try to marry successfully.

Although these girls also straddle the gang and the mafia they have a more subordinate position in the gang than 'wives' and must always be prepared to face the consequences (being beaten up or having money taken from them) if they fail in their roles. They have no bargaining power in these situations.

Sexual relationships are conducted only with 'their own' lads and it is very rare for these girls to sink to prostitution. They consider it their duty to 'look after' the lads in the gang who 'work hard'.

Girl fighters (*boitsy*) are the girls of male fighters or, less frequently, fighters themselves. They take responsiblity for preparing gang gatherings but rarely participate in important fights. They are sometimes used as look-outs and have been known to participate in group rapes of other women. There are two broad types of girl 'fighters'. First there are those who try to be exactly like boys. These girls tend not to wear makeup at all, have short 'boyish' hairstyles, practice body building and combat sports, and use obscene language (*mat*) in their speech. They tend to be students of vocational-technical colleges (PTU) or sixth formers from schools in new districts. They rarely have female friends from outside the gang, preferring a kind of male friendship with other girls in the gang. Above all, they make friends among the male gang members. Indeed, many first enter the gang as a result of a relationship with a lad from the gang. Although partially subjected to fashion norms, there are some persistent elements to the dress style of the fighters, in particular, wide trousers or, alternatively, long, wide black skirts.

The second type of girl fighter is rarer and, in appearance, completely opposite to the first type. These girls emphasize what they consider to be 'feminine' particularly by the application of incredibly obvious make-up (almost clown-like), which is an immediate indicator of gang membership. In other ways they are similiar to the first type: the same level of culture, use of *mat* and heightened aggression. In a strangely distorted form, this kind of girl has a maternal relationship to the fighters. They are genuinely unselfish in their concern and tenderness for the lads and sexual relations are entered into only 'for love'.

'Common girls' (*obshchie devochki*) are considered to belong to the gang and can be used sexually by its members. They are treated purely as sexual objects, not women in their own right, and it is almost impossible to rise in the hierarchy of the group and become, for example, a 'prestigous girl'. 'Attached girls' (*pristegnutie devochki*) are simply friends hanging out with the gang who often take care of gang members after fights. 'Common girls' and 'attached girls' have a marginal position in the gang and it is difficult to distinguish clearly between them. 'Attached girls' have somehow been drawn into the gang but are often the object of teasing. They have a very low level of culture and are reserved and unsociable. 'Common girls', on the contrary, have generally already passed through the stage of being 'attached' and tend to be rather loud and vulgar. They are unable to explain why they entered the gang and appear to have neither fighting skills nor the ability to conduct any 'ideological' struggle with their enemies.

Among these girls the level of venereal disease is high, as is the rate of abortion. This is often the result of sexual use and abuse of such girls in the gangs and thus it would be inaccurate to label them 'prostitutes'; their sexual activity is either involuntary or conducted out of curiosity and not for material gain. The incidence of gang rape (of non-gang girls or of girls who have broken gang rules) is high, and such rapes often are conducted in order to subjugate girls who, it is feared, know too much. As a consequence of their negative sexual experience in the gangs, however, these girls may become prostitutes after leaving the gang.

Prostitutes or 'cheap tarts' (*deshevie davalki*) are relatively rare in the gangs and usually leave the gang after only a short period, preferring the 'street life'. They sometimes develop friendships with more experienced, older women.

CONCLUSION

In place of a conclusion, a number of hypotheses about the future direction of the gangs (in Ul'ianovsk and other similar provincial cities) are offered. These hypotheses have been generated from the survey of experts conducted as well as from the author's own observations.

The first hypothesis is advanced primarily by political scientists and lawyers and suggests that a further fusion with the mafia will occur, resulting in a gradual dissolution of the gangs into the internal mafia hierarchy. This would turn the gang into the youngest and most mobile unit of 'order maintenance' in the city. If this were to materialize, the space occupied by girls in the gangs would disappear, leaving only roles as expensive prostitutes, permanent or temporary lovers of racketeers or, more rarely, mafia 'wives'. Girl fighters would not remain within the mafia structure and thus gangs would become exclusively male (although if this were to happen, purely female gangs of the old kind would probably also re-emerge). In fact, the author would suggest, this is an unlikely scenario, since the use of gangs by the mafia is a temporary phenomenon caused by the specific Russian road to the market, while gangs themselves are a manifestation of deeper cultural and psychological aspects of relations of gender and generation. Moreover, the closed structure and clearly criminal orientation of the mafia fits uneasily with values of openness, risk, independence and the desire to stand out which appeal to teenagers. Thus, although criminal behaviour is rising among teenagers currently, it is unlikely to spread to all those young people in gangs (membership of which is significantly higher than the numbers suggested by police statistics on teenage crime). The gang, therefore, has been and remains a kind of middle path between 'informal youth associations' (which require a higher cultural level and associate on a less primitive basis than the defence of territory) and more or less covert, anti-social activities which are, in any case, only anti-social in so far as teenagers are seen to be violating the accepted notion of 'normal youth'.

The second hypothesis is one of 'permanent war', in which relations between various gangs are aggravated but there is no total fusion with the mafia. This hypothesis is suported above all by workers in the juvenile affairs department of the police and may lead, in their opinion, to serious criminal conflict in the course of which many may suffer death or injury. However, in the subsequent period gangs might gradually, if only temporarily, disappear in the city. Since the position of girls in gangs today is relatively marginal, then, given this scenario, only fighters would remain in the classic gang; some girls would leave of their own acccord ('prestigious girls' and 'wives') and some would be forced to leave (prostitutes and 'attached girls').

The third hypothesis is that these 'terrible' gangs will disappear and be replaced by a renaissance of the 'classic' gang. This envisages that the majority of teenagers will gradually move away from current gangs, and is a view supported above all by psychologists. This loss of gang members might be caused by increasing criminality and fusion with the mafia and would lead to a temporary disappearance of the gangs before they re-emerged in their original form. Gradually, small gangs based on individual blocks (*dvor* gangs) whose aim was to defend their own territory from invasion by outsiders would reappear. Girls, in this scenario, would occupy their original positions; they would either create their own purely female gangs or become equal members of male ones.

Regardless of which of these visions of the future materializes, one thing is certain; the gang is not a temporary phenomenon and is more than just a form of 'deviant' behaviour. It is a perfectly natural accompaniment to unbalanced urbanization which has created an incredible disjuncture between space and culture. The classic Western descriptions of gangs in the context of race and class relations and, above all, the processes of urbanization in America (Campbell 1984; Griffin 1993) thus do not wholly apply to Russian, especially provincial Russian, gangs. The specificities of Russian gang culture might be summarized as follows:

- the absence of ethnic origin as the basis for the formation of gangs;
- the significance of an almost complete lack of urban cultural infrastructure in the cities in which gangs thrive (there is not even elementary provision of bars, pubs or cafés).
- the absence of the concept of 'social work' with difficult teenagers in Russia – this means the only people working with these kinds of young people are the police, drugs specialists and lawyers (which explains why the literature on gangs focuses on 'the struggle agianst deviance').

Youth gangs in Russia are thus unlikely to become gangs (*bandy*) of the Western type. It is more likely that they will remain a unique, though changing, phenomenon of the Russian provinces; both an expression of and a means of reproducing provincial Russian rural-urban culture.

NOTES

1 The Russian word here is *gruppirovka* but the term 'group' in English does not distinguish the phenomenon adequately from other youth cultural groups and thus is translated here as 'gang'. However, the *gruppirovka* is not a 'gang' (*banda*) in the sense used in Western sociological literature. This distinction is taken up in the concluding section to this chapter.

2 In the course of the research, interviews were conducted with a number of gang members who were assured complete confidentiality. This means that neither their names nor other personal details may be given. It was also agreed that the results of the study would be published only in the West.

3 'Cleaners' (*sanitarnie*) is a generic term for youth groups which see their mission as being to 'clean up' the city of 'undesirable elements'.

4 This is particularly noteworthy given the declared intention of discussing the issue from a 'feminist poststructuralist' perspective.

5 'Sleeper districts' are suburbs in a negative sense; there is little infrastructural development and poor communications with other areas and the centre of town means that they are reduced to 'places to sleep'.

6 Up to 16 years of age.

7 Between 16 and 20 years of age.

8 Secondary Vocational-Technical College.

9 This was at the end of 1993 to the beginning of 1994 and at the time was the equivalent of between $1 and $10.

10 This was primarily in order to recognize each other but the choice of white bows may relate to a symbol adopted by a male gang – black hats.

11 The Russian term is '*zhena v zakone*' which is analagous to 'thieves within the law' (*vory v zakone*), that is, a woman who is known within this distinct community and must not be 'touched' by anyone else.

12 For a fuller explanation of the origin of this term see Chapter 13.

13 For further discussion of the role of *fenechki* in youth cultural groups see Shchepanskaia 1991: 6–9 and Pilkington 1994a: 266.

13 Farewell to the *Tusovka*

Masculinities and femininities on the Moscow youth scene

*Hilary Pilkington**

In November 1994, referring to a mapping of youth cultural groups drawn up by this author on the basis of a study of the Moscow scene between 1988 and 1991 (see Appendix 1 p. 259), one interviewee noted:

> that diagram would have to be all rubbed out now and [the categories] all mixed up ... because earlier there was a purity in style but now the *tusovka*[1] of so-called 'new Russians' has appeared.

(1)[2]

She is absolutely correct; the fundamental socio-economic and socio-cultural changes which Russia has experienced since 1992 have disrupted and reformed youth cultural hierarchies and differentiations. In addition to the 'market' (producing the 'new Russians' of which the interviewee talks), however, four other factors have been central to this:

- the penetration of drugs into the youth scene in Moscow;
- the Westernization of the youth scene (in particular, the blossoming of the club scene);
- the rise of chauvinist politics;
- and the 'coming out' of sexuality as a key identifier among youth.

Some of these factors might have been anticipated; the author herself had concluded on the basis of material gathered in 1991 that the traditional Russian *tusovka* was being threatened by the growing influence of market relations, Western images and the, as yet unrealized, potential impact of drugs on the Russian youth scene (Pilkington 1994a: 300–2). This chapter seeks to define the parameters of this post-*tusovka* world and the gender strategies employed by young people negotiating their way around it. The first half of the chapter considers the general impact of the market, drugs and images of the West on youth cultural activity in Moscow, while the second half explores issues of gender identity and chauvinist politics via case studies of two current youth cultural formations.[3]

Money, mafia and masculinity: the *gopniki* come of age

the world has started to be ruled by money... it has become more difficult to live... No matter how much money you have it's never enough.

(2)

The advent of market relations has brought both positive and negative changes for *tusovka* members. On the positive side, there are new freedoms to become fully fledged cultural producers and thereby to shape the youth scene for themselves. The slippage on the cultural and political planes between formal and informal worlds characteristic of the late Soviet period has thus been extended to the economic sphere in post-Soviet Russia. A number of interviewees expressed their desire or plans to open business ventures associated with their youth cultural style. What Igor' Zaitsev[4] had done for biker fashion, for example, others felt they could do for biker symbolica, accessories, cafés and clubs.

However, the space for *tusovka* members to realize these ideas remains limited. They are inhibited, first by old enemies (the police and other political authorities), and second, by new enemies – gangsters (*bandity*), racketeers or worse. The difficulties arise from the fact that in order to act in the newly legal and formal world of business in contemporary Russia, illegal and informal means must be adopted. New ventures (such as youth cafés or clubs) must secure, and pay for, their protection (*krysha*). Indeed, this is not resented since it is preferable to falling victim to the more dangerous, internally unregulated and opportunistic racketeers who work in small groups outside their home cities.[5]

The market has also facilitated the fusion of the old *gopniki*[6] and those 'doing business' (see Appendix 1) into a new animal on the youth scene, the *byk* or, when in packs, *bych'e*.[7] The *byk* is a genetic descendent of the *gopnik*, being primarily a territorial animal (defending its space frequently by aggression) and most respondents referred to them as simply 'grown-up *gopniki*' (3). They retain the

very short hairstyles and macho (iron-pumping) image associated
with *gopnik* strategy, but now clothe this in long leather coats, often
a cap and 'wheels'.[8] They are not 'new Russians' but they have made
money in the new commercial sphere and are more threatening than
the *gopniki*, in that they are older and have money attached to their
territory. Thus, although those on the youth cultural scene (former
tusovka members) continue to look down on the *bych'e*, the latter
can directly limit the ability of the former to realize opportunities
provided by new economic freedoms. They do this by throwing
them out of meeting places, preventing them from opening business
concerns or directly extorting money.

It is the 'legal racket' conducted by the police which caused
the most outrage amongst interviewees, however. Described as 'the
worst gangsters', the police, it was suggested, frequently sup-
plemented their meagre wages by taking bribes for turning a blind
eye towards illegal acts, especially the possession of weapons (often
discovered when cars are stopped). One of the founders of an
alternative night-club in Moscow noted that the police had tried on
numerous occasions to close the club, subjecting it to raids during
which property was damaged or confiscated and people beaten up
as they searched for knives, drugs, pistols and knuckle-dusters (2).
For many this simply signifies the fact that *plus ça change*:

> just like in the old days, if a person doesn't look like he should
> do, they assume there is something up ... in the city [Moscow]
> there is police mayhem ... The police get money from
> prostitution ... They control a lot ... They have the power, the
> weapons. You can't reason with them ... [if you complain] The
> investigation proceeds like this: [question to the policeman] 'Did
> you beat him?', [Answer] 'I didn't beat him', [conclusion]
> 'There you see, he didn't beat you', and that's it.
>
> (2)

Indeed in Spring 1995 this club (the Sexton) burned down – fortu-
nately without injury to anyone – amid rumours that the fire had
been started deliberately. Two leading organizers of the club claimed
on television that even if it was 'criminal elements', rather than
political actors, who had directly caused the fire, then nevertheless
they had no doubt that the action had been sanctioned 'from above'.
To support their claim they cited staged extreme right-wing gatherings outside the club (at which fascist flags and slogans were waved)
designed to portray the bikers as a fascist movement (Abramov and
Lutkovskii 1995).[9]

Thus, the advent of the market provides the possibility for some to turn their cultural practice into a steady income;[10] it makes more tangible the slippage between formal and informal worlds. However, young people are also aware of the risk involved in following this (Western) path:

> Now music is infused with commercialism...before...there were two basic enemies: the cops [*menty*] and the *liubera*.[11] But now the enemy is money.
>
> (1)

The tarnishing of the authenticity of the youth cultural scene for some signifies the cultural consequence of economic 'freedom'.

The West, 'new Russians' and the club scene

> America has arrived...We waited a long time for it in this country, now it's come everyone has gone mad.
>
> (2)

The impact of Westernization in the post-Soviet period has been massive and deserves much lengthier and separate consideration which would take into account all the channels employed: media, film, video, computer technology and games, music, style, fashion and advertising. Here only one element of the Westernization process will be discussed; the re-siting of city centre youth cultural activity and the implications of this for youth cultural strategies in general.

By 1991, only one Western institution had achieved any real impact on the distinctive *tusovka* gatherings; McDonald's. The common use of McDonald's on Pushkin Square (at the time, the only McDonald's in Moscow) by a number of previously distinct *tusovki* had begun to blur boundaries between *tusovka* members and between them and the *mazhory*.[12] By 1994, a much more significant phenomenon had seriously disrupted the *tusovki*; the emergence of a club scene.

Clubs were originally opened in Moscow with the intention of using the new commercial freedoms to establish more comfortable environments for *tusovki* to gather, away from the street, metro or basements of the past. It was hoped that the Hermitage, which opened at Easter 1993, for example, would provide a gathering place for the bohemian set in Moscow. The reality of the market environment, however, has meant that these goals have been only partially realized. In its original form the club was not profitable; the cultural intelligentsia has no great spending power. In addition, the reality of the Russian market is that commerce means racket; paying for protection immediately devours 25–50 per cent of profits. This is even before state institutions, such as the police, the fire service and other officials, are paid for their services or bribed for their approval. Perhaps not surprisingly then, the Hermitage quickly re-profiled into an acid-house disco with a reputation primarily associated with the drugs scene.

The Sexton club was also a joint venture between the formal and informal world; investment came from a financial backer who had experience in running cafés and from the Night Wolves,[13] who saw it not primarily as a commercial enterprise, but as somewhere to relax and listen to their kind of music. For the first few months of its existence, the Sexton really was the centre of the biker *tusovka*, but a refurbishment and reorientation towards music and concerts undertaken in 1994 did not meet the approval of some of the original clientele, who saw it as symbolizing the move away from the 'underground' to the world of business which they felt had been made by many of the club's founders.

Although the club scene has exploded in the last three years, there are still relatively few clubs and they remain exclusive.[14] This is manifest, not in strict dress policies (in this sense the Moscow scene is much more democratic than its equivalents in the West) but with the excessive prices charged for entrance and for drinks. The Hermitage is the cheapest of the central clubs – charging (in autumn 1994) $10 in either hard currency or roubles – and, accordingly, has the youngest regular public. Others (such as the Pilot, the Manhatten Express, Moscow Club, the 2X2 and the Metelitsa), which have newer and better interiors, cost $20–$50. Some clubs have policies of letting girls and/or foreigners in free on all or some nights. Central clubs, therefore, are dominated by Westerners and 'new Russians', who are the only people in Moscow able to afford either the entrance fee or the price of drinks. Nevertheless, *tusovka* connections still work and all those interviewed by the author in the present study used these to obtain free entrance. In any case, those who have been on the *tusovka* scene for a while, consider it a matter of principle that they do not pay entrance to any concert or club and would rather not attend than go as an ordinary punter.

Alongside these central clubs there also exist more 'underground' establishments (the old basement hangouts) which continue to house peripheral or risky scenes, such as the emergent gay and lesbian club scene,[15] and also hard punk and skinhead hangouts and bohemian *tusovki* such as the Pitlura.

Drugs: 'It's one thing to try them – another to be on them'

In 1991 drugs were used regularly in a number of *tusovki*; by 1994 drug use had become virtually universal on the youth scene.

> Now virtually everyone here smokes drugs, hashish or something more serious, cocaine, they sniff or inject intravenously . . . sometimes [they take] acid, some are not choosy.
>
> (5; 4)

Although most *tusovka* members admit to having tried drugs (including hard drugs such as cocaine and heroine) they are quick to distinguish their drug use from that of drug 'addicts' and frequently recall former friends and acquaintances who have ended up as addicts. The use and abuse of medical drugs remains common; chemical cocktails are concocted and petrol-based substances employed.

Accessing drugs is not difficult; their sale and use in clubs is virtually uncontrolled. At the Hermitage (still the club most heavily associated with acid) the sale and use of drugs (mainly LSD, ecstasy and to a lesser extent cocaine and hashish) is open, and drugs were seen being taken openly in a number of central Moscow clubs in the autumn of 1994. Periodically the drug scene quietens down when dealers 'disappear'. However, at least ten regulars of the Hermitage are known to have died from drug abuse since its opening; some from overdoses, others from drugs-related suicide. Consciously 'alternative' clubs claim to control the use of drugs more strictly; the size of the toilets in the Sexton, for example, was significantly reduced during refurbishment last year in order to inhibit drug users (syringes had been found). Anyone found using drugs, it was claimed, would be 'dealt with' by the management, although it was recognized that it was impossible to prohibit people already under the influence of drugs from entering the club (2).

Like club entrance, affording drugs is a problem. Although 'home-grown' drugs (mainly from the Central Asian republics of the former Soviet Union) are relatively cheap, the most prestigious drugs are those associated with the Western youth cultural scene. These are much more expensive; LSD and ecstasy cost around $60 per 'score' while cocaine (which is becoming increasingly widespread) costs $150–200 per 'score'. The opening up to the West provides not only the desire, but also the means of satisfying that desire; when asked how people afforded their drug habit, one interviewee said:

> some sell stuff [*utiuzhat*], some rip off foreigners, some work somewhere ... Some spend all the money they earn on drugs.
>
> (5)

Farewell to the *tusovka* ...

It was clear from interviewees' statements in 1994 that they felt that the old *tusovki* had been re-sited off the streets and into clubs:

> now people here hang out at clubs [*tusuiutsia po klubam*] ... I consider myself to be on the scene [*tusovochnii chelovek*], and this is associated with the Hermitage ... what it was like before doesn't exist any more.
>
> (5)

This respondent went on to note that this might not be a problem for the likes of her – she and her friends welcomed the club scene – but younger kids (especially girls) with no permanent income or past connections allowing them free entrance were effectively left with nowhere to go, since they would not be able to afford the entrance fee. Another female respondent spelled out the ambivalence felt towards the changes on the scene:

> Then the Sexton opened and everybody stopped hanging out at the Margarita[16] although it was an ideal place for a *tusovka* ... I could go there at 2 in the morning ... and know that I would definitely meet somebody there ... someone would be asleep on the benches, already drunk, that was normal, we drank, wandered around, had fun ... Then the Sexton opened and at first it was really cool there, really brilliant. It was our club, for me it was like a second home. We went there every day ... The first six months at the Sexton were really brilliant, (it captured) the atmosphere of the *tusovka* itself, which you can't put into words.
>
> (1)

Putting the *tusovka* into words sealed its own fate; when bottled and marketed for general consumption it lost its original appeal. This, is not surprising since the essence of the *tusovka* was an embodied communication expressed through style, music, dance and play which was constantly reshaped and recreated in different ways by its participants. Once packaged and moulded by a combination of the advent of the market, drugs and the new Western-orientated model of youth cultural activity, the meanings of the *tusovka* were lost and the form itself became associated by interviewees with a past Soviet reality (*sovkovaia deistvitel'nost'*[17]) no longer in existence. The *tusokva* had become the *tu*-sovka.

Masculinities and femininities on the post-*tusovka* scene

Youth cultural practice has never been either sub, counter or parallel to 'dominant' culture but constantly interwoven and interacting with it. Changes in the macro socio-cultural environment clearly shape youth cultural activity, therefore, in as much as they determine wider relations of domination and subordination. Thus, it is essential to employ micro-studies of youth cultural groups in order to trace the processes at work in the negotiation of these changes.

Such a micro-study of the *stiliagi*,[18] conducted between 1988 and 1991 suggested, for example, that this particular *tusovka* had been destroyed from within as male members of the group became increasingly dissatisfied with the weak masculine identity the group offered. This led them to leave the scene altogether (entering education, work or business) or to choose harder masculine identities, aspiring first to the *rokabilly* (rockabilly) and then the *rokery* (bikers). This left *stiliagi* girls with nowhere to go, since they saw biker groups as incompatible with their feminine identity, which was centred in a 'good girl' positioning which allowed them to experiment with image and style whilst not threatening their femininity (Pilkington 1993: 184). This gender strategy was possible to implement only at the expense of girls in other subcultural groups who had to be differentiated as vulgar, stupid and sexually loose.

The importance of gender identity in shaping youth cultural strategies has not diminished; if anything, it has increased. The re-masculinization of Russian society (often misnamed the 're-sexualization' of post-Soviet society) around confrontational politics and macho marketization has thrown up new challenges to young people, and the playing out of their possible futures often takes place via style, music and other youth cultural practices. The micro-study undertaken in 1994 sought simply to trace the youth cultural careers of those original interviewees still on the scene.[19] The aim was to assess how the changes described in the macro-environment may have impacted on masculine and feminine codes on the youth cultural scene and the strategies developed by young people to negotiate them. The form these youth cultural careers have taken means that two youth cultural groups are discussed below; (bikers) *rokery*[20] and (skinheads) *skinkhedy*.[21]

From 'good girls in trousers' to bad girls in leather jackets?

Ironically, leather jackets were finally donned by the girls from the *stiliagi* – who in 1991 had stressed their fears of and distaste for biker culture – rather than the lads who had persistently aspired to the *rokery*.[22] Why?

The girls' self-explanations focused on:

- style (which had always been the centre of their youth cultural practice – they were simply attracted to the uniform black leather jackets of the *rokery*;
- the *tusovka* – their own had collapsed and the biker *tusovka* based at the *TsDKh*[23] had been a welcome replacement. They had been introduced there by *rokabilly* friends and had been accepted quickly. The girls' ultimate recognition in the biker crowd came with their movement into the Sexton (where they spent the autumn and winter of 1993) since the core of the crowd there was the extremely prestigious Night Wolves biker gang.

Did this mean the girls were forced to abandon their 'good girl' strategy which they had so carefully fostered in the *stiliagi*? Biker strategy was certainly more risky; a fact symbolized by one girl's fear of telling her mother that she had bought a motorbike. However, the girls claimed they had managed to find space for themselves in the biker crowd. Initially, this was achieved by two of them buying a motorbike together which enabled them to participate fully in the *tusovka*; prior to this they had been dependent on one of the lads taking them on the back of his bike. As all of them noted, however, the lads could not be relied on, since they generally took other lads first and frequently the girls would be left without a ride (5). Buying their own bike gave the girls both independence from the lads and a focus for their own identity; they were now not just girls hanging round the biker *tusovka* but bikers in their own right:

a girl biker (*rokersha*) – is a girl who rides her own motorbike.

(3)

However, just a year later the girls openly discussed the limits they felt to the space available to them within the group and all had consciously moved away from the Night Wolves and the Sexton. Their unease centred on the lack of fit between biker style and culture and their own sense of femininity. This was expressed in two ways. First, the bike itself fitted more easily with a masculine style and way of life: it was heavy and difficult to pick up when it fell on them; biking was dirty, and they sometimes got bored with never being able to look good; and biking was very dangerous (central to one girl's decision to give up her share in the bike was a fatal accident involving one of the *tusovka* members). Second, dissatisfaction with the coarseness of masculinist biker culture was expressed:

> from 14 I always wanted to have a motorbike, loved leather jackets and so on ... but this ideology of life, it's not really part of me, [I mean] the coarseness and so on.
>
> (5)

This 'coarseness' manifested itself in the extensive use of mat[24] and heavy drinking, but, above all, in a disrespectful attitude to women. Interestingly, the girls attributed this to the adoption and adaptation of the images of *Western* bikers now commonplace in Moscow. They were particularly concerned about films which showed girls being used 'in common' and which rarely portrayed positive images of families on the road together. The violence used towards women was also discussed and clearly felt to be threatening. One girl biker recounted how one of her friends had her hand banged against railings by her boyfriend (4). This young woman also noted, with irony, that the male bikers would seek sympathy, claiming that they had all been hurt by love, and somehow seeing this as giving them the right to act violently. The sense that this attitude to girls had Western roots was also articulated in the girls' explanations of it as stemming from the lads' attitude to them as being their 'property' to be handled as they liked; the word used was a Russification of the English rather than any of the perfectly adequate Russian words available.

Despite this, all the biker girls interviewed said that these attitudes could be resisted. The strategy they had adopted they called:

> a system of 'how you are treated depends on how you assert yourself'. We had girls who got on to the back of a bike in order to fuck afterwards but we were not that type.
>
> (3)

This is reminiscent of their old *stiliagi* strategy, which blamed the girls for their treatment by the men. On the other hand, the promiscuity of male bikers was joked about affectionately; their leader

Table 13.1 Biker groups in Moscow: organizational differences

	TsDKh Bikers	'Night Wolves'
Type of org.	'tusovka'	'banda'[25]
Membership	open, girls accepted	closed fraternity[26]
Hierarchy	authoritative figures but no 'leader'	long apprenticeship, acknowledged 'leader'
Average age	around 19	around 30 (youngest 'Night Wolf' is 22)
Uniting factor	'friends with common interests'	common business interests requiring 'mutual protection'[27]

Khirurg, for example, was described as a 'Don Juan' who, besides his two wives, had numerous 'chicks' (*telki*) and said he was capable of loving more than a dozen women at once (1). Thus, the girls revealed neither a prudishness nor a naivety in relation to male–female relationships left over from their *stiliagi* days; overt sexism (including a 'Miss Breasts' competition) at the main biker event of 1994 – a biker rally held just outside Moscow in August – caused amusement rather than outrage. However, when it came to attitudes towards them as individuals, they wanted space to command the respect they deserved.

At what point, therefore, did the girls perceive this space to have closed down to such a degree that they took the decision to move away from the biker *tusovka*? Analysing the girls' statements it would appear that this moment came with the disintegration of the TsDKh biker *tusovka* which was a very different formation from the Night Wolves (see Table 13.1).

Until the summer of 1993 the TsDKh *tusovka* and the Night Wolves (whose gatherings became focused around the Sexton club) were completely separate, and although many of the former had contacts with the Wolves, there were latent conflicts centring on the perceived desire of the Wolves to remain the only biker gang in Moscow (1). The closed fraternity of the Night Wolves was symbolized by their emblem (*nashivka*), which only they were allowed to wear. Even those girls who were very close to the Wolves met resistance when on two occasions there were attempts to set up girl gangs by the most established women bikers (one gang to be called the Wild Vixens, the other the Panthers).[28] When this became known, the girls were immediately warned by the Wolves that they would not be allowed to wear any emblem of their own unless it read 'property of the Night Wolves' (4).

Growing up and looking back

By the winter of 1994, the biker girls appeared to have decided to move out of the everyday *tusovki* of the bikers. This was partially because they felt excluded from the key symbols of the *rokery*. As one interviewee put it:

> the emblem signifies that they are brothers ... it is a male gang. Of course girls can't be in it.
>
> (1)

However, they had also had begun to have doubts about whether the gang structure was really what they wanted. A gang required trust, authority and readiness to defend one another, which the girls themselves said they did not really feel. At the same time, the gang structure was a limitation of personal freedom and necessitated involvement in semi-legal activities (*krutie dela*) which was a long way from the biker style and way of life that they saw as central to their own activity. Thus, the girls criticized the Wolves for having begun to dress in fashionable clothes, drive cars rather than motorbikes and be more interested in making money than in the romance of the biker lifestyle.

Moreover, the girls had developed new needs which were not being satisfied. For some, the scene at the Sexton had simply become too threatening,[29] while others expressed the need for different forms of communication and more permanent and secure relationships than were on offer in post-*tusovka* circles.

> I know that every Saturday and Sunday, they gather at the Tishinskii market. They are always happy to see me when I turn up. We have a beer together, hang out a bit ... but I don't want to meet with them every day any more.
>
> (4)

> I simply stopped being interested in talking with many of them. If I just want to drink myself stupid, I could do that with anyone ... and the relations there have become cruder, more cynical ... generally I just meet up with the people I enjoy seeing ... they are simply my friends ... but I don't really believe

much in the movement any more because with every year I see a decline, a real decadence.

(1)

This reorientation may reflect the gendered nature of youth cultural practice which has been described as the tendency of boys to form hierarchical groups or gangs based on common physical activities and competitive performance while girls establish private zones in public places (or within a particular subculture) based on close girlfriend relationships which continue the mother–daughter relationship (Ganetz 1995: 85; Roman 1988: 152–3). The girl who had moved furthest away from the bikers by 1994 put this particularly starkly:

people betray you, your best friends. . . . they simply betray you . . . I am afraid now to say about someone that they are my friend . . . this is a lesson which *tusovka* life teaches you well.

(5)

In contrast to the interviews of 1988–1991, it was noticeable that the girls felt much more marginalized on the biker scene. To some extent this fed into a nostalgia for the days with the *stiliagi*:

I would hang out in that *tusovka* with pleasure if it was there . . . there is a new one but its not the same, I don't think they are as close as we were – we were like one big family.

(3)

For all the former *stiliagi*, however, envy of the possibilities open to the new generation of *stiliagi* to create the kind of style of which they themselves had always dreamed was diluted by a recognition that the new post-*tusovka* environment also took away some of the space for the kind of 'embodied communication' which they had so cherished in the *stiliagi*.

I haven't seen any [new] *stiliagi*. The *stiliagi* probably have a *tusovka*. . . . like we had *Ploshchad' Revoliutsii*, the Catacombs. But I am 100 per cent sure that there isn't such a place in the centre. . . . We had the 'rock and roll day (*stilnii den'*) at the *Prospekt* and the *Moloko*,[30] but they haven't got anything like that it seems to me.

(4)

Above all, however, in looking to their future, the girls were beginning to accept their own process of 'growing up' and each was finding a unique balance between different aspects of their lives (work, personal life, friends, family) and their youth cultural activity. The *rokery* had facilitated that growing up process:

> when we were *stiliagi* there weren't that many adults, the oldest was only 23. It was purely about being really into music, fans of rock'n'roll music... whereas the *rokery* is broader, there are motorbikes, new acquaintances, here people are growing up.
>
> (4)

The future youth cultural strategy of the girls, therefore, will focus on clawing back the space they have lost with the bikers,[31] whilst trying to take with them what they missed from the *tusovka* environment.

> that we will create our own *tusovki* is definite... we will simply hang out and talk with friends.
>
> (1)

Politics, masculinity and skinhead style

By 1991 many *stiliagi* lads had already become dissatisfied with the masculinities offered to them by the *tusovka* and had begun moving into groups with harder images, aspiring eventually to becoming bikers. However, of those relocated on the scene in 1994, none had become fully fledged bikers, but had gravitated rather to a group of clean-shaven, designer-conscious skinheads.[32]

Listening to articulated explanations by skinheads of their activities one might be tempted to conclude that what was taking place on the Moscow youth scene was a 'Zhirinovskyfication' of Russian youth, expressed in desires for an 'iron hand' and a restoration of national pride. As one interviewee (a former *rokabilly* turned skinhead) put it:

> I don't need this democracy, it's not for us... I am in favour of strong power... of the native population of the country.
>
> (6)

Despite this, the skinheads interviewed,[33] it will be argued, were not natural allies of, nor a ballast for, the Liberal Democratic Party or indeed any other neo-right or neo-fascist political grouping in Russia.

This is apparent first of all in the territorial dimension of skinhead strategy, which is based not on a restoration of empire accompanied by an imperialistic and colonizing consciousness but on a 'defence' of territory expressed in metaphors of invasion, threat and disempowerment.

> about 20,000 Chinese are living here without visas, 20,000 ... they are robbing my country, they don't even pay taxes ... I don't want to see this nigger scum ... or the Chinese and Vietnamese. There are a lot of them here. There are whole gangs here.
>
> (7)

The threat is especially associated with the perceived monopolization of money-making positions by non-Russians.

> Here the commercial operators [*kommersanty*] are generally blacks [*chernomazie*] ... Why don't we like them? Because they live here in the capital as if they own everything and we are second class ... They are rich, they have money, they have expensive cars, limousines, and we are second class Russians.
>
> (6)

Thus, counter to Zhirinovsky's typically colonial surface commitment to harmonious inter-ethnic relations in a re-established Russian empire, Moscow skins articulate open racial hatred:

> For me it is the colour of the skin that is important – white ... I have talked to people who said that Hitler's problem was that he emphasized the German nation, Germans ... when it should have been white power ... because there are less and less of us and more and more of them. That's the problem ... if there were black racists ... I wouldn't have a negative attitude towards them ... they want there to be blacks only, blacks to mix among themselves ... that is normal ... the same goes for the Jews, the racist Jewish sect ... It's right that they observe purity.
>
> (7)

Not only the ideology but also the political strategy of the skins differs from that given mainstream articulation. Politics, for the young skins interviewed, was palatable only outside the spectrum of 'normal' Russian politics:

> I don't vote at all. Those like me[34] would not go and vote out of principle. It is stupid, nobody will take account of us anyway.
>
> (8)

This is not just apathy; scepticism about formal political parties on the far right is a central part of skinhead identity:

Zhirinovsky is just a mad man ... and he is a Jew as well ... we think that he has been put there specially, that he is backed by Jewish money.

(7)

Thus, approaches made to the skins for cooperation were largely rejected. This is partially because the skins feel used; they are a valuable asset as both 'evidence' of the existence of a youth section and, more importantly, as a heavy mob when there is likely to be violence at a meeting. It is also because formal political parties are seen to be out of tune with the new political realities.

there is the National Front in Russia, they want us to work with them but the thing is, they consider our music to be Satanic ... They are like the fascists of the thirties ... that's the past, but there should be some kind of future ... people should have some kind of modern appearance ... I don't want to be like them.

(7)

The skins, therefore, are not prepared to wait for a right-wing political victory but prefer to involve themselves in direct action centring on attacks on targeted groups and individuals (blacks, foreigners, Jews and gay men). The movement is territorially based and strongest in those districts with the highest population of foreigners. Territory is also important in that some areas are more conducive to attacks than others:

if the district is a negro one ... then we know that the police are all racists and we can do what we want.

(7)

However, the commitment to 'body politics' did not rule out, for the most politicized at least, the possibility of developing a political organization in the future. One interviewee declared his intention to earn enough money to set up a party. Nevertheless, he said, he would want to be not the political leader of such an organization but the leader of the stormtroopers he would send, for example, to South Africa.

Racing the *tusovka*: style and political expression

Racist violence is only sometimes the product of an overtly political agenda however. As Willems' study of collective acts of violence against foreigners in Germany in the 1990s shows, the right-wing, politically motivated type is a minority among perpetrators of such acts. More frequently participants in attacks are: xenophobic youths in various violent youth subcultures; criminal marginalized youth; and even 'fellow-travellers' from middle-class families involved in music or leisure cliques whose primary motive in participating in racist attacks is a desire to prove oneself in front of others (Willems 1995: 510–14).

Amongst those skins interviewed in Moscow in 1994 the politically motivated and articulate individuals described above were also exceptions to the rule. What was striking, in contrast, was their close ties to the leisure-based *tusovka* world and the continued centrality of music and style to their activity. All those interviewed had long *tusovka* histories (as *stiliagi*, *rokery*, *rokabilly*, heavy metal fans or just generally on the scene) and used *tusovka* slang with an expanded racist vocabulary. Although no strict rules of inclusion and exclusion based on style and music were followed, their choices of both these reflected the central ideas of the group. A number of Russian bands were considered fascist bands (*Tankovaia diviziia SS-Gitlera, Krek, Koroziia metalla*) and Oi music was popular with some.[35] Perhaps more important, however, is the fact that music knowledge retained the role it had played in the *tusovka* as a kind of cultural capital. Music use among skins also involves 'letting go' in *tusovka* style; skins like to 'move, dance, shout and drink beer' at concerts and this often led to 'certain excesses', later defined as being 'when people get beaten up' (7).

The dress style adopted might best be described as 'designer skinheadism': jackets, boots, shirts and braces have to be from a particular range (all Western) and the group had their own tattooist. As in the West, skinhead style expresses the 'simpleness' of the skinhead,[36] as well as his commitment to cleanliness. It is also convenient; more fashionable long hair gets in the way when you are fighting.

Although there is some disagreement among skins themselves on attitudes to other 'informals' (ranging from seeing them as being 'like us' to viewing them simply as objects for attack), some youth cultural styles are universally disliked:

> we despise the punks for their dirtiness, for their unwashed necks. . . . dirtiness is not a protest.
>
> (7)

This interviewee noted that they had also beaten up young skins at a recent concert; the reason given was that they were scruffy and had emerged out of the punk movement. On the other hand, particularly good relations were maintained with the *rokery*, who are seen in general to have similar right-wing and racist views.[37]

Masculinity, the street and skinheads

Although the skins articulated their behaviour in terms of participation in a pan-European neo-right youth movement, off-tape conversations and observations reinforced or suggested other motivations. The most striking statement was that made by the most politicized of the skins interviewed:

> I like football and I like music even more. But the most important thing for me is that my daughter grows up and marries a white person ... That's why I am a skinhead ... that is the most important thing. It is probably politics.
>
> (7)

Indeed, gender politics was a recurrent theme in the skins' talk; the most common motif of which was that the lads were repulsed by the thought or sight of (white) Russian women having relations with 'black' men. In an untaped interview one skin explained his dislike for Azerbaijanis by saying that he didn't like the fact that white girls sleep with black men (8). A common complaint was that transcaucasian men harassed Russian women when they should 'keep a mile away from them' as it 'violated all laws of nature'(6). On a number of occasions the story of how the group had done an 'experiment' to prove this was recounted; they had put a Russian girl at a bus stop and sure enough, they claimed, she was immediately hassled by 'some nigger'.

The ritual fighting[38] of the skinheads is also significant; it offers young men a much harder street position than that they had been able to adopt in other *tusovki*. As one interviewee put it:

> skinheads win, we have never lost.... a crowd of these freaks ... I don't even know what to call them, who go around in caps – gangsters, hooligans ... They are sure of themselves, they feel that it is their city. They feel like that because all the *neformaly*, the rest of the informal groups are very cowardly ... they can't respond as they should, they never do sport, they don't know what it is.
>
> (7)[39]

The concern with body image and preference for the muscular

mesomorphic body (the muscle-man-type body characterized by well-developed chest and arm muscles and wide shoulders tapering down to a narrow waist) plays a central role in men's self-esteem in late modern societies (Mishkind *et al.* 1987: 39) and is becoming increasingly visible as the tendency to relegate bodily concern exclusively to the female sex-role stereotype is challenged (47). Fighting does not only provide a focus to the evening but constitutes a whole culture centred on masculinist banter and beer-drinking in the build-up to 'fights' and the formation of a group narrative based on the recounting of past fights. It is also a form of personal development, raising prestige and position within the group; when there is nobody else to fight, the skins will fight amongst themselves.

Fighting is not the sole determinant of internal hierarchy, however. Position is based on a mixture of fighting prowess, intelligence and other 'masculine qualities'. Unlike *gopnik*-type territorial gangs, having served a prison sentence does not necessarily give prestige; you should not be stupid enough to be caught. However, being sentenced for Article 74, that is, for inciting racial hatred, is viewed positively.[40] Interviewees also emphasized the principle of quality over quantity ('better fewer but better') in the process of inclusion in and exclusion from the group. In total, it was estimated that there were 150–200 skinheads in the whole of Moscow, based in different districts of the city but with an elite 'core' to which others aspire and to which access is restricted. Those who are not considered worthy of attention, referred to as 'duffers' (*tupari*) or 'queers' (*pedarasty*) are simply ignored.

Of course, pumping up the masculine, means suppressing the feminine; one of the lads was ribbed for not having left his wedding ring at home when he came out to fight, and for being under the influence of his wife who was trying to turn him into a 'domesticated man, who stayed in'. And, those men who are seen to be expressing the feminine are targets of attack; 'queers have always been the enemy of skins' (7). This is not surprising given Kimmel's argument that one of the sources of the apparent 'muscular backlash' on the part of men is women's increased participation in the public sphere, which has reduced cognitive, occupational and lifestyle differences between men and women and thus accentuated body image as one of the few areas in which men can differentiate themselves from women (Kimmel 1987b: 16).

Women themselves are seen primarily as a motivation for action (territory to defend) rather than as co-participants. Indeed, one of the group noted that having girls in the group would just create 'unnecessary problems' (8).

Although there are reportedly about ten skingirls in Moscow, the group of skins interviewed associated them with the 'punk' element of the movement and chose not to mix with them, describing them as, 'a bit dirty' (7). None of the interviewees objected in principle to the idea of skingirls but found it difficult to imagine: 'what would they look like?' (6)

They viewed more positively girls (especially girlfriends or wives) who supported male skins' views but who 'naturally' were not going to cut their hair. There was one woman 'active' in the group – an American – who, the skins explained, would not dare touch 'niggers' at home but who was a useful asset in a surprise attack or mollifying police when out fighting (8; 7). Despite claims that she was treated as 'one of the lads', she did not escape objectification; at a group gathering where she was not present, the lads discussed who she had slept with out of the group and ribbed one of the lads about being her 'favourite' before a core member of the group gave him 'permission' to sleep with her, if he so wished. Thus, the girls around skin circles were invited along for a single reason:

> There are no sound [*ideinie*] girls as a rule. There are girls who we simply use to spend time with. We invite them along, although few know what they're talking about, or understand anything ... They are stupid ... as a rule they are common [*obshchie*] ones.
>
> (9)

On the other hand, girls, it was claimed, were never the objects of violence; after all, 'fights' were meant to test strength and show white superiority. However, one story was recounted of how two Vietnamese girls had been thrown out of a bar (for refusing to leave when told to and for talking in their 'stupid, pidgin language') (7). When challenged on this, the explanation given for the attack on these girls sums up the relationship between race and gender politics for skinheads: 'we don't consider these girls to be girls'(7).

CONCLUSION

On the surface, former *stiliagi* girls who moved into the *rokery* and former *stiliagi* lads who moved into the skinheads appear to have little in common. However, analysis of their youth cultural careers suggest that both were seeking more grown-up *tusovka* identities in a post-*tusovka* world which raised new questions about gender identity.

For former *stiliagi* girls this was expressed through a movement into the grown-up world of the *rokery*, which offered an alternative identity to that of the 'new Russians' but without the weak masculinity of the *stiliagi* lads which female *stiliagi* had also found inadequate (3).[41] The *rokery* provided an alternative identity, focused on romantic, subcultural poverty which contrasted the culture of the new 'cynical generation'(1), which the girls did not feel part of.

Their new youth cultural positions protected the former *stiliagi* girls in a second crucial way; by remaining in the *tusovka* world the girls had access to clubs and the kind of lifestyle they desired without needing to pay for it in cash or services rendered. One biker girl stressed her dislike of the common practice among non-*tusovka* young women of 'screwing men for money' (*vykruchivat'*) or seeking 'sponsors' for the night. If she could not afford to go out, she said, she would rather stay in than risk her independence. Cultural capital, it appears, could substitute economic capital in some circumstances.

Nevertheless, the girls faced an apparently irresolvable dilemma. The independence they so valued could only be ensured by material security, which meant that earning money had to be high on their agenda. This, on the other hand, threatened their alternative image. The solution which many saw to this problem was to use the growing space between formal and informal worlds and set up a small business somehow connected with their youth cultural interests. However, the girls were much less confident about their ability to carry their ideas through than were their male counterparts, reflecting a popular belief that women cannot survive in business because of the dangers and threats associated with this world in contemporary Russia. This difficult positioning between worlds, together with more mundane concerns about the influence of new boyfriends and jealousies of other female friends left the biker girls feeling increasingly vulnerable about their identity.

Although expressed in a completely different form, this vulnerability was also evident among skinhead lads. One former *stiliaga* turned skinhead, in a rare moment of nostalgia for his former life, noted that when he had been a *stiliaga* everyone always seemed to have money, whereas now everyone was involved in commerce and nobody had any time (8). Although his own material needs were modest, he claimed, his job (in a theatre) did not really pay enough. Another noted that his (fittingly working-class) profession was not lucrative and that he had a problem with earning money. Those who did earn well did so by compromising themselves – working as bodyguards for Western firms, which, as one of them acknowledged, equated them socially to black men in Western Europe or North America.

Inability to earn in the land of supposed new opportunities threatens masculinity, especially given the general context of a society in which the cultural stereotype of girls evaluating men by the size of their wallet is omniscient and the youth cultural scene has been re-sited away from the streets and into controlled environments to which access also depends on the wallet. The answer some former *tusovka* lads have found in skinheadism is not a hidden, subcultural resistance but takes up current themes of the dominant discourse and re-works and embodies them: the re-masculinization of politics in the post-Soviet space and the media beating of the folk devil of the Transcaucasian male (*litso kavkazskoi natsional'nosti*). Their own masculinity is reinforced in an aggressive, street position articulated through a politics of racial, ethnic, spatial and sexual superiority whose targets are depressingly familiar: 'black scum', 'dirty hippies', 'hen-pecked' husbands and gay men. These young men are not 'marginals' who have chosen an imaginary (and dangerous) solution to their 'problems', they are directly interacting with the cultural codes of modern, industrialized societies.

This superiority complex (expressed frequently in references to the superiority of and need to defend Moscow) is what sets skinhead strategy apart from the dominant aggressive street masculinity of the Soviet period, the *gopniki*. While their activities (attacks on those who are ideologically 'unacceptable') and their strategies (aggressive masculinism) appear similar, their origins and positionings on the youth scene are quite different. If the *gopniki* were natural products of the inequalities generated by the Soviet modernization project (Pilkington 1994a: 255–63), then the skins are more the product of the postmodern culture of global borrowings and displacements. Their style and language is littered with globalisms: white laces in Doc Martin shoes are borrowed from German skins to show hatred of foreigners; phrases such as *'Ausländer raus'* and 'Skins on your bikes' decorate speech; references to the Australian cult film 'Romper Stomper' abound; positive political preferences are orientated to the French neo-right around Le Pen. But cultural displacements create political ambiguities, and the attempts of skins to rework the 'old-fashioned' fascism which they criticize into a postmodern identity is problematic. In terms of racial politics, this was evident in deep ambiguity over Russianness and its place in world culture. One interviewee for example, declared that he would never touch 'a negro' in Moscow because,

> their civilization is higher than ours ... especially if a negro is an English person or an American.
>
> (9)

Another noted:

> I am not against Jews, not against Chechens ... there are Tatars, even Chechens who are like Russians ... [and Ukrainains] they are okay, they consider themselves to be Russians ... Russians and Belorussians are one Slavic people, Slavs ... we have a common religion.
>
> (6)

Interviewees also frequently noted their own mixed nationality or acceptance of non-Russian friends; post-Soviet society is multi-ethnic and this visibly challenges skinhead positions.

In terms of sexual politics, the male, heterosexual exclusivity of the skin movement in Moscow will also inevitably be challenged from within. There are signs of this already; if white laces need to be adopted to show 'hatred of foreigners' this suggests that other kinds of 'skins', based on consciously alternative femininities and masculinities – taken up often by young lesbians and gay men – may already be challenging a single meaning of skinheadism, even if at the moment this is coming mainly from without rather than within. Moreover, the origins of Moscow skins in central *tusovki* provide a wide previous experience of permissive and liberal cultures and interactions with broad groups of people. This was reflected in the fact that the sexuality of others was a constant theme of discussion. It might be expected that the decreasing stigmatization of gay men as effeminate, 'failed' men, and the replacement of this stereotype with the new stereotype of gay macho body-builder as has occurred in the West (Kimmel 1987: 16), may also challenge the body image of skinheads.

This chapter has attempted to identify how socio-economic and socio-cultural changes in post-Soviet society have impacted on the youth scene in Moscow. The micro-study described has shown how Westernization and marketization have linked Russian youth more materially into global youth cultures but at the same time displaced and uprooted distinct *tusovka* identities (a process which might perhaps mirror the global displacement of Russian culture in

APPENDIX 1

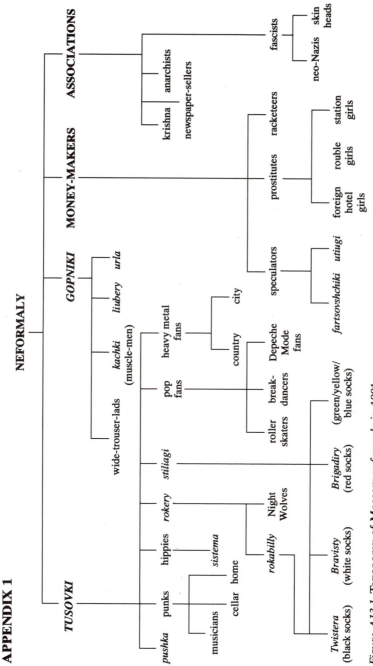

Figure A13.1 Taxonomy of Moscow *neformaly* in 1991

general). This has left young people active on the Moscow scene in search of new post-*tusovka* identities, a process in which the reforging of gender identities has been central. Although feminine and masculine strategies vary distinctly, nevertheless for both young men and women, these identities remain firmly rooted in style and body politics and in the regaining of power relinquished in the displacement process.

APPENDIX 2: LIST OF INTERVIEWEES

1 Biker, female aged 22, not interviewed in 1991.
2 'Night Wolf', male, aged 25, on *tusovka* scene since 1985, known since 1988.
3 Biker, female, aged 22, former *stiliaga*, not interviewed but met in 1991.
4 Biker, female, aged 22, former *stiliaga*, interviewed repeatedly in 1988–91.
5 Biker, female, aged 22 former *stiliaga*, interviewed repeatedly in 1988–91.
6 Skinhead, male, aged 24, former *rokabilly*, known but not interviewed in 1991.
7 Skinhead, male, aged 27, previously non-aligned *neformal*, known since 1992.
8 Skinhead, male, aged 21, former *stiliaga*, known since 1991.
9 Skinhead, male, aged 22, football fan and musician, not known previously.

NOTES

* The author would like to thank the young people interviewed in the course of this study for the generosity with their time and the openness with which they talked. I would also like to thank participants in the ESRC 'Seminar on Women and Gender Relations in Russia and Eastern Europe', The University of Birmingham, February 1994 for their comments on an earlier draft of this chapter.
 1 The *tusovka* was the basic unit of youth cultural activity in major cities of Russia in the late Soviet period. For a fuller discussion of the nature and significance of the *tusovka* see Pilkington 1994a: 226, 234–302.
 2 For a list of interviewees see Appendix 2. Hereafter interviewees will be referred to by number only.
 3 Sexual identity is considered only in as far as it is significant in the two groups studied and is discussed in its own right by Lynne Attwood in Chapters 6 and 8 of this volume.
 4 The son of the famous fashion designer Slava Zaitsev, who is also an

active member of the biker scene in Moscow and frequently featured in the media.

5 For a more detailed discussion of the relationship of mafia structures to youth groups see Chapter 12.

6 *Gopnik* is a generic term for peripheral or provincial males whose activity is associated with 'raids' on central youth cultural haunts and the 'snatching' of girls (see Appendix 1).

7 The gender significance of '*byk*', literally meaning a male, horned animal (usually a bull), but having a wider cultural sense of a brawny but brainless male, should be noted here.

8 They generally drive domestically produced cars rather than the expensive, imported cars associated with the mafia.

9 This version of events was disputed by informants in Moscow in July 1995, however. One informant claimed the club had shut down because its founders had decided they wanted to make profit for themselves rather than devote their lives to the club (2), whilst another said that the fire had been caused by a simple cigarette butt (5).

10 The gender implications of this are discussed further below.

11 *Liubera* were the most famous of the *gopniki*; they originated from the city of Liubertsy to the south-east of Moscow and became notorious during the perestroika period for their attacks on *neformaly* (especially punks, hippies and heavy metal fans).

12 *Mazhory* was the term used to describe the sons and daughters of highly placed people whose parents' privileges allowed them to dress in Western styles and therefore to stand out, but who were not considered by *tusovka* members to be part of the alternative youth cultural scene.

13 The Night Wolves is a biker gang in Moscow which will be discussed in greater detail below.

14 Since writing this article a number of new clubs have opened in Moscow whose aim has been precisely to move away from the exclusive and expensive image of the capital's club world. One of these is the Ptiuch club which makes claims to be the new centre of the rave scene and is reportedly popular with young, less well-off ravers (5).

15 See Chapter 6 of this volume.

16 A cafe at the Patriarch's Pond in central Moscow where bikers hung out prior to the opening of the Sexton.

17 The adjective '*sovkovii*' from *sovok* meaning 'Soviet Union', or 'Homo Soveticus' is colloquially used to describe that which relates to Soviet mentality (see Pilkington 1994b: 17).

18 The *stiliagi* are rock and roll fans reviving and reworking style, music and lifestyles of the 1950s and early 1960s.

19 The majority of interviewees in 1988–91 were *stiliagi*. For a full list of original interviewees see Pilkington 1994a: 311.

20 *Rokery* here is translated as 'bikers', since the symbolic focus of the group is the motorbike. However, they are also loosely united by an interest in heavy rock music, dress style and 'alternative' way of life. Many, especially young bikers in Moscow do not have their own bikes and for them the latter, together with the aspiration towards the former, are probably most important.

21 The preliminary comments here draw on interviews (eight individual,

one group interview) with members of skinhead and biker *tusovki*. All but two of these respondents had been interviewed or known during 1988–91. In addition, untaped conversations were held with around half a dozen former *tusovka* members and observation carried out at clubs, cafes, bars and concerts, mainly in November and December 1994. One interview was conducted with the head of security at a central Moscow club. The strategy of following through original interviewees, however, means that the studies cannot be directly compared, since the people talked to in late 1994 are of course older than they were in 1991. The views they now express and identities they adopt reflect not only a new environment but their different positioning in it, since they are now either the *stariki* (older, respected members) of the *tusovka* world or mix youth cultural activity with a 'civilian' (family and professional) life.

22 This section is based on interviews with four girls who identified themselves as *rokersha* (girl bikers), three of whom had been *stiliagi*. One member of the Night Wolves was interviewed who had been interviewed in 1988–9 although had never been a *stiliaga*. Photographs and videos of key biker events since 1991 were also employed in the study.

23 The TsDKh (Tsentral'nii Dom Khudozhnika is an arts complex (gallery, café, bar, cinema) opposite the Gorky Park main entrance in Moscow.

24 '*Mat*' is swearing whose level of obscenity goes far beyond its equivalent in the English language.

25 Outsiders generally consider the Night Wolves to be the Moscow branch of the Hells Angels, although the Wolves themselves deny this and call themselves the Motoclub Moscow Night Wolves (2).

26 There are currently fifteen Night Wolves. The gang is gender exclusive; they have their 'girls' (i.e. girlfriends) but no woman would be accepted as a member (5). When asked if there are girls in the group, one of the Wolves missed the point altogether and interpreted the question as being about the moral principles of the group:

> Of course there are: there are wives and children ... they live together. They are a family ... I think that nevertheless a family is a family. Of course you can go out with a girl if you haven't got a family. Why not? (2)

27 Any connection with mafia structures is denied, of course, and the Night Wolf interviewed even denied that the Sexton club had to pay protection money.

28 The Panthers was the idea of Khirurg's own sister, while the Wild Foxes was the dream of one of the girls who had been around the biker scene since its earliest gatherings at the sports complex at the Luzhniki.

29 One interviewee recounted a story of a (female) friend who had been beaten up at the Sexton and almost raped after going drinking there on her own.

30 The *Prospekt* and *Moloko* were cafés where the *stiliagi* hung out in the mid to late 1980s.

31 Two of the girls talked about how to get round the exclusivity of the Wolves's emblem; they would devise their own. This, they said, might be a sign of the Urals motorbike, which is what they rode, or 'Tour Moscow–Leningrad', since once you had done that tour you had the right to wear such an emblem.

32 The suggestions made here are based on individual interviews with three skins and one group interview with six skins in addition to participant observation at a number of gatherings. One interviewee was a former *stiliaga*, one a former *rokabilly* who had hung out with the *stiliagi*, one a former *roker* friend of *stiliagi* girls in 1992, one a non-aligned 'informal' whom the author met in 1992 through *stiliagi*, and one was a football fan and musician previously not known.

33 The conclusions put forward here can only be accepted as valid for the group of skinheads interviewed, who consciously disidentified from those they termed '*Natsskiny*' (Nazi skins) and who were more interested in participation in established far-right groupings. Nevertheless, it is suggested, the 'designer skinheadism' this group represents is an important element of a pan-European neo-fascism and worthy of serious attention.

34 Defined elsewhere in the interview as 'informals' and 'skins like me'.

35 One interviewee described 'their' kind of music as generally hardcore, i.e. 'hooligan music, industrial . . . not music for poseurs' (8).

36 'Simple' replaces 'working-class' here because, as one of skins himself noted, it is almost impossible to talk about the skins as a 'working-class movement' because of the difficulty of determining class in Russia. Thus, he described the milieu from which skins are drawn as:

> those who work . . . somewhere and receive honest money and have parents who also work in jobs and earn honest money . . . a lot of us work in security, mainly . . . few work in commerce. (7)

37 It was noted that relations with the Night Wolves had been damaged temporarily after an incident in which a skin had cut off the ear of one of the Wolves. After talks with the Wolves, however, the problems had been sorted out!

38 Interestingly, attacks are generally referred to as 'fighting', less frequently 'beatings', which confirms that this practice is written into skin culture as defence of invaded territory. Attacks such as fire-bombs and knifings, common in other parts of Europe, were not discussed.

39 This interviewee also noted that he had originally been attracted to the skinhead movement back in 1982 when a group had descended on a central *tusovka* where young people went to exchange records and tapes.

40 One member of the gang who had recently been taken into the core had served two months for beating up the ambassador of Guinea Bissau.

41 *Stiliagi* lads persistently refuted and continue to refute that they failed to protect their girls against attacks by *gopniki* (8). The girls' version is given added confirmation by an article in *Ogonek*, however, about two women kick-boxers, themselves former *stiliagi*, who explained their new youth cultural practice as being a natural continuation of being a *stiliaga* since they had always had to defend *themselves* from *gopniki* (Bykanova 1992).

14 The body encoded

Notes on the folklore of pregnancy

Tat'iana Shchepanskaia

This article considers an urban subculture defined by gender and generation but invisible to all but those who are part of it; mothers. It is a woman's first pregnancy which acts as an 'initiation' rite into the subculture's secret tradition, since it is in this period that the popular beliefs, rituals, customs of mutual help and norms of communication, whose assimilation precedes the acquisition of motherhood status, are learned. Only one central aspect of this tradition is discussed here: symbolism of the body. Such a discussion entails, first, an analysis of the role of bodily symbols in organizing relations and consolidating the communicative system of what is termed here 'the female – maternal – community'. Second, it will consider how this bodily code is reproduced by looking at its assimiliation in the period of first pregnancy. Central here is maternal folklore (advice and taboos, symbols and portentious signs (*primety*)) which codify the body. The phenomenon of 'maternal erotica' or 'eroticism of the belly' forms part of this discussion, since this is passed on by maternal culture also and is shaped and strengthened in folklore. Finally, the cultural taboos which make the bodily language of maternal culture difficult for the uninitiated to understand, and thus semiotically invisible from without, are explored.

The material presented was gathered from 1990 in large Russian cities (Moscow and St Petersburg) primarily among Russian women (although many have Ukrainian, Belorusian, Tatar, Bashkiri or Kazakh roots and relations). However, there are clear correlations between contemporary urban traditions of motherhood and those, usually referred to as 'traditional' or 'archaic', observed by ethnographers in Russian villages since the end of the nineteenth and beginning of the twentieth centuries. The present research suggests that there is no rupture between the two; they share a single system of symbols, and many of the same popular beliefs are frequently encountered. This suggests that the contemporary urban tradition refers back to earlier village ones; indeed, it is constantly replenished from localized village traditions which are interchanged in the city.

THE FEMALE COMMUNITY

I am walking along Nevskii[1] (it is already obvious that I am pregnant). From behind somebody takes my arm – a middle-aged woman, 'You mustn't step over any dog ... Have you got a dog at home? If you do the baby may be born hairy.'

(St Petersburg, 1990)[2]

This is a typical example of advice offered to women during pregnancy. Communication with those who are pregnant has certain distinct forms; most frequently that of advice and prohibitions. Advice is received in huge quantities and the fact that the same advice is encountered so frequently indicates that its function is to pass on female popular belief and tradition.

A second characteristic genre form is portentious signs, in particular, various signs employed in guessing the sex of the unborn child:

On my travels I ended up in Pechory [Pskov region]. I was already eight months pregnant and I spent the night at Anna's, a local old woman. As soon as we were left on our own, Anna asked, 'Which side is the baby kicking – to the left or right?', and looked at my belly. 'I think to the right', I answered. 'Then it will be a boy. Mine always kicked to the left and both were girls.'

(Pechory, Pskov region, 1990)

This portentious sign was encounted more than once in St Petersburg as well and indicates the importance of the belly as the symbol via which information significant for women is made available to others (the advice and portentious signs come only from women who have had children).

It is important here to note the role played by the physical appearance of a pregnant woman, more precisely by her belly, in the episodes described. The belly removes interpersonal barriers and helps overcome the alienation typical of a large city. Complete strangers approach and ask which side the baby is kicking on, advise you not to step over a dog, not to eat sunflower seeds or not to sleep with your husband. At first their behaviour feels overfamiliar but soon it is seen as normal. The usual barriers between people are broken down among women who have had children, which lends a real depth to contact in their milieu. This localized concentration of contacts is one of the determinants of communality and in this sense it is possible to talk about a 'maternal community'. The belly acts as a symbol and mediator creating the possibility for contacts where otherwise they would be unlikely.

The maternal tradition is not only an informational network for pregnant women, it also has a well-developed set of customs, in particular, of mutual help.

> I wrote to my friend in Magadan and told her I was pregnant. Her first reaction was, 'I received your news that you are expecting a child... Write and tell me how you are feeling. Perhaps you need some help? I will gladly do whatever I can. Have you got the baby things?'
>
> (Nina R., teacher, Magadan-St Petersburg 1958)

Other women reacted in the same way, as a result of which the majority of things for my first child were donated by friends, close relatives and even distant acquaintances. Indeed, this has a ritual significance. There is a popular belief that a pregnant woman should not sew, knit or buy the baby things herself; if she does the baby may be still-born or not live long. Buying baby things in a shop, therefore, is treated almost as a lack of respect for the custom. Since this belief[3] means effectively that one has to rely on presents and help from other women, it serves the purpose of guiding a pregnant woman towards expecting support from the female community and not fussing with preparations herself.

This practice continues after the birth of the child, via a system of passing on to younger chidren those clothes which older children have grown out of. This is referred to as the 'queue'. The 'queue' means that each woman has her own regular donors and recipients.[4] In effect, this is a system of exchange between a woman and the maternal community; you give and receive. But, in each case, it appears, and is experienced as, a gift, and thus relations are tinged with tender gratitude. It should be noted that partners in the 'queue' are sought usually by the donor not the recipient; for the former the practice solves the problem of getting rid of children's things which have become too small and no longer useful, but are not yet worn out. Masha S. explained how the 'queue' works perfectly:

> A child is a double joy; at the start when people bring [things] to you, and then later when you can give them away and free some space.
>
> (St Petersburg, 1992)

The customs of mutual help are not restricted to less well-off mothers, and the exchange itself has more a symbolic than a utilitarian value. Indeed, mothers are often very superstitious about their children's things and avoid throwing them out at all costs. Sometimes, when clothes are given, they said: 'If it doesn't fit, give it to somebody else or throw it out.' If somebody else throws it out, it is better. Many mothers also avoid selling clothes, even if they are completely new, or giving them to strangers:

> Take them ... I don't want just anybody to wear them. Who knows who could end up with them. It would be better for your son to wear them. I would be happier.
>
> (St Petersburg, 1994)

This is associated with the fear that if clothes which your child has worn end up on a bad person then this might bring harm to your own child. This might be compared to the traditional belief that a person can be 'cursed'[5] via their things. Thus, children's clothes are sacred, symbolic objects whose significance stems from their symbolic representation of the relationship of the mother to the body of the child. When they are passed on, therefore, the mother almost transfers her own relationship to the child to the child of her friend. Maternal mutual help is thus not only material support but also a demonstration of kindness and communality. Children's clothes act as symbolic mediators – an intermediary link between women – and these links are preserved even after clothes cease to be exchanged (usually when the child is about 3 years old).

Clothes are thus bodily attributes acting as symbolic mediators between parents and children and this explains why, traditionally, from the birth of a child, especially a first child, the father washes the nappies and rompers. It is a popularly believed that this will make him love the child more. Mothers sketch around the hands and feet of their small children on paper and send the tracings in letters to relatives. They measure the height of their children with thread and enclose the thread in the envelope. This is done so that relatives living far away can 'get to know' the baby. Many mothers keep the shoes in which the baby first walked on its own and locks of hair from the first hair-cut (usually around the age of 12 months).

Bodily attributes – clothes and shoes, hair, silhouettes of feet and hands, the measures of height – mediate and symbolize the relations into which the new-born child is being incorporated (with the father, mother and other relatives).

The bodily nature of these symbols is central to the female community. Symbolic acceptance into this comunity takes place after the birth of one's first child and, significantly, is also mediated by a bodily symbol – the tradition of giving symbolic presents.[6] Women (those who have children) visit the new mother and bring a present (jumpers, slippers, toy frogs, rattles, etc.) for the infant. This practice stems from an earlier village tradition. Indeed, in the villages sometimes the birth shirt of the woman who had given birth would be hung out on a pole over the bath house (*bania*) to signal to the neighbours that the birth had been successful and that it was possible to visit the mother. Only married women with children came and brought home-made pies, pancakes and other snacks (in some places they were brought to the mother, in others to the baby) (Zelenin 1991: 322). This all symbolized initiation, acceptance into the female community, and was particularly significant upon the birth of a first child.

The same significance is attached to conversations on the subject of the 'belly' (pregnancies, births, infancies) among women themselves. As mothers with prams go for walks around their block, there gradually develops a constant group – a community centred on that block. The mothers, as a rule, do not know each other personally, so they call each other by the names of their children: 'Masha's mum', or 'Grisha's mum'. In effect, the children become their symbolic mediators.

The signal for interaction is the pram. Women with prams freely strike up conversation with one another, often about quite intimate subjects such as childbirth. Indeed, this is characteristic of a first acquaintance and the conversation leads both mothers to become excited, interrupt one another and laugh. It seems that such conversations create an emotional communality, bring to life a common experience and in this way give rise to a feeling of intimacy which is at the heart of the maternal community of the block. In some cases these non-personal links grow into personal friendships.

The Russian philosopher (and father of four children at the time) V. Rozanov referred to the magical power of conversations about 'the belly' and their influence on women. Having witnessed, at the theatre, the excited reaction of a usually prim woman to a comment about motherhood, he was inspired to note in his diary that:

An interest in 'the belly' immediately reduces barriers and distance between people, the socializing role of the belly is striking, touching, generous, sublime.

(Rozanov 1990: 180)

THE BODILY CODE

What is under consideration, therefore, is a communicative network which is consolidated via bodily symbolism. This bodily symbolism is also the chief means of communication and the central element of its language.

During pregnancy a woman develops a characteristic self-perception based on what Emily Martin describes as 'the signals' sent to her by her body (Martin 1987: 77). A pregnant woman listens to the sensations and conditions of her body and encodes them. The woman's own body and its sensations are a sign of the child and her body thus exists not only in the material world but also in a parallel symbolic world where the image of this future individual is formed.

This encoding of the body is not formed spontaneously but is heavily influenced by female tradition expressed in maternal folklore, especially the advice and portentious signs mentioned above. Kicking to one side or the other is a symbol of the sex of the future child. Stepping over dogs, cats or various other objects is said to encourage miscarriage or the child becoming entangled in its umbilical cord. Holding your belly is said to give the baby a birthmark. Each piece of advice symbolically links a particular gesture or movement to a possible complication (strangulation by the umbilical cord, hairiness, still-birth, etc.) with the baby.

The advice and portentious signs – which you hear dozens of times every day during pregnancy – have not only a concrete content but provide a system of understanding one's own body, movements and states as symbols in themselves. In this way a pregnant woman ceases to distinguish between herself and her child, and mothers (and even future mothers) constantly interpret things happening to their own bodies as signs about the child. Thus, female tradition, even during pregnancy, 'teaches' the future mother its own language and cultural code; with the help of portentious signs and advice it encodes bodily phenomena. The issue of precisely which aspects of 'bodilyness' enter the symbolic world of maternal culture, however, is best explored via an analysis of the image of the body in this female tradition.

The pregnant belly

The belly attracts, perhaps, the most attention:

- Form – if it is an even belly which juts out sharply in front (referred to as 'turnip', 'melon' or 'cucumber' shape), then this is taken to be a sign that a boy will be born; if it is broad, visible from behind and uneven in form, this is to be a sign of a girl.
- Size – if the belly is small, it will be a boy; if it is large, plump and the woman has a generally swollen figure, then it will be a girl.
- Positioning of the foetus – on the right, or if kicks are felt to the right it means a boy; kicks to the left indicates a girl.
- The belly must not be clutched (especially in fright) otherwise the child will be born with a birthmark.

Breasts (and how they change during pregnancy)

- If the nipples stick out, and are pointed, it will be a boy; if they are sunken or flat, a girl.
- In the ethnographic literature another portentious sign is noted: if the nipples darken during pregnancy, it will be a girl; if they are 'white', a boy (Popov 1903: 330).

Legs and gait

> even the nurse says . . . I carry myself like a sausage when one should glide like a swan, and that this is important for the child.
> (Natasha A., Moscow 1991)

- In ethnographic literature the encoding of the 'waddling' typical of a pregnant woman is noted, as is the significance of certain poses. Stepping out left foot first, means a boy; right first, a girl whilst, if when sitting, the right leg is stretched out, it means a boy; stretching out the left leg means a girl (Dal' 1993: 126–7).
- The strict rules concerning stepping over objects (objects from dogs to axes are prohibited) has already been mentioned. Moreover the act of 'stepping over' draws attention not so much to the legs as to the genital opening and is traditionally associated with intercourse or birth. Probably the prohibition against sitting on doorsteps, noted by the contemporary ethnographer M.V. Sementsov in Krasnodar region, is also related to the vagina

(Sementsov 1992: 10). Prohibitions on kicking domestic animals (cats, dogs) were also noted by the author (St Petersburg, 1990.)[7]

Arms

The arms receive less attention.

- The author was often told not to raise her arms above her head and not to reach up when hanging out washing (St Petersburg, 1990), since the child might get entangled in the umbilical cord or lie incorrectly in the belly (feet or side first).
- A similar prohibition – against putting your arms behind your head during sleep – is noted among the Kuban Cossacks (Sementsov 1992: 10). It would seem that these prohibitions are not designed to regulate arm movements themselves, but rather the pressure these place on stomach muscles; they are prohibited for the same reason that lifting weights is.

Face and head

- If the face of a pregnant woman is thin, pinched, but clear and rosy, this is a sign of carrying a boy; if the face is puffy and of poor complexion, it is a girl.[8]
- It is said that if a pregnancy makes a woman beautiful she is carrying a boy; if it makes her ugly then it is a girl, because 'a girl steals all the mother's beauty' (St Petersburg, 1990).
- A pregnant woman is warned not to clutch at her face since, like clutching the belly, it will give birth marks to the child.
- Of all the facial features the *mouth* is singled out for particular attention. If the lips swell, then a boy will be born.
- Eating sunflower seeds or spitting out peel is advised against, since it will mean the child will dribble a lot (St Petersburg, 1990; Natasha A., Moscow, 1991)
- Particular attention is also paid to *hair*. Hair should not be cut or even trimmed during pregnancy (since it might lead to a miscarriage or still-birth). In village tradition there is even a pro-hibition on brushing hair on holidays and Fridays (this is seen to bring about a difficult birth and the child being lice-ridden) (Popov 1903: 329).

Feelings of 'weakness' and 'heaviness'

These are characteristic of pregnancy and are encoded by female tradition thus:

- Severe weakness in the later stages of pregnancy and a feeling of heaviness in the womb are signs of the birth of a boy (Stepanov 1906: 224).
- If the first three months of pregnancy are easy, it will be a boy; if this period is difficult, a girl (Dal' 1993: 126–7). However, there is no consensus on this; the author was also told the opposite; that is, severe morning sickness suggests a boy, whilst late illness, a girl.

Food cravings

- If a pregnant woman eats well, a boy will be born. The author was advised, 'if you eat everything and a lot of it, it will be a boy' (St Petersburg, 1990).
- If she craves salty and spicy foods, such as herrings or salted tomatoes, it will be a boy; if she wants sweet things and fruit, radishes or beetroot, then a girl (Popov 1903: 330).[9]
- It is sometimes said that if a mother longs for fresh fish, then the child will not live long (Loginov 1993a: 30).

We thus have a picture of the image of the body in maternal culture. Above all it is a feminine and pregnant body: a large belly (attention is paid to its size, form and sensations), swelling nipples, changing pigmentation, a rolling gait, enforced ways of standing and sitting, arms pinned to one's sides like an aleolithic Venus (because you are afraid to raise them, in case the baby suddenly starts lying wrongly and thus the birth be complicated). There are also unaccustomed feelings: heaviness, weakness, sudden sleepiness, unexpected desires and changing tastes. These physical attributes and sensations are fixed by maternal culture and act as the signs of its unheard language. Its meanings and texts exist only in the presence of a pregnant body, since the signals for their actualization are the sensation of pregnancy or the sight of a pregnant woman (causing others to approach and proffer advice).

THE EROTICA OF THE 'BELLY'

> For some reason people ask about my belly; whether it is big (if they haven't seen me). And they sigh that I have lost weight and am losing weight and that I have 'eyes like an owl' as if this is bad ... many try to touch my belly ... One woman wanted to determine the sex of the child by it, but I wouldn't let her.
>
> (Natasha A., Moscow, 1991)

Women seem to be drawn to the belly; they approach and begin speaking to pregnant women, discussing its form and size. There is a clearly erotic attraction to the belly which is characteristic of women who have had children of their own. It is even said that 'A woman without a belly is like an oven without a flame' (Moscow, 1977). Pregnant woman are, it would seem, extraordinarily beautiful and even the news of pregnancy makes women (who have their own children) unaccountably happy. Throughout her pregnancy a woman is immersed in a peculiar, warm and tender atmosphere created by the euphoric condition of herself and the women around her.

> at last ... I have decided to have a child ... I have been floating in an euphoric state of tender pregnancy for almost five months ... I don't really understand myself what I have done, but, so far, I am in the happiest state ever.
>
> (Rita P., Moscow, 1994)

This euphoric, erotic experience of pregnancy is created by maternal tradition which is transferred in the same way as the codes and information discussed above; it is an erotic reinforcement of bodily symbolism. But how exactly does the maternal tradition form and strengthen the erotica of motherhood? It does so using the 'advice-giving' function referred to above. Advice is a means of making some symbols taboo, of driving them out of the symbolic world of maternal culture, or rather of preventing them coming into contact with the body of a pregnant woman. Thus, harm ensues from looking at or stepping over an object which is taboo, or from a pregnant woman becoming frightened, or rather from transferring that fright to the pregnant body. No distressing emotion must be associated with the bodily manifestation of pregnancy.

What precisely is banished from the symbolic world (myth) of motherhood?

Death

The taboo on contact with the symbols of death is the most persistent. A pregnant woman must not: be present when a coffin is brought in or out of a house; wash the body of a dead person (this was forbidden even to village midwives who helped at births); accompany the body to the graveyard or throw earth onto the grave. If these rules are not obeyed the unborn child may die or, at the very least, be pale, blue in the face and unattractive (Loginov 1993a: 28). These prohibitions remain today; even crossing a road along which a body is being carried is seen to threaten an unborn child, since, it is said, the blood will clot causing a birthmark (Popov 1903: 329).

A pregnant woman should not even think about death, therefore, and, it seems, this prohibition preserves the erotic, euphoric experience of pregnancy. In maternal culture, that which threatens the erotic serenity of motherhood – the fear of death – is banished.

Distressing Experiences

Distressing experiences such as anger, sadness, offence and, above all, fright, are taboo. It is said that if a mother is frightened during pregnancy, then the child may be born dumb, mentally deficient, unsociable, nervous, insomniac or will not survive at all. If you are frightened by a wolf, the child will be marked and covered in hair (Popov 1903: 329); if by a cow, the child will be afraid of cows; if by a dog, then it will be afraid of dogs. If the pregnant woman is frightened by water, the child born might drown (Arkhiv MAE 1989: 1.2). Under no circumstances should a pregnant woman argue with anybody, since this might cause the child to be still-born or deformed (the words falling on the mother's ears carry harm to the baby). What is feared is 'the evil eye', since an unborn child is particularly subject to such dangers.

Maternal culture seeks to strengthen positive emotions and banishes all negative emotions and stresses which must not come into contact with the pregnancy. Thus, a pregnant woman is advised to surround herself with beautiful things; hanging a portrait of a beautiful person over the bed of a pregnant woman, for example, is said to mean the baby will look like that (St Petersburg, 1990). On the other hand, it is not recommended to look at blind or crippled people; the author was even advised to remove a book on teratology from the shelf.

Sex and external erotica

Finally, maternal culture protects its erotica by banishing any 'external' erotica. Erotic attention must be concentrated on the pregnant body (later this will be transferred to the body of the new-born baby) and thus erotic attraction to the male body is made taboo; the erotica of the 'belly' pushes out the erotica of intercourse.

A pregnant woman must not sleep with her husband otherwise the baby will have eyes ... which are not quite right ...
(Moscow, 1991)

Ethnographers of the nineteenth and early twentieth centuries noted a similar banishment. G. Popov suggests the following motivation: during the second half of pregnancy, an angel is believed to bring the infant a soul. If this is hindered (by intercourse), then the angelic spirit will not be able to enter the body. The result is mental deficiency and a mean child (Popov 1903: 332). Hence the 'eyes which are not quite right', no doubt.

The objects which must not be stepped over by a pregnant woman are all attributes of male occupations: axe, reins, saddle, horse collar, cobbler's stand (Dal' 1993: vol. 3: 614; Loginov 1993b: 72; Popov 1903: 329–30), which are all used as male symbols in rituals. For example, when cutting the umbilical cord, a boy had it cut traditionally with an axe or on a cobbler's stand, while for a girl symbols of women's occupations – a distaff or spindle – were used (Zelenin 1991: 321). It was also prohibited to step over phallic objects such as a shaft or a yoke (for carrying buckets).

The taboo on intercourse with a man or its symbolic representation (stepping over male attributes) pushes out the competing ('male') erotica and thus maintains the image of the erotic 'purity' of motherhood. Just as these 'texts' (and their signs) excite and attract women with children, however, with the same force they repulse the uninitiated.

THE ANGELS ARE FLYING

The symbolic world (bodily code) of maternal culture is not confined to the encoding of the female body nor is the erotica of motherhood restricted to an 'attraction to the belly'. Pregnancy only prepares a woman for that which she will experience once she has become a mother. Female culture forms patterns of understanding and encoding the body and, after the birth, this is projected onto the infant.

The relationship of the mother to the new-born baby is clearly erotic. According to Freud:

> his mother ... regards him with feelings that are derived from her own sexual life: she strokes him, kisses him, rocks him and quite clearly treats him as a substitute for a complete sexual object.
>
> (Freud 1991: 145)

Sexual attraction is accompanied by 'intellectual infatuation' which is manifest in the the sexual overvaluation of the qualities and perfection of the object of attraction. Freud makes the provision that this phenomenon is more apparent among men while women generally fail to exhibit any sexual overvaluation towards men, although 'they scarcely ever fail to do so towards their own children' (ibid.: 63). The Russian saying formulates this more succinctly: 'Every first-time parent thinks their child is the most beautiful and clever in the world' (Dal' 1993: 138).

Maternal culture supports and stimulates the erotica of motherhood. Formulaic ways of addressing the infant – 'sweety-pie' ('*detkakonfetka*'); 'bunnykins' ('*zaichik moi*'); 'my little sunbeam' ('*solnyshko moe*'); 'my little sweetie' ('*sladkii moi*'); 'little flower' ('*tsvetochek*'); and 'little berry' ('*iagodka*') – all emphasize warmth, sweetness and gentleness.

Folklore also surrounds a child's smile. A researcher at the beginning of the twentieth century, Divil'kovskii, observed among village residents of the Russian North a practice amongst mothers of trying to see how the baby smiled in its sleep. According to popular belief, at this moment the guardian angel caresses and sings lullabies to the infant, thereby setting the child on the righteous path. At this time the child must not be disturbed, otherwise the angel may leave and the child's soul will be taken over by evil forces (Divil'kovskii 1914: 596). To this day, every time she sees a sleeping child, one of my older relatives says blissfully, 'when children sleep the angels fly'. An infant's smile is a source of incredibly sweet feelings for parents, and especially for the mother, but also for women with children in general. This is expressed by parents in the following way:

> When he smiles, I can't bear it, it's such a trusting, blinding smile.
>
> (Natasha A., Moscow, 1992)

> Sania smiled and I was stupified by his smile.
>
> (Ivanov 1990: 5)

'I cannot bear it' and 'I was stupified' are uncontrollable, bodily feelings, and those who have experienced them then try to elicit a smile or laugh from the baby. The maternal tradition provides certain ways of making a baby smile. This is a genre of folklore called 'baby-talk' (*pestushki*).[10] In this practice mothers unite verbal statements and tender manipulations of the infant's body; the baby is tickled, stroked, rocked and kissed.

> I am travelling with my small son on a trolleybus. He is not talking yet, he is only 6 months old. A woman is sitting opposite, she is about 40 years old, she touches his fingers, and smiles: 'What sweet little fingers!' Then she puts out two fingers as if they were horns: 'A goat with horns is coming . . . I will butt, butt, butt!'. As she says the last words she tickles the child with the 'horns' and he laughs joyfully. There is no less joy on the woman's, and my, face.
>
> (St Petersburg, 1991)

In such 'baby-talk' an unaccountable attraction, a desire to touch, stroke and caress the baby, as well as to see its magical smile, is given an outlet and is strengthened verbally.[11] It is important to note that the physical contact engaged in during 'baby-talk' focus on the most sensitive places of an infant's body – palms, soles, tummy and (the most ticklish of all) the underarms – and is thus clearly associated with erotic stimulation.

Maternal attraction to the infant is important for female tradition and is used by it. The child's body like that of the pregnant mother, is encoded and now becomes the basic source of signs:

> I was in a shop with my 8-month-old son, when suddenly he shouted out. 'What a loud voice', commented a woman standing next to me, 'He will be a captain!'
>
> (St Petersburg, 1991)

A second time this happened it was read as being a sign of a future career as an opera singer. Other predictions which were noted included: 'a tsar', when he was demanding chocolate loudly; 'a sportsman', when tried to run away from me; 'an artist', when he got covered in paint; 'mummy's little helper', when he tried to wash his own plate after lunch; 'a driver', when he reaches out to touch a car he has seen; 'an inventor', when he tried to take my typewriter apart; 'a climber', when he fell off the sofa (St Petersburg, 1992).

This is a widespread customary reaction to gestures, movements or cries of the baby, and it is used by people not only to 'predict' the future but to wish something nice on the child. The essence of this genre is the encoding of gestures, qualities, shouts of the child, which are interpreted as signs of the child's future fate. The body of a child and its experiences in early childhood exist not only in the material, but also the symbolic, world. Everything is interpreted as a sign of his future fate.

The invisible world

The bodily code of maternal culture is completely inaccessible to the uninitiated. Without the corresponding bodily experience, they neither see these signs nor want to see them. The bodily nature of birth repulses. These feelings are most succinctly expressed by the Russian philosopher Berdiaev in *Samopoznaniia* (*Self-knowledge*):

> Pregnant women repulsed me. This grieves me and seems evil. I had a strange sense of fear and an even stranger sense of guilt. I cannot say that I did not like children, I probably did like them. I was very concerned about my nephews and nieces. But childbirth always appeared hostile to the individual, to threaten its integrity. Like Kierkegaard I sensed the sin and evil of birth.
> (Berdiaev 1991: 88)

The fear and guilt are part of a rejection complex and are just as inexplicable as the 'attraction to the belly' noted among women who have had children. It suggests the existence of an emotional barrier inhibiting the understanding of the bodily language of maternal culture. This can be overcome only by personal bodily experience of motherhood (or coming into very close contact with it). However, many cultural taboos render the bodily side of motherhood hidden and inaccessible to those outside. Customs of confinement allow only women who have had children (and sometimes the father as well) to see the pregnant and infant body. Corresponding erotic feelings and bodily contacts are also made taboo.

The confinement begins during pregnancy; a pregnant woman is advised against using common crockery or utensils, participating in common labour or rituals or undertaking journeys and visits (Baiburin 1993: 89). Men avoided pregnant women walking their way; they believed that if a pregnant woman stepped over any part of the horse's harness then their journey would not be successful.

A pregnant woman's sexual confinement – especially in the second half of pregnancy – has already been mentioned and this effectively isolated her from society, especially male society. Nobody was to know of her pregnancy, except for women who had their own children – and they, on the contrary, were to be told as soon as possible (since the sooner they knew, the sooner the child would start talking). But the information was to remain within the maternal community. In the same way, the moment of birth was kept secret from all but the mother, mother-in-law and midwife, that is, those who embodied the community of mothers into which, from this moment (if it was a first child) the mother giving birth would enter. If virgins, women who had no children, old maids, or men found out then, according to popular belief, it would be a terribly difficult and tortuous birth; the more people found out, the more difficult. The new-born was also hidden; until forty days (now up to two months) after the birth the child was not shown to anybody. Pregnant women and new-born infants were believed to be particularly susceptible to the 'evil eye', by which is meant a harm-bearing influence brought by a, sometimes unintentional, look or word from an outsider. This popular belief remains influential. A month after her first son was born, Natasha A. wrote:

It will be a month tomorrow and we are ill ... the child has fractured his left collar-bone. I don't understand how it happened. Nothing unusual happened. I did not drop him, did not shake him, and suddenly – a fracture appears! It is as if someone has put the evil eye on him. Just before this I had shown him to my aunt and cousin (but now I won't show him to anyone until the forty days are up).

(Natasha A., Moscow, 1992)

The fear of the evil eye makes a pregnant woman and a woman just having given birth avoid contacts. Popular belief about her ritual 'impurity' made others avoid her. Together they rendered, and continue to render, the bodily nature of motherhood a secret which may not be taken beyond the maternal community. Even the mother herself, after a period of time has elapsed after the birth, becomes estranged from her acquired bodily experience. This is reinforced by taboos on the appearance of the pregnant woman and the new-born: traditionally, neither are allowed even to look in the mirror and thus fix their appearance. Village tradition also limited erotic contacts with the infant: it was advised not to kiss (especially on the lips) or fuss over the child, (i.e. practice the 'baby-talk' referred to above) or to sleep with the baby in the same bed. It is not advised to step over a small child (this will stunt growth) or to breast-feed the baby for too long (more than 18 months). It is also warned that if a child has to be weaned off the breast twice, then he will have an evil eye (i.e. he might put the evil eye on others) (Baiburin 1993: 89; Dal' 1993, vol. 3: 614; Divil'kovskii 1914: 596; Uspenskii 1991: 27). Such taboos facilitated a gradual estrangement of the woman from the bodily experience of motherhood. She (and with her the child) are extracted from the influence of the bodily code and brought into the world of verbal communication. Thus, it is no coincidence that prohibitions are often justified by suggesting that otherwise 'the child will not start talking until late' (the prohibition on kissing, breast-feeding for a long time, looking in the mirror). Virtually all these prohibitions (except perhaps kissing) remain current in the urban enviroment today.

Conclusions

It has been suggested that the language of maternal culture is based on an encoding of various characteristics, movements, conditions of the pregnant body of the mother and the body of the infant. This bodily symbolism has an erotic reinforcement, moreover, the erotic feeling and attraction (probably connected with hormonal processes) is fixed and strengthened by maternal culture. As a result of the uaccountable attraction to the 'belly' and then to the child, the attention of the mother is constantly fixed on the bodily signs of this culture and, consequently, on its texts. This change of code is not all that a woman experiences during pregnancy; it is simply one consequence of the acceptance by her of the maternal folklore surrounding her. At the same time, the structure of the symbolic world itself changes: from a binary myth the woman moves into a concentric myth (Shchepanskaia 1994). Here a multitude of signs envelope a single central symbol which is the core of this myth – the child. This transformation requires more detailed explanation for which there is no space here, as do other aspects of 'female initiation' (the change in behaviourial norms, the restructuring of relations with the outside world, etc.). But we might conclude, at least, that what is being explored here is a change of myth, the model of the world as a whole. What is experienced by the pregnant woman is a movement into another communicative system and, as a result, into another culture.

NOTES

1 Nevskii Avenue – the main street in St Petersburg.
2 Evidence drawn from the personal archive of the author will henceforth be indicated in brackets citing the place and year of its recording. If the evidence has come from other women, the name, profession and date of birth of the respondents are given.
3 The prohibition is not strict and nobody observes it fully; its meaning is, above all, symbolic.
4 The terms used are 'to join a queue' (*pristroit'si v ochered'*) or 'to be in the queue' (*byt' v khvost*) of your benefactor.
5 The verb used is '*isportit'*' from the root '*porcha*' meaning 'magic spells', 'sorcery' and here meaning 'to put the evil eye on someone'.
6 The term 'symbolic' is used here in the sense of 'small', that is, significant not in material terms but in the 'giving' itself. The term used in the original Russian is '*podarki na zubok*'.
7 This prohibition is noted among village residents of the Russian North, see Loginov 1993: 29–30.
8 This is also noted by Popov (Popov 1903: 330).
9 Variants of these superstitions were met by the author on a number of occasions during pregnancy.
10 This is not a direct translation but indicates the essence of the term '*pestushki*' which is a peculiar form of relating to a baby designed to evoke a reaction from it.
11 There are a huge number of *pestushki* which have been collected and published in a recent anthology of folklore connected with infancy, see Anikin (1991).

Bibliography

ENGLISH LANGUAGE SOURCES

Abrams, M. (1959) *The Teenage Consumer*, London: London Press Exchange.

Andrew, C., Coderre, C. and Denis, A. (1990) 'Stop or go: Reflections of women managers on factors influencing their career development', *Journal of Business Ethnics*, 9, 4–5: 361–7.

Attwood, L. (1990) *The New Soviet Man and Woman: Sex-Role Socialization in the USSR*, London: Macmillan and Bloomington, Ind.: Indiana University Press.

—— (1994) 'Confronting sexuality in school and society', in A. Jones (ed.) *Education and Society in the New Russia*, Armonk, NY and London: M. E. Sharpe.

Aukutsionek, S. and Kapeliushnikov, R. (1994) 'The Russian labor market in 1993', *Radio Liberty, Radio Free Europe Research Report*, 3: 26–30.

Bekhtereva, N. (1988) 'I like dance music', *Moscow News*, 10.

Belkin, A. (1975) 'Masculine, feminine or neutral?', *The Unesco Courier*, August–September: 58–61.

Bernard, M. and Meade, K. (eds) (1993) *Women Come of Age: Perspectives on the Lives of Older Women*, London: Edward Arnold.

Blaxter, M. (1983) 'The causes of disease: Women talking' *Social Science And Medicine*, 17, 2: 59–69.

—— (1990) *Health and Lifestyles*, London: Routledge/Tavistock.

Bondarev, Iu., Belov, V. and Rasputin, V. (1988) 'Young people: Discarding flattery and demagogy', *Moscow News*, 6: 5–6.

Brannen J. *et al.* (1994) *Young People, Health and Family Life*, Buckingham: Open University Press.

Bridger, S. (1989) 'Rural youth', in J. Riordan (ed.) (1989).

Bridger, S., Kay, R. and Pinnick, K. (1995) *No More Heroines? Russia, Women and the Market*, London: Routledge.

Bruno, M. (1995) 'The second love of worker bees: Gender, employment and social change in contemporary Moscow', in *Women in Post-Communist Russia* (edited by Sue Bridger), *Interface: Bradford Studies in Language, Culture and Society*, no. 1, Spring 1995.

Buckley, M. (1991) 'Gender and reform', in C. Merridale and C. Ward (eds) *Perestroika: The Historical Perspective*, London: Edward Arnold.

—— (ed.) (1992) *Perestroika and Soviet Women*, Cambridge: Cambridge University Press.

Campbell, A. (1984) *The Girls In the Gang*, Oxford: Basil Blackwell.

Carter, E. (1984) 'Alice in the consumer wonderland', in A. McRobbie and M. Nava (eds) (1984).

Chelnokov, A. (1993c) 'Children of the market', *Current Digest of the Post-Soviet Press*, 45, 32: 24.

Clarke, S. (1994) 'Privatisation: The politics of capital and labour', in S. White, A. Pravda and Z. Gitelman (eds) *Developments in Russian and Post-Soviet Politics*, London: Macmillan.

Clarke, S., Fairbrother, P., Burawoy, M. and Krotov, P. (eds) (1993) *What about the Workers? Workers and the Transition to Capitalism in Russia*, London: Verso.

Cohen, P. (1986) *Rethinking the Youth Question*, London: Post-16 Education Centre, Institute of Education.

Connell, R. (1987) *Gender and Power*, Cambridge: Polity Press.

Cook, L. (1993), *The Soviet Social Contract and Why it Failed*, Cambridge, Mass.: Harvard University Press.

Corrin, C. (ed.) (1992) *Superwomen and the Double Burden: Women's Experience of Change in Central and Eastern Europe and the Former Soviet Union*, London: Scarlet Press.

Davison, C., Davey-Smith G. and Frankel, S. (1991) 'Lay epidemiology and the prevention paradox', *Sociology of Health And Illness*, 13: 1–19.

De Melo, M. and Ofer, G. (1994) 'Private service firms in a transitional economy: Findings of a survey in St Petersburg', *Studies of Economies in Transformation*, Paper 11, Washington D.C.: The World Bank.

d'Houtaud A. and Field, M. (1987) 'The image of health', *Sociology of Health And Illness*, 6: 30–60.

Easton, P. (1989) 'The rock music community' in J. Riordan (ed.) (1989).

Einhorn, B. (1993) *Cinderella Goes to Market: Citizenship, Gender and Women's Movements in East Central Europe*, London: Verso.

Fagenson, E. and Horowitz, S. (1985) *"Moving Up": A List of the Person Organisation-Centred and Interactionists Perspectives*, Academy of Management Best Papers Proceedings.

Fain, A. (1990) 'Specific features of informal youth associations in large cities', *Soviet Sociology*, 29: 1.

Feltham, A., Murcott, A. and South, J. (1994) 'Beliefs about reproductive health among young Russian women,' *Working paper submitted to the ODA*, London, (April).

Fong, M. (1993) 'The role of women in rebuilding the Russian economy', *Studies of Economies in Transformation*, Paper 10, Washington, D.C.: The World Bank.

—— (1994), 'Russia: The role of women in rebuilding the economy', *Russia: Social Protection and Beyond*, Report no 11748–RU, Washington, D.C.: The World Bank.

Fornäs, J. and Bolin, G. (eds) (1995) *Youth Culture in Late Modernity*, London: Sage.

Freud, S. (1991) *On Sexuality: Three Essays on the Theory of Sexuality*, (The Penguin Freud Library, vol. 7) London: Penguin Books.

Funk, N. and Mueller, M. (eds) (1993) *Gender Politics and Post-Commu-*

nism: *Reflections from Eastern Europe and the Former Soviet Union*, London: Routledge.

Ganetz, H. (1995) 'The shop, the home and femininity as a masquerade', in J. Fornäs and G. Bolin (eds) (1995).

George, A. and Murcott, A. (1992) 'Research Note: Monthly strategies for discretion: shopping for sanitary towels and tampons', *The Sociological Review*, 40, 1: 207–24.

Gesson, M. (1994) *The Rights of Lesbians and Gay Men in the Russian Federation*, San Fransisco: International Gay and Lesbian Human Rights Commission.

Greer, G. (1995) 'A phallocentric view of sexual violence', *The Guardian*, 3 April: 20.

Griffin, C. (1985) *Typical Girls? Young Women from School to the Job Market*, London: Routledge.

—— (1993) *Representations of Youth: The Study of Youth and Adolescence in Britain and America*, Oxford: Blackwell.

Hall, R. (1985) *Ask Any Woman: A London Inquiry into Rape and Sexual Assault*, Bristol: Falling Wall Press.

Hall, S. (1989) 'The meaning of new times', in S. Hall and M. Jacques (eds) *New Times: The Changing Face of Politics in the 1990s*, London: Lawrence and Wishart.

Hoggart, R. (1957) *The Uses of Literacy*, London: Chatto & Windus.

Homer, H. (1970) *Femininity and Successful Achievement: A Basic Inconsistency: Feminine Personality and Conflict*, California: Brooks/Cole.

Hudson, B. (1984) 'Femininity and adolescence', in A. McRobbie and M. Nava (eds) (1984).

Institute of Personnel Management (1993) 'Age and employment: Policies, attitudes and practices', London: IPM Series.

Jenson, J. (1992) 'Fandom as pathology: The consequences of characterization', in L. Lewis (ed.) *Adoring Audience: Fan Culture and Popular Media*, London and New York: Routledge.

Johnson, L. (1993) *The Modern Girl: Girlhood and Growing Up*, Buckingham and Philadelphia: Open University Press.

Jones, A. and Moskoff, W. (1991) *Ko-ops: The Rebirth of Entrepreneurship in the Soviet Union*, Bloomington, Ind.: Indiana University Press.

Kanter, R. (1977) *Men and Women of the Corporation*, New York: Basic Books.

Karmaza, O. (1992) 'Child labour in Russia: Prostitution', *Current Digest of the Post-Soviet Press*, 44, 42: 22–3.

Kimmel, M. (ed.) (1987a) *Changing Men: New Directions in Research on Men and Masculinity*, Newbury Park, Cal.: Sage.

—— (1987b) 'Rethinking "masculinity": New directions in research', in M. Kimmel (ed.) (1987).

Konovalov, V. and Serdiukov, M. (1984) 'Foreign-made mirage', *Current Digest of the Soviet Press*, 38, 12: 21,39.

Kraminova, N. (1993) 'Group portrait with lady', *Current Digest of the Post-Soviet Press*, 45: 24–5.

Lapidus, G. (1978) *Women in Soviet Society: Equality, Development and Social Change*, Berkeley, Calif.: University of California Press.

Lees, S. (1986) *Losing Out: Sexuality and Adolescent Girls*, London: Hutchinson.

Lindsey, K. (1979) 'Madonna or whore?', *ISIS International Bulletin*, 13: 4–5.

Lopez, I. (1987) 'Sterilisation among Puerto Rican women in New York City: Public policy and social constraints', in L. Mullings (ed.) *Cities of the United States*, New York: Columbia University Press.

Luce, E. (1994) 'ILO alleges free-marketeers are concealing Russia's jobs crisis', *The Guardian*, 1 November: 16.

McAuley, A. (1981) *Women's Work and Wages in the Soviet Union*, London: Allen and Unwin.

McClelland, D. (1975) *Power: The Inner Experience*, New York: Irvington Publishing.

McRobbie, A. (1994) *Postmodernism and Popular Culture*, London and New York: Routledge.

McRobbie, A. and Garber, J. (1976) 'Girls and subcultures – an exploration', in S. Hall and T. Jefferson (eds) *Resistance Through Rituals: Youth Subculture in Post-war Britain*, London, Hutchinson.

McRobbie, A. and Nava, M. (eds) (1984) *Gender and Generation*, London: Macmillan.

Martin, E. (1987) *The Woman in the Body: A Cultural Analysis of Reproduction*, Boston: Beacon Press.

Martin, P., Harrison, D. and Dinitto, D. (1983) 'Advancement for women in hierarchical organizations: A multi-level analysis of problems and prospects', *Journal of Applied Behaviourial Science*, 19, 1: 19–33.

Martin, S. (1993) 'The women have their work cut out for them', *The Irish Times*, 15 February: 7.

Meliksetian, A. (1990) 'The social causes of deviant behaviour in young women', *Russian Education and Society*, February: 82–95 (originally in *Sovetskaia Pedagogika* (1990), 10: 53–8.)

Mies, M., Bennholdt-Thomsen, V. and Von Werlhof, C. (1988) *Women: The Last Colony*, London and New Jersey: Zed Books.

Mishkind, M. *et al.* (1987) 'The embodiment of masculinity: Cultural, psychological and behaviourial dimensions', in M. Kimmel (ed.) (1987a).

Moore, J., Tilson, B. and Whitting, G. (1994) 'An international overview of employment policies and practices towards older workers', *Employment Department Research Series*, 29.

Nava, M. (1992) *Changing Cultures: Feminism, Youth and Consumerism*, London: Sage.

Paiva, V. (1993) 'Sexuality, condom use and gender norms among Brazilian teenagers', *Reproductive Health Matters*, 2: 98–109.

Picchio, A. (1992) *Social Reproduction: The Political Economy of the Labour Market*, Cambridge: Cambridge University Press.

Pilkington, H. (1992), 'Whose space is it anyway ? Youth, gender and civil society in the former Soviet Union', in S. Rai, H. Pilkington and A. Phizacklea (eds) (1992).

—— (1993) ' "Good girls in trousers": Codes of masculinity and femininity in Moscow youth culture', in M. Liljeström, E. Mäntysaari and A. Rosenholm (eds) *Gender Restructuring in Russian Studies*, Tampere: Slavica Tamperensia II, 175–91.

—— (1994a) *Russia's Youth and Its Culture: A Nation's Constructors and Constructed*, London: Routledge.

—— (1994b) '*Tusovka* or *tu-sovka*? What does youth slang tell us about contemporary Russian youth culture?', *Rusistika*, 9: 10–21.

—— (1996) 'Young women and subcultural lifestyles: A case of "irrational needs"?', in R. Marsh (ed.) *Women in Russia and Ukraine*, Cambridge: Cambridge University Press.

Pill, R. and Stott, N. (1982) 'Concepts of health and illness causation and responsibility', *Social Science and Medicine*, 16: 42.

—— (1985) 'Choice or chance: Further evidence on ideas of illness and responsibility for health', *Social Science and Medicine* 20: 981–91.

Pollock, K. (1988) 'On the nature of social stress: Production of a modern mythology', *Social Science and Medicine*, 26, 3: 381–92.

Poole, M. (1983) *Youth: Expectations and Transitions*, Melbourne.

Popov, A., Visser, A. and Ketting, E. (1993) 'Contraceptive knowledge, attitudes, and practice in Russia during the 1980s', *Studies in Family Planning*, 24, 4: 227–35.

Posadskaya, A. (1994a) 'A feminist critique of policy, legislation and social consciousness in post-socialist Russia' in A. Posadskaya (ed.) (1994).

Posadskaya, A. (ed.) (1994b) *Women in Russia: A New era in Russian Feminism*, London: Verso.

Punamäki, R-L. and Kokko, S. (1995) 'Reasons for consultation and explanations of illness among Finnish primary-care patients', *Sociology of Health and Illness*, 17, 1: 42–64.

Putnam, L. and Heinen, S. (1976) *Women in Management: The Fallacy of the Trait Approach*, MSU Business Topics, 24, 3: 47–53.

Radley, A. (1994) *Making Sense of Illness*, London: Sage.

Rai, S., Pilkington, H. and Phizacklea, A. (eds) (1992) *Women in the Face of Change: The Soviet Union, Eastern Europe and China*, London: Routledge.

Reimer, B. (1995) 'Youth and modern lifestyles' in J. Fornäs and G. Bolin (eds) (1995).

Riordan, J. (ed.) (1989) *Soviet Youth Culture*, London: Macmillan.

Roman, L. (1988) 'Intimacy, labor, and class: Ideologies of feminine sexuality in the punk slam dance', in L. Roman and L. Christian-Smith (eds) *Becoming Feminine: The Politics of Popular Culture*, London: The Falmer Press.

Russia: Social Protection and Beyond (1994) Report no 11748–RU, Washington, D.C.: The World Bank.

Schein, E. (1973) 'The relationship between sex role stereotypes and requisite management characteristics among female managers', *Journal of Applied Psychology*, 7: 89–105.

Sedaitis, J. B. and Butterfield, J. (eds) (1991) *Perestroika from Below: Social Movements in the Soviet Union*, Boulder, Colo.: Westview Press.

Seidler, V. (1994) *Unreasonable Men: Masculinity and Social Theory*, London: Routledge.

Shlapentokh, D. (1992) 'Lovemaking in the time of perestroika: Sex in the context of political culture', *Studies in Comparative Communism*, 25, 2 (June): 151–76.

Shlapentokh, V. (1989) *Public and Private of the Soviet People: Changing Values in Post-Stalin Russia*, Oxford: Oxford University Press.

Shreeves, R. (1992) 'Sexual Revolution or Sexploitation? The Pornography and Erotica Debate in the Soviet Union', in S. Rai, H. Pilkington and A. Phizacklea (eds) (1992).

Stimson, G. (1974) 'Obeying doctors' orders: A view from the other side', *Social Science and Medicine*, 8: 97–104.

Stoltzman, S. (1986) 'Menstrual attitudes, beliefs, and symptom experiences of adolescent females, their peers, and their mothers', in V. Olesen and N. Woods (eds) *Culture, Society, and Menstruation*, New York: Hemisphere.

Terborg, J. (1981) 'Interactional psychology and research in human behaviour in organizations', *Academy of Management Review*, 6, 4: 569–76.

Terkhov, V. (1993) 'Russia's farm women can't raise the corps on their own', *Current Digest of the Post-Soviet Press*, 45, 32: 25–6.

UNICEF (1994) *Crisis in Mortality, Health and Nutrition*, Florence: UNICEF.

Waldron, I. (1983) 'Sex differences in illness incidence, prognosis and mortality', *Social Science and Medicine*, 17: 1107–23.

Watson, P. (1993a) 'The rise of masculinism in Eastern Europe', *New Left Review*, 198: 71–82.

—— (1993b) 'Eastern Europe's silent revolution: Gender', *Sociology*, 27, 3: 471–87.

Weedon, C. (1987) *Feminist Practice and Poststructuralist Theory*, Oxford: Basil Blackwell.

Wellings, K., Field J. and Whitaker, L. (1994) 'Sexual attitudes', in K. Wellings *et al. Sexual Behaviour in Britain*, Harmondsworth: Penguin.

Willems, H. (1995) 'Right-wing extremism, racism or youth violence? Explaining violence against foreigners in Germany', *New Community*, 21, 4: 501–23.

Williams, R. (1983) 'Concepts of health: An analysis of lay logic', *Sociology of Health and Illness*, 17: 185–204.

Worobec, C. (1991) *Peasant Russia*, Princeton, N.J.: Princeton University Press.

Yakov, V. (1993) 'Ministry of internal affairs warns that an increase in sex crimes has begun', *Current Digest of the Post-Soviet Press*, 45, 32: 24–5.

Zborowski, M. (1952) 'Cultural components in responses to pain', *Journal of Social Issues*, 8: 16–30.

Zola, I. (1973) 'Pathways to the doctor – from person to patient', *Social Science and Medicine*, 7: 677–89.

RUSSIAN LANGUAGE SOURCES

Abramov, O. and Lutkovskii, N. (1995) 'Neformaly – 10 let spustia', *Tema*, Ostankino Television, July 19.

Afanas'eva, T. (1988) *Semia*, Moskva.

Agarov, S. (1991) 'O sekretakh intimnoi zhinzni', *Vospitanie Shkol'nikov*, 6: 59–62.

Alekseev, N. (1994) 'Gruppiorovki – eto ser'ezno', *Pravoporiadok*, 3 March: 1–2.

Alekseenkov, S., Baranov, S. and Nevar, S. (1993) 'Molodezh': Komu ona nuzhna?', *Nezavisimaia Gazeta*, 3 March: 6.

Alekseeva, K. and Iur'eva, A. (1990) 'Sneg iz-pod sapog', *Moskovksii Komsomolets*, 26 October: 2.

Aleshina, Iu. and Volovich, A. S. (1991) 'Problemy usloveniia rolei muzhchiny i zhenshiny', *Voprosy Psikhologii*, 4: 74–82.

Analiticheskaia sluzhba 'KP' (1993) 'Pochem vy, devochki?', *Komsomol'-skaia Pravda*, 12 May: 3.

Anikin, V. (ed.) (1991) *Mudrost' Narodnaia: Zhizn' Cheloveka v Russkom Fol'klore. Vyp.I. Mladenchestvo, Detstvo*, Moskva: Khudozhestvennaia Literatura.

Antonian, Iu., Pertsova, L. and Sablina, L. (1991) 'Opasnie devitsy (Onesovershennoletnikh prestupniksath)', *Sotsiologicheskie Issledovaniia*, 7: 94–9.

Arkhiv MAE (1989) f.K-I, op.2, d.1647, (Arkhangel'skaia obl., Pinezhskii r-n).

Arshavskii, A. and Vilks, A. (1990) 'Antiobshchestvennie proiavleniia v molodezhnoi srede: Opyt regional'nogo prognoza', *Sotsiologicheskie Issledovaniia*, 4: 57–65.

Aslamova, D. (1992) ' "Elegantnie devushki – kruglosutochno" ', *Komsomol'skaia Pravda*, 1 September: 4.

'Assotsiatsiia informiruet' (1991) *SPID-info*, 7: 2.

Avdeeva, K. (1993) 'Molodoi muzh', *Ogonek*, 38 (July): 24–5.

Avilov, V. (1987) 'Rok ili urok?', *Komsomol'skaia Pravda*, 12 March: 2.

Babich, D. (1990) 'Potomu, chto liubliu', *Komsomol'skaia Pravda*, 10 July: 4.

Baiburin, A. (1993) *Ritual v Traditsionnoi Kul'ture: Strukturno-semanticheskii Analiz Vostochnoslavianskikh Obriadov*, Sankt Peterburg: Nauka.

Baklanova, E. (1993) 'Vokzal dlia mal'chishek i voskresnii klub dlia devochek', *Rabotnitsa*, April: 22–3.

Balon, V. (1993) 'Lesbiiskaia liubov' k iskusstvu', *Gumanitarnii Fond*, 2 (24–179): 4.

Barabash, N. (1994) 'Okhotnitsy za muzh'iami, pomnite: Eti zhivotnie vsegda khodiat staiami', *Komsomol'skaia Pravda*, 18 February: 9.

Belaga, L. (1994) 'Razdevaius' i drazniu', *SPID- info*, 11: 11–12.

Belskaia, G. (1977) 'Otkuda berutsia plokhie zheny', *Literaturnaia Gazeta*, 7 September: 12.

Berdiaev, N. (1991) *Samopoznanie*, Leningrad: Lenizdat.

Bernshtam, T. (1991) 'Sovershennoletie devushki v metaforakh igrovogo fol'klora (traditsionnii aspekt russkoi kul'tury)', in *Etnicheskie Stereotipy Muzhskogo i Zhenskogo Povedeniia*, Sankt Peterburg: Nauka.

Bogdanova, L. (1993) ' "Uzh zamuzh . . ." ili novoe pokolenie vybiraet?', *Rabotnitsa*, 6: 28–9.

Bogoliubova, K. (1991) in 'Pochemu my vmeste?', in *RISK*, January: 14.

Bol'shaia Sovetskaia Entsiklopediia (1939) volume 41, Moskva: OGIZ RSFSR.

Boguslavskaia, Z. (1992) ' "Devushkoi mozhno byt' tol'ko raz v zhizni', *Moskovskii Komsomolets*, 2 October: 2.

Borisov, I. (1991) 'Koe-chto o rokerakh' in K. Igoshev and G. Min'kovskii (eds) *Po Nepisanim Zakonam Ulitsy*, Moskva: Iuridicheskaia Literatura.

Breslav, G. and Khasan, B. (1990) 'Poloviie razlichiia i sovremennoe shkol'-noe obrazovanie', *Voprosy Psikhologii*, 3: 64–69.

Bualvintsev, N. (1994) 'Soldat Katiusha', *Rossiiskaia Gazeta*, 23 February: 1.

Budartseva, S. (1994) 'Romantika zla ili romantika dobra, chto sil'nee?', *Moskovskaia Pravda*, 14 July: 2.

Burgasov, P. (1986) 'Spid: Voprosov bol'she, chem otvetov', *Literaturnaia Gazeta*, 7 May: 15.

Bykanova, N. (1992) 'Bei bez promakha krasavitsa!', *Ogonek*, (February) 8: 24–5.

Chelnokov, A. (1993a) 'Uidia ot "krasnikh", rokery popali k "korichnevim"', *Izvestiia*, 12 November: 6.

—— (1993b) 'Rokery mezhdu dubinkoi i fashizmom', *Izvestiia*, 25 December: 6.

—— (1993d) ' "Trudnie" podrostki ispytaiut zabotu gosudarstva', *Izvestiia*, 10 September: 4.

—— (1994a) 'Molodoi natsist p'et gor'kuiu i chitaet "Mein kampf" ', *Izvestiia*, 15 January: 7.

—— (1994b) ' "Chernaia sotnia" sobiraet svoiu chern'', *Izvestiia*, 16 February: 1.

Cherednichenko, V. (1989a) 'SOS! Nedobrosovestnost'', *Sem'ia i Shkola*, 1: 25–6.

—— (1989b) 'Chtoby semeinaia zhizn' byla schastlivoi', *Vospitanie Shkol'nikov*, 6: 128–39.

—— (1990a) 'Starsheklassnitsa stala meter'iu', *Vospitanie Shkol'nikov*, 1: 68–72.

—— (1990b) 'Starsheklassnitsa stala meter'iu', *Vospitanie Shkol'nikov*, 3: 70–2.

Cherkasova, N. (1993) 'Russkaia Madonna – Inna Erofeeva', *Pul's*, 2: 22–3.

Chistiakov, V. and Sanachev, I. (1988) 'Troianskii kon', *Nash Sovremennik*, 10: 126–41.

D'iachenko, A. (1994) Speech at conference 'Zhenshchiny, molodezh', nasilie' Moscow, October 1993, published in *Vy i My. Dialog Zhenshchin*, 9.

Dal', V. (1993) *Poslovitsy Russkogo Naroda: Sbornik V. Dalia v Trekh Tomakh*, vol. 2, Moskva: Russkaia Kniga.

'Deshevka-2' (1992) *SPID-info*, 7 (July): 5–7.

Divil'kovskii, (1914) 'Ukhod i vospitanie detei u naroda', in *Pervoe Detstvo*, Izvestiia Arkhangel'skogo obshchestva izucheniia russkogo severa, 18: 589–60.

Dlia Vas, Devochki (1993) Novosibirsk: Detskaia Literatura.

Dodolev, E. (1993) 'Muzheubiitsy', *Novii Vzgliad*, 24: 1.

Dorno, I. (1981) 'Muzhchina za 30', *Zdorov'e*, 5: 18.

Dukarevich, M. (1993) 'U menia bol'she pretenzii k vracham', *Ty*, 2: 23–4.

Dzhaginova, E. (1993) 'Muzhchina i zhenshchina', *Megalopolis-ekspress*, 21 April.

Editorial (1993) *Ogonek*, February 6: 35.

Efremov, A. (1994) 'Eto moe delo', *Gazeta Dlia Zhenshchin*, 18, 38: 6–7

Egorova, A. (1994) 'Deti podzemel'ia', *Pravoporiadok* (Ul'ianovsk), February.

Egorova, A. and Zimina, V. (1994) 'Zagnannie v ugol', *Pravoporiadok* (Ul'ianovsk), February: 4–5.

Egorova, E. (1994) 'Gadkii utenok', *Moskovskii Komsomolets*, 14 October: 2.

El, A. (1990) 'Shershe lia fam!', *Moskovskii Komsomolets*, 3 February: 2.

Eremin, V. (1990) 'Seksual'naia vsedozvolennost' pronikaet v podrostkovuiu sredu', *Vospitanie Shkol'nikov*, 6: 25–8.

—— (1991) 'Vorovskoi orden', *Nedelia*, 13: 16–17.

'Etika i psikhologiia semeinoi zhizni' (1983) *Vospitanie Shkol'nikov*, 3: 28–36.

Fedorov, N. (1994) 'Bez krovi', *Simbir'skii Kur'er* (Ul'ianovsk), 20 January.

Filinov, Iu. (1986) 'Na konverte pishite "ABV" ', *Komsomol'skaia Pravda*, 15 January: 4.

Fromm, E. (1991) *Iskusstvo Liubit'*, Moskva: INION AN USSR.

Gareev, E. and Dorozhkin, Iu. (1993) 'Molodezh' industrial'noi Rossii: Zhiznennie i sotsial'no-politicheskie orientatsii', *Sotsiologicheskie Issledovaniia*, 1: 123–5.

Gilinskii, Ia. (1989) *Sotsiologiia Nasil'stvennoi Prestupnosti – Teoreticheskie Problemy Izucheniia Territorial'nikh Razlichii v Prestupnosti: Sotsial'nie i Pravovie Aspekty Nasiliia*, Tartu: Uch.Zap.Tart.un-ta.

—— (1990) 'Sotsial'noe nasilie i . . . smysl zhizni', in *Sbornik: Issledovanie Soznaniia i Tsennostnogo Mira Sovetskikh Liudei v Periode Perestroiki Obshchestva*, Moskva: INION.

Golovakha, E. (1988) *Zhiznennaia Perspektiva i Professional'noe Samoopredelenie Molodezhi*, Kiev.

Gordeeva, L. (1994) 'Vooruzheny. Kto planami, a kto pistoletom . . .', *Sem'ia* (Ul'ianovsk), 12 February.

Goskomstat RF (1992) *Obraz Zhizni Detei i Podrostkov RF*, Moskva: Respublikanskii informatsiono-izdatel'skii Tsentr.

Grigor'eva, E. (1991) 'Pochemu my vmeste?', *RISK*, January: 14.

Grishin, A. (1990) 'Izgoi', *Rabotnitsa*, 11: 26–7.

Gromov, A. and Kuzin, O. (1990) 'Neformaly: Kto est' kto?', Moskva: Mysl'.

Gromyko, M. (1986) *Traditsionnie Normy i Povedeniia i Formy Obshcheniia Russkikh Krest'ian XIX Veka*, Moskva: Nauka.

Gyne, I. (1960) *Iunosha prevrashchaetsia v muzhchinu*, Moskva.

Iagodinskii, V. (1990) 'O devich'ei chesti i supruzheskoi vernosti', *Vospitanie Shkol'nikov*, 5: 61–5.

'Ia k vam pishu' (1992) *Delovaia Zhenshchina*, 16: 4.

Ivanov, S. (1990) *Gde Vash Dom, Deti?* Leningrad: Lenizdat.

Ivanova, V. (1990) 'Cheboksarskie "Amazonki" ', *Sovetskaia Chuvashiia*, 24 November: 2–3.

Kachaeva, M. (1994) 'Speech at meeting of F-1 Club', April 1994, (audio tape recording).

Kamalina, L. (1993) 'O polovom razvitii i vospitanii', *Vospitanie Shkol'nikov*, 1: 63.

Kashelkin, A. (1990) 'Nasilie kak forma antiobshchestvennogo povedeniia molodezhnikh gruppirovok', in I. Karpets (ed.) *Kriminologiia o Neformal'nikh Molodezhnikh Ob'edineniiakh*, Moskva: Iuridicheskaia Literatura.

Kataev, S. (1986) 'Muzykal'nie vkusy mdodezhi', *Sotsiologicheskie Issledovaniia*, 1: 105–8.

Kharitonenkov, M. (1992) 'Mat'-ubiitsa', *Kuranty*, 28 April: 8.

Khotkina, Z. (1994) 'Gendernie aspekty bezrabotitsy i sistemy sotsial'noi zashchity naseleniia', in M. Malysheva (ed.) (1994).

Khlebnikov, G. (1992) 'Eshche odna!', *Spid-info*, 7: 10–11.

Khripkova, A. (1979) 'Neobkhodima mudrost', *Sovetskaia Rossiia*, 16 December: 3.

Khripkova, A. and Kolesov, D. (1981) *Devochka-Podrostok-Devushka*, Moskva.

Klimova, K. (1994) 'Infanty strashnie', *Stolitsa*, 10: 35–7.

Kodzaeva, L. (1993) 'Devochka plachet' *Rabotnitsa*, March: 28.

Kofyrin, N. (1991) 'Problemy izucheniia neformal'nikh grupp molodezhi', *Sotsiologicheskie Issledovaniia*, 1: 82–5.

Kolesov, D. (1980) *Besedy o Polovom Vospitanie*, Moskva.

Kon, I. (1991a) 'Erotika: eto khorsoho ili plokho?', *Eros*, 1: 5–7.

—— (1991b) *Vkus Zapretnogo Ploda*, Moskva.

—— (1991c) 'Voina ob''iavlena. Odene'tes.', *Novoe Vremia* 1: 48.

Konysheva, L. (1988) *Sudebno-psikhologicheskaia Ekspertiza Psikhicheskogo Sostoianiia Nesovershennoletnei Zhertvy Iznasilovanniia* (Avtoreferat dissertatsii), Moskva.

Kornilovskaia, T. (1994) 'Kak poimat' ptichku?', *Moskovskii Komsomolets*, 21 January: 8.

Kotliar, A. (1986) 'Muzhskaia otvetsvennost', *Vospitanie Shkol'nikov*, 4: 69–71.

Kotovskaia, M., Zolotukhina, M. and Shalygina, N. (1993) *Zaviduite, Ia Zhenschina!?*, Moskva: Larisa Servis.

Kovalev, A. (1983) *Lichnost' Vospityvaet Sebia*, Moskva.

Kozlov, A. and Lisovskii, A. (1986) *Molodoi Chelovek: Stanovlenie Obraza Zhizni*, Moskva: Politcheskaia Literatura.

Krashennikova, E. (1990) 'Kak sokhranit' liubov'', *Vospitanie Shkol'nikov*, 2: 65–7.

Kruglov, A. (1993) 'Kak eto bylo so mnoi', *Ty*, 2: 22–5.

Kulik, D. (1994) 'Khorosha Natasha, da ne nasha, da ne nasha', *Komsomol'-skaia Pravda*, 6 April: 6.

Lavskii, V., Naidenko, A. and Semenchenko, F. (1991) *Potrebitel'stvo Kak Nedostatok Tvorcheskogo Nachala i Prichina Degumanizatsii Zhizni Molodogo Pokoleniia*, Kherson: Ministerstvo Vysshego i Srednego Spetsial'nogo Obrazovaniia USSR, Kherson Industrial'nii Institut.

Lebedev, V. (1994) 'Akh, eti devushki v triko – oni snimaiutsia legko!', *Komsomol'skaia Pravda*, 25 May: 6.

Lelekov, V. and Prokhorov, Iu. (1994) 'Molodezh': Kriminal' naia aktivnost' i problemy resotsializatsii', *Sotsiologicheskie Issledovaniia*, 8–9: 109–15.

Letter (1989) *Moskovskii Komsomolets*, 30 June: 4.

Levada, Iu. (ed.) (1993) *Sovetskii Prostoi Chelovek*, Moskva: Intertsentr.

Levitskaia, A., Orlik, E. and Potapova, E. (1991) *Konfliktnie Orientatsii Molodezhnogo Soznaniia v Usloviiakh Demokratizatsii Obshchestva: Sotsiologicheskii Analiz*, Vladimir: Vladimir Politekhnicheskii Institut.

Loginov, K. (1993a) *Semeinie Obriady i Verovaniia Russkikh Zaonezh'ia*, Petrozavodsk: Izd-vo Karel'sokgo Nauchnogo Tsentra RAN.

—— (1993b) *Material'naia Kul'tura i proizvodstvenno-bytovaia Magiia Russikikh Zaonezh'ia*, St Petersburg: Nauka.

Maksimov, A. (1992) 'Nagota spaset mir?', *Sobesednik*, 13, 1 April: 15.

Malenkova, L. (1990) 'Slovar' semeinogo vospitaniia: Materinstvo', *Vospitanie Shkol'nikov*, 2: 67–70.

Malysheva, M. (ed.) (1994) *Gendernie Aspekty Sotsial'noi Transformatsii*, Moskva: Institut Sotsial'no-ekonomicheskikh Problem Narodonaseleniia RAN.

Mashkova, L. (1992) 'Izmennik. Izmennitsa. Pochemu my ikh liubim i proshchaem?', *Chas Pik*, 10 August 1992: 13.

Medvedkin, K. (1991) 'Za prekrasnikh dam prikhoditsia poroi platit' svobodoi', *Moskovksii Komsomolets*, 7 February: 2.

Mikhailov, I. (1994) 'Kroshka syn v karman zalez...', *SV* (Ul'ianovsk) 19 March.

Mikhailovich, S. (1993) 'Prostitutki podorozhali', *Kuranty*, 13 February: 5.

Min'kovskii G. (1992) *Sovremennaia Sem'ia Problemy, Resheniia, Perspektiv Razvitiia* (conference proceedings), Moskva.

Mkrtchian, G. and Chirkova, A. (1986) 'Dinamika professional'nikh orientatsii moskvichei', *Sotsiologicheskie Issledovaniia*, 3: 162–7.

Mladshii, A. (1991) 'Golobie – tozhe liudi!', *Moskovskii Komsomolets*, 3 August: 4.

Molodezh RSFSR. Statisticheskii Sbornik (1990) Moskva.

Moroz, O. (1989) 'Spravedliva li kara?' (interview with I. S. Kon) *Literaturnaia Gazeta*, 10: 47–55.

Musina, M. (1992) ' "Davno, ustalii rab..." ', *Rabotnitsa*, 7–8: 14–15.

'Na voliu vyshla drugoi' (1993) *SPID-info*, 7: 14.

Nekrasov, S. (1991) *Zhiznennie Tsenarii Zhenshchin i Seksual'nost'*, Sverdlovsk: Urals University Press.

Nevskii, A. (1992a) 'Ne liubliu besstrastnykh!' *SPID-info*, 7: 29.

—— (1992b) 'Zhenshchina vashei mechty', *SPID-info*, 8: 7–8.

Nikolaev, V. (1991) 'Mezhdu erotikoi i pornografiei', *Argumenty i Fakty*, 2: 6–7.

OMRI Daily Digest (1995) 1, 4, 5 January.

Orlov, S. (1991) 'Osobie primety: glaza naglie', *Komsomol'skaia Pravda*, 12 March: 2.

Osheverova, A. (1994) ' "Gop-stopnik" Misha. Rossiiu zakhlestyvaet volna detskoi prestupnosti', *Izvestiia*, 8 February: 5.

Plesko, G. *et al.* (1936) *Devushki Tekstil'nogo Poselka*, Moskva: Molodaia Gvardiia.

Plotnikov, A. (1991) *Vzaimosviaz' Ob"ektivnikh i Sub"ektivnikh Faktorov Formirovaniia Molodezhnoi Kul'tury'*, Avoreferat dissertatsii, Moskva: Institut Sotsiologii.

'Pochta *SPID-info*' (1992) *SPID-info*, 8 August 1992: 5.

Podkolodnii, F. (1991) 'Bania', *SPID-info*, 7: 10.

—— (1992) 'Kak uznat' golubogo?' *SPID-info*, 7: 8–9.

Pokrovskii, V. (1991) 'Ekh, "Pazovym" da esche raz!', *Spid-info*, July 1991: 3.

Poliakov, V. (1994) 'Propala devochka', *Livenskaia Gazeta*, 20 July: 4.

Polupanov, V. (1994) 'Vseleii ekipazh "Dvukh Samoletov" ', *Argumenty i Fakty: Ia Molodoi*, 22: 4.

Popov, A. (1989) 'Eta drevniaia igra', *Moskovskii Komsomolets*, 18 August: 4.

Popov, G. (1903) *Russkaia Narodno-bytovaia Meditsina: Po Materialam Etnograficheskogo Biuro kn. V. N. Tenisheva*, Sankt Peterburg.

Popova, N. (1994) 'Dva chasa na ostrove lesbos', *Rossiiskie Vesti*, 17 November: 8.

Potekhina, I. (1992) 'Nashi mamy stanoviatsia vse molozhe i molozhe', *Komsomol'skaia Pravda*, 17 October: 3.

Priglashaem na rabotu (1994): 2.

'Proekt. Doklad o vypolnenii v Rossiiskoi Federatsii konventsii o likvidatsii vsekh form diskrimnatsii v otnoshenii zhenshchin' (1994) Moskva.

Reklamnoe prilozhenie (1993) no. 35: 6.

Repin, L. (1994) 'Malen'kie deti, zato problemy...', *Komsomol'skaia Pravda*, 9 April: 2.

Rezanov, G. and Khoroshilova, T. (1992) 'Sdelal telo – guliai smelo', *Komsomol'skaia Pravda*, 17 April 1992: 4.

Rimashevskaia, N. (ed.) (1991), *Zhenshchiny v Obshchestve*, Moskva: Nauka.

Rozanov, V. (1990) 'Opavshie list'ia. Korob pervii', in V. Rozanov *Sochineniia*, Leningrad: Vasil'evskii Ostrov.

Rutkevich, M. (1984) 'Reforma obrazovaniia, potrebnosti obshchestva, molodezh'', *Sotsiologicheskie Issledovaniia*, 4: 19–28.

Rzhanitsyna, L. (ed.) (1993) *Rabotaiushchie Zhenshchiny v Usloviiakh Perekhoda Rossii k Rynku*, Moskva: Institut Ekonomiki RAN.

Sadykova, Z. and Gorobtsova, O. (1994) 'Muzhchiny i zhenshchiny', *Vestnik* (Ul'ianovsk), 14 October: 6.

Samuseva, A. (1994) ' "Sestry" dlia iznasilovannikh' *Argumenty i Fakty*, 24: 3.

Sarkitov, N. (1987) 'Ot "khard-roka" k "khevi-metallu": Effekt oglupleniia', *Sotiologicheskie Issledovaniia*, 4: 93–4.

Savel'ev, V. (1994) 'Bros' vyzov svoemu nasil'niku', *Vecherniaia Moskva*, 4 February: 3.

Savichev, V. and Sargin, A. (1994) 'Rossiia beremenna prestupnost'iu', *Argumenty i Fakty*, 15:1.

Sbornik: Molodezh Rossii: Tendentsii, Perspektivy (1993) Moskva.

Sbornik: Problemy Bor'by s Deviantnim Povedeniem (1989) Moskva: INION.

Semashchko, L. (1992) 'Otvety na voprosy uchastnikov "kruglogo stola" ', *Materialy Mezhdunarodnogo Seminara 'Sovremennaia Sem'ia': Problemy, Resheniia, Perspektivy Razvitiia*, Moskva: Institut Molodezhi.

Semenov, L. (1992) 'Kak pomoch' molodezhi?', *Pedagogika*, 1–2: 22–9.

Sementsov, M. (1992) *Narodnaia Meditsina Kubasnkikh Kazakov: V Pomoshch' Rabotnikam Kul'tury i Narodnogo Obrazovaniia*, Krasnodar.

Shashkova, T. (1994) 'Khochu muzha!!!', *Kuranty*, 18 June: 5.

Shavyrin, D. (1989) 'Tak rebriata, ne poidet!', *Moskovskii Komsomolets*, 16 June: 4.

Shchepanskaia, T. (1991) 'Zhenshchina, gruppa, simvol (na materialakh molodezhnoi subkul'tury)' in *Etnicheskie Stereotipy Muhskogo i Zhenskogo Povedeniia*, Sankt Peterburg: Nauka.

—— (1994) 'Mir i mif materinstva. Sankt Peterburg, 1990–3 gody (ocherki zhenskikh traditsii i folklora)', *Etnograficheskoe Obozrenie*, 5: 15–27.

294   *Bibliography*

Shubkin, V. I. (1970) *O Sotsial'nom Prognozirovanii Shansov Molodezhi na Poluchenie Obrazovaniia*, Moskva.
—— (1978) *Professional'naia Orientatsiia Molodezhi v Sotsialisticheskom Obshchestve*, Moskva.
—— (ed.) (1992) *Vstuplenie Novikh Pokolenii v Trudovuiu Zhizn' v Usloviiakh Politicheskikh i Sotsial'no-ekonomicheskikh Reform*, Moskva.
Snegireva, T. (1984) 'Ne predopredlenie, a vybor', *Literaturnaia Gazeta*, 23 May: 12.
Sovetskii Entsiklopedicheskii Slovar' (1980), Moskva: Sovetskaia Entsiklopediia.
Sovremennaia Sem'ia: Problemy, Resheniia, Perspektivy Razvitiia. Materialy Mezhdunarodnogo Seminara (1992), Moskva.
Stepanov, V. (1906) 'Svedeniia o rodil'nikh i krestinnikh obriadakh v Klinskom uezde Moskovskoi gub', *Etnograficheskoe Obozrenie*, XX-XXI, 3–4.
Sukhareva, L. and Kuindzhi, N. (1992) 'Zachem devushke muzhskoe litso?', *Meditsinskaia Gazeta*, 26 (3 April): 11.
Surkov, V. (1994) 'Okaiannoe remeslo', *Nedelia*, 30: 3.
'Sut' liubvi: dialog docheri – desiatiklassnitsy Svetlany i ottsa – pisatelia Iuriia Borisovicha Riurikova' (1989) *Vospitanie Shkol'nikov*, 5: 122–30.
Suvorova, T. and Geiges, A. (1990a) 'Liubov' vne plana', *Sobesednik*, 8 (February): 12.
—— (1990b) 'Liubov' vne plana', *Sobesednik*, 9 (February): 12.
Sviadoshch, A. (1991) *Zhenskaia Seskopatologiia*, Moskva.
'Syn soldata' (1965) *Rabotnitsa*, 9: 18–19.
Sysenko, V. (1980) 'Zhenshchina i muzhchina', *Zdorov'e*, 1: 14–15.
Tarkhova, T. (1993) 'Vospitat' muzhchinu', *Vospitanie Shkol'nikov*, 2: 13–18.
Tartsan, N. (1992) '80–e gody: Obrazovanie kak faktor integratsii molodikh pokoleniii' in V. I. Shubkin (ed.) (1992).
Tikhonova, O. (1992) 'Devushka telookhranitel' ishchet rabotu', *Kuranty*, 19 August: 8.
—— (1993a) 'Zhenshchiny gotovy na vse', *Kuranty*, 5 March: 16.
—— (1993b) 'Zamuzh za 'kvartiru' ne poidu', *Kuranty*, 20 October: 7.
Timoshchenko, L. (1978) *V Sem'ye Rastet Doch'*, Moskva.
—— (1980) 'O vospitanie devochki, *Vospitanie Shkol'nikov*, 6: 37–40.
—— (1992) 'Posovetite devushkam', *Vospitanie Shkol'nikov*, 1–2: 44–6.
Tiurina, I. (1994) 'Pomogite emu vliubit'sia v vas', *Kuranty*, 11 May 1994: 7.
Tiuriukanova, E. (1994) 'Migratsiia zhenshchin iz Rossii: eshche odna "strategiia uspekha?" ', in M. Malysheva (ed.) (1994).
Toktalieva, G. (1989) 'Olia + Iulia', *Sobesednik*, 48: 11.
'Tselii chemodan novostei' (1992) *SPID-info*, 7: 3.
Uspenskii, D. (1991) 'Rodiny i krestiny, ukhod za rodil'nitsei i novorozhdennim', *Mudrost' Narodnaia: Zhizn' Cheloveka v Russkom Fol'klore. Vyp.I. Mladenchestvo; Detstvo*, Moskva: Khudozhestvennaia Literatura.
Vasil'ev, Iu. (1994) 'Metodologicheskie aspekty izucheniia deviantnogo povedeniia v molodezhnoi srede', in *Tsennostnii Mir Sovremmoi Molodezhi: Na Puti k Mirovoi Integratsii*, Moskva: Sotsium.
Vasil'ev, V. L. and Mamaichuk, I. I. (1993) 'Analiz lichnost' nesovershennoletnikh prestuplenii', *Voprosy Psikhologii*, 1: 61–8.
Vasilov, A., Kupriianov, A. and Cherniak, I. (1986) 'Muzyku zakazyvaet raikom', *Sobesednik*, 20: 8–10.

Veselkin, V. (1991) 'Rok protiv terrora', *Spid-info*, 7: 6–7.

Viukova, N. (1968) 'O materinskom schast'e', *Rabotnitsa*, 7: 1–2.

Volskaia, L. (1992) 'Kakoga sveta balet?', *SPID-info*, 8: 5.

'V teni kryli tvoikh ukroi menia' (1991) *SPID-info*, 7: 7.

Zabelina, T. (1994) 'Obzor "Itogi seminara v Institute Molodezhi" ', *Vy i My* 9: 24–7.

Zelenin, D. (1991) *Vostochnoslavianskaia Etnografiia*, Moskva: Nauka.

Zotova, A. Ui (1994) 'Komy nuzhen seks-telefon?', *Sotsiologicheskie Issledovaniia*, 1: 59–68.

Index

Abkhazian-Georgian conflict 181
abortion 10–11, 152–3; beliefs about
  162–3; juveniles 176, 232
Abramov, O. 238
Abrams, M. 195
accountancy courses 25
'accountant', gang 221
Adelfi 111
'administrative leave' 21
advertisements, job 23, 30
advice (pregnancy) 265, 269, 273
Afanas'eva, T. 97, 100
Africa 109
Agarkov, S. 107
Agarov, S. 100
age 41; discrimination in labour market
  23–8; gangs and 219, 227; *see also*
  generation
aggressive subcultures 202–3
aggressiveness, gangs and 219–20
AIDS 102; influence on behaviour
  141–3; information about 107, 109,
  141
alcohol/drunkenness 51, 63–4, 165
Alekseenkov, S. 3, 8, 202, 203
Alekseeva, K. 197
Aleshina, Iu. 112–13, 203
alienation 216
'Anima' Centre, Ekaterinburg 179, 181
anomie 217
anti-social activities 233
Antonian, Iu. 13
Argumenty i Fakty 172
Armenian pogroms, Sumgait 181
arms 271
Aslamova, D. 209
assertiveness 51–5
Association of Russian Crisis Centres
  for Women 181
association of teenage clubs 204

associations 259
'attached girls' (*pristegnutie devochki*)
  228, 232
attitudes: to employment 29–30, 35,
  36–7; to homosexuality 102–12, 119,
  130, 131, 144–7, 149; school-leavers' to
  higher education 75–91; young
  people's to sex roles and sexuality
  132–51
attractiveness 30–1, 267–8
Aukutsionek, S. 47
authoritarianism 69, 127
automatic job assignment 28
Avdeeva, K. 15

Babich, D. 199
babies: abandonment and killing 176;
  new-born 275–8, 279–80; *see also*
  children
babushka (grandmother) 28
'baby-talk' (*pestushki*) 277, 281
Baiburin, A. 278
Baklanova, E. 206
bania (bathhouse) 108
banking 25–6
Barabash, N. 16
Baranov, S. 3, 8, 202, 203
bargaining power 55
bay leaves 163
BBC 195
'beautiful life' 208
beauty contests 33
behavioural models 52, 57
behavioural patterns: girls in gangs
  229–32
Bekhtereva, N. 197
Belaga, L. 118
beliefs, health 152–68
Belkin, A. 100, 102

'belly' 265–6, 268–9, 270; erotica of 273–5
Belov, V. 197
Belskaia, G. 96
Berdiaev, N. 278
Bernshtam, T. 193–4
bikers (*rokery*) 202–3, 214, 237, 243, 253, 261; masculinities and femininities 244–9, 256; Sexton Club 240, 244
birth 279
birth control 11, 160–2, 167
birth-rate 96
bodily attributes 30–1, 267–8
body 10–11, 264–81; bodily code 269–72; erotica of the 'belly' 273–5; new motherhood 275–80
body image 253–4
Bogdanova, L. 35, 207, 208
Bogoliubova, K. 104
Boguslavskaia, Z. 15
Bondarev, Iu. 197
books 140–1
Borisov, I. 196
boss-men (gangs) 222, 224, 228, 229
Brannen, J. 156
breasts 270
Breslav, G. 99–100
Bridger, S. 8
Britons 156–7
Bruno, M. 48
Bualvintsev, N. 15
Budartseva, S. 176
Burgasov, P. 105
Buriatiia 178, 186
business trips 72
business ventures 24, 237, 256
bych'e 237–8, 261
Bykanova, N. 15

calculation 207–10, 211
Campbell, A. 191
career: family/career dilemma 64–7; 'initiating' type 123–4, 125, 128, 129; school-leavers' expectations 7–8, 86; women's career patterns 57–74; *see also* work
CARITAS 179
Carter, E. 190
Catacombs 248
'Cats' (*'Koshki'*) 226
censorship 110
central gatherings *see tusovki*
Centre of Ethno-Gender Research 122
chauvinist politics 236, 243–55, 257–8
'cheap tarts' (*deshevie davalki*) 228, 232–3 *see also* prostitution

Chechnia 181; appeal against violence towards women 184–6
Chelnokov, A. 202–3, 205, 207
Cherednichenko, V. 97, 100–1, 101–2
Cherkasova, N. 15
childcare training 29
children 170; campaigns to persuade women to have children 96; and crime 203–5; 'initiating' type and 128–9; street children 203–4, 214; young people's expectations 148, 149, 164, 165; *see also* babies, family
children's clothes 266–7
China 209
Chirkova, A. 78, 81
Chistiakov, V. 197
citizenship 43, 100
Clarke, S. 44
class rule 169–70
'classic' gangs 233–4; *see also* gangs
'cleaners' (*sanitarnie*) 216, 235
clothes, children's 266–7
clubs: gay 110; Moscow club scene 239–41, 261
coarseness 245
cocaine 241
Cohen, P. 195
coil, contraceptive 161
cold water treatment 152, 157
collectivism 95
commercial sector 25–6
Committee for Combating Organized Crime 226
'common girls' (*obshchie devochki*) 228, 232
condoms 143, 161, 162
confinement 273–5, 278–80
conflict: gangs and 216; inter-ethnic and military 181; management of 69
Connell, R. 9
conservatism 229
consumerism 195
consumption 190–1, 192, 211; gender and 196–201; of girls 200–1; style and 196, 198–9; youth and 193–5
contraception 11, 160–2, 167
Convention on the Rights of the Child 176
Cook, L. 49
corruption 44–5, 238, 240
cottage industry 24–5, 48
counselling 27
CPSU (Communist Party of the Soviet Union) personnel policy 71
creative self-realization 123–4, 125
crime 199; gangs and 217, 222, 224–6,

233; increase in 173; marginalization and market 203–5, 206–7, 214; organized 222, 224–6, 227, 233, 237–9; street crime 165
Criminal Code 103, 104
crisis centres 178–81
crude language 63, 245, 262
cultural capital 81–2
cultural dislocation 4–6
cultural practice 12–14; *see also* youth culture
culture, dominant 43

Dal', V. 272, 276
dancers 107
death 274
defence: object of 218–19; of territory 249–50
degradation 2–4
Delovaia Zhenshchina 31, 171, 172
democratic institutions 42–3
democratic orientation 130, 130–1
dependency 134, 148–9
designer skinheadism 249–55, 263
de-skilling 23–4
devaluation of education 89
development 129
deviance 217, 234
D'iachenko, A. 174–5
difference 9, 14–15, 17
direct action 251
discrimination: age 23–8; against homosexuals 103–4, 106; sexual 22–3, 25–6, 30–1, 36–7, 70–2, 183; UN Convention 171
dismissal 103, 104
distressing experiences 274
diversity 58–9
Divil'kovskii, 276
Dodolev, E. 177
domestic life 126–7, 128; *see also* family
domestic skills 24–5
domestic violence 176–81
domestic work 50; male and female roles 113, 135; sexual equality and 147–8; women's dual burden 66, 165
Dorozhkin, Iu. 204
dress: consumption and 198–9; gangs 227–32 *passim*; skinheads 252; *see also* style
drugs 205, 236, 241–2
drunkenness 51, 63–4, 165
Dubna Employment Centre 27, 37
Dzhaginova, E. 16

Easton, P. 198, 213

ecstasy 241
education 7–8; devaluation of 88–9; higher *see* higher education; school-leavers' expectations 75–91; sex-role socialization 96–7; *Trud* (labour) class 147; women managers 59–60
Efremov, A. 115
Egorova, A. 204–5
Egorova, E. 106–7
Ekaterinburg 179, 181
El, A. 14–15, 199
Elenovskaia, M. 111
emancipation 136
employment *see* career; work
Employment Centres 27
entrepreneurs 30
equality: in academic writings 9, 99–100; education as means to 84–6; students' attitudes 147–8, 149
equipment, gang 222
Eremin, V. 117, 200
erotica 264; of the belly 273–5; external 275; new motherhood 275–8
'Ethics and Psychology of Family Life' course 96–7
ethnographic interviewing 153–5
'evil eye' 279
Evseeva, E. 37
exchange of children's clothes 266–7
exclusion from school 205
experimentation in sex 130
extortion 204, 205, 206, 238; gangs and 222

face 271
Fain, A. 199
'fake resistance' 173
family 75, 90; domestic violence 176–81; 'initiating' type and 126–7, 127, 128–9, 130, 130–1; partnership model 64–5, 66 school-leavers' expectations 8, 77, 79, 85–6, 87–8, 89–90; sex-role socialization 96–7, 98–9, 99, 101; Soviet campaigns 96; trainee teachers' attitudes 135, 135–6, 139–40, 148–9; women managers 62–3 (family/career dilemma 64–7)
fandom 191, 197–8, 213
father, role of 267
feasibility study 153–5
fel'dsher 160, 167
female sexuality 118, 191–2
feminine management style 67–70
feminist literature 150
femininity: images of 15, 57, 134–8;

sexuality, power and 9–12; variants on Moscow youth scene 243–55, 256–7
feminization of poverty 21–2
fenechki 229
'fighters', gang 221, 225, 228
fighting, skinheads and 253, 254, 263
Filinov, Iu. 197
focus groups 79–80
folklore, pregnancy 264–81
Fong, M. 47
food cravings 272
foreign firms 41–2, 49–51, 52–4, 55
foreign husbands 34–5, 37–8, 208
foreign workers 41–2
Freud, S. 276
fright 274
frivolity 199, 209–10, 211
future, images of 138–40

Gaidarenko, N. 176–7, 180
gait 270–1
game tests 122
Ganetz, H. 191, 192
gang rape 13, 117, 175
gangs 13, 117, 216–35, 247, 248; activity in Ul'ianovsk 13, 222–33; classification 218–20; consumption of girls 200; girls in gangs 226–32, 233; hypotheses about future developments 233–5; influence 221–2; 'Kazan' phenomenon 217–18; membership 220, 220–2; and organized crime 224–6; specificities of culture 234; territorial 200, 204–5, 218–22, 234
Garber, J. 191
Gareev, E. 204
gatherings (*sbor*) 221
gay clubs 110
gay/lesbian movement 109–10
gay/lesbian press 110–11
Gazeta dlia Zhenshchin (The Women's Gazette) 115
Geiges, A. 103
gender 1; classification of gangs 219; consumption, irrational needs and 196–201; and coping with change 41; employment and unemployment 46–8; generation and identity 14–17; identities on Moscow youth scene 237, 243–55, 255–60; identity, cultural practice and 12–14; and images of contemporary Russia 164–5; images and violence 170–2; lack of attention to in Russian writings 79; and school-leavers' expectations 77, 90–1; and

youthful subjectivities 190–3; *see also* femininity, masculinity
gender relations: impact of market 112–16; Soviet writings 96–102
gender roles *see* sex roles
gender stereotypes: school-leavers' expectations 87–8, 90; sex-role socialization 97–9; students' attitudes 134–8, 140–3; and violence 170–2
general health 155–9
generation 1–4; gender, identity and 14–17; labour market and 21–38; women managers 61–2; *see also* age
Georgian–Abkhazian conflict 181
Germany 251–2
Gesson, M. 103, 104, 106, 109–10
'girl fighters' (*boitsy*) 228, 231–2
girls: bikers 244–5, 246–7, 247–9, 256; consumption of 200–1; in gangs 226–32, 233; skinheads 254–5; *see also* women, young women
glamour industry *see* sex industry
glasnost 170
globalization 2
Golovakha, E.I. 76, 77
gopniki 229, 237–8, 257, 259, 261
Gordeeva, L. 204
graduates 28–9
grandmother (*babushka*) 28
Greer, G. 12
Griffin, C. 1, 78, 190
Grigor'eva, E. 102
Grishin, A. 105–6
Gromov, A. 200
Gruppa (Group) fund 204
gynaecological problems 11, 158
Gyne, I. 103

hair 271
Hall, R. 11
Hall, S. 2
handwork skills 24–5
'harmonious' type 131
head 271
health beliefs 10–11, 152–68; general health 155–9; images of contemporary Russia 164–5; reproductive health 10–11, 159–63
health policies 153
heaviness, feelings of 272
hegemonic patriarchal ideology 58
help, mutual 266–7
Hermitage Club 239–40, 240, 241, 242
'high-class' prostitution firms 209
higher education 91; attitudes to 75, 76–86, 88–90 (male attitudes to

women's education 86–8; motives for continuing 81–6); labour market and 28–9, 75, 83; women in 76
'highlife' group (*mazory*) 199, 239, 261
Hitler, A. 107–8
HIV infection 109; *see also* AIDS
Hoggart, R. 195
home 126–7; *see also* domestic work, family, marriage
home remedies 157, 166
homosexuality: AIDS and 143; attitudes to 102–12, 119, 130, 131, 144–7, 149; gay clubs 110; gay/lesbian movement 109–10; gay/lesbian press 110–11; skinheads and 254, 258
hospitalization 103, 104
housing 182
Hudson, B. 191–2, 200–1
humanistic framework 121
husband/spouse: foreign husbands 34–5, 37–8, 208; and wife's promotion 62; work status 48–9; *see also* marriage

Iagodinskii, V. 98, 99, 101
identity 1; gender, cultural practice and 12–14; gender identities on Moscow youth scene 237, 243–55, 255–60; generation, gender and 14–17; jobs and new sexual identities 51–5, 55; young people and sexual identity 95–120
images: body image 253–4; of feminine and masculine 134–8; of ideal 14–17, 18
indispensability 54
industrialization 129
industry: women managers 57–74
informal sector 48
informal youth groups (*neformaly*) 201, 213, 233, 259
information: reproductive health 159–60; on sex 140–3
Ingushetia 184–6
inherited constitution 155
'initiating' type 10, 122–31
Institute of Ethnology and Anthropology 122
institutions, democratic 42–3
intellectual infatuation 276
intelligence 134
inter-ethnic conflict 181
Interperiodica 46, 55–6
intimidation 221
'iron hand' 249
irrational needs 196–201
Iur'eva, A. 197

Ivanov, P. 157
Ivanov, S. 276
Ivanova, V. 200

Jenson, J. 197–8, 213
job advertisements 23, 30
job prospects 83–4, 89–90
jobs: and sexual identities 51–5; *see also* work
judges 174

Kachaeva, M. 173
Kamalina, L. 97, 102
Kapeliushnikov, R. 47
Karabakh conflict 181
Karmaza, O. 208, 210
Kashelkin, A. 200
'Kazan' phenomenon' 217–18
Ketting, E. 153
Kharitonenkov, M. 207
Khasan, B. 99–100
Khirurg (biker leader) 245–6
Khlebnikov, G. 107–8
Khoroshilova, T. 207
Khotkina, Z. 26
Khripkova, A. 96, 98, 99
Kimmel, M. 9, 254, 258
Klimova, K. 117
Kodzaeva, L. 11
Kofyrin, N. 200
Kolesov, D. 98, 99
Kollantai, A. 98
Kol'tso 58
Kometa 58, 69, 74
Komsomol 3, 194, 197, 212
Komsomol'skaia Pravda 172
Kon, I. 105
Konovalov, V. 207
Konysheva, L. 174
Kornilovskaia, T. 16
Kotliar, A. 99
Kovalev, A. 95
Kozlov, A. 195
Kraminova, N. 207
Krashennikova, E. 98
Krest'ianka 171
Kuban Cossacks 271
Kuindzhi, N. 201
Kulik, D. 209
Kulikov, A. 176
Kuzin, O. 200

labour law, draft 90
labour market 21–38, 44–8; gender, employment and unemployment 46–8; generational differences 45–6;

and higher education 28–9, 75, 83; older women 23–8; survival 6–9; younger women 28–35; *see also* work

labour productivity 49–50

language, crude 63, 245, 262

Lavskii, V. 195

law: and sexual violence 173–6, 182

Law on the protection of socialist property 1932 169

laziness 50

Le Pen, J.M. 257

learning 58–9

Lebedev, V. 209

Lees, S. 192, 193

legs 270–1

leisure 141; young people's 194, 199, 204, 206

Leningrad 200

lesbianism 103, 104, 104–5, 108; gay/lesbian movement 109–10; gay/lesbian press 110–11; *see also* homosexuality

Levitskaia, A. 201

Lewis, L. 191

Liberal Democratic Party 249

Libin, A. and Libin, A. 117

lichnost' (individual) 41, 195

lifestyle: consumption and 198–9; and health 155, 157

Lisovskii, A. 195

liubera 239, 261

'lieutenants' ('right-hand men') 223, 226, 228, 231

Loginov, K. 272, 274

LSD 241

'lumpen teenagers' 202

Lutkovskii, N. 238

mafia 222, 224–6, 227, 233, 237–9

mail-order brides 34–5, 37–8

Maksimov, A. 113–14

male attitudes 87–8

male pride 201–7

Malenkova, L. 98

Mamaichuk, I.I. 117

Mamin, Y. 39

management: feminine style 67–70; women managers in industry 57–74

Manhattan Express club 240

manhood, glorification of 137–8

manipulation 68; youth culture 207–10, 211

Margarita café 242, 261

marginalization 201–7, 212

market: impact on crime 173; impact on gender relations 112–16;

marginalization and male pride 201–7, 212; money-making and youth culture 237–9; new market environment 6–9; women and 192

marriage 121, 227; foreign husbands 34–5, 37–8, 208; 'initiating' types 126, 128, 130, 130–1; for money 207, 208; promotion of 101; school-leavers' expectations 79, 84–6; students' attitudes 148–9; young women's expectations 164, 168; *see also* family, husband

Martin, E. 269

Marxism–Leninism 169–70

masculinity: corruption and 44–5; crisis of 15; images of 134–8; market and 112–13, 237–9; rise of masculinism 43; youth culture and 203, 237–9; variants of masculinity on the Moscow youth scene 243–55, 256–60

masculinity complex 16, 122–31

Mashkova, L. 16

mat (swearing) 245, 262

maternal community 13–14, 265–9

mazhory (highlife group) 199, 239, 261

McDonald's 239

McRobbie, A. 14, 191, 192, 212

media *see* press

medical care 157, 166

Medvedkin, K. 200

Melikian, G. 38

Meliksetian, A.S. 114

men: attitudes to women's education and work 87–8; and contraception 162; domination of management 63; and laziness 50; rape of 186; seasonal migration 129; seen as principal breadwinner 134; and unemployment 49

'Men Killers' 172

Metelitsa Club 240

migration, seasonal 129

Mikhailov, I. 204

Mikhailovich, S. 209

military conflict 181

military service 82–3, 89

Min'kovskii, G. 174

Mir Zhenshchiny 171

Mishkind, M. 254

Mkrtchian, G. 78, 81

Mladshii, A. 106

mobility, female managers' 58–9

modelling 33

MOLLI (Moscow Association of Lesbian Literature and Arts) 111

Molodtsova, V. 116–17

Moloko Café 248, 262
money: Moscow youth scene and 237–9, 250, 256–7, 259
morality: literature on gender relations 100–2; market, marginalization and moral degeneration 206–10; symbolic role of youth 3–4; Westernization and 116–17; women's role 104, 114–15
Moroz, O. 105
mortality rates 167
Moscow 89, 91; gay/lesbian movement 109–10; prostitution 208, 209; responses to violence against women 178–81 *passim*, 183–4; service sector 39–56; youth scene 236–63
Moscow Club 240
Moscow Pedagogical University 132
Moskovskii Komsomolets (MK) 15, 106–7, 141, 199
motherhood 164; eulogization 98; pregnancy folklore 13–14, 264–81; *see also* children, family
motivation for continuing education 81–6
murders 172, 177, 182
muscularity 253–4, 254
music: MOLLI concert 111; popular 107, 197–8, 213; skinheads 252; youth culture 197–8, 213
Musina, M. 207
mutual help 266–7
muzhik ('bloke') 225
My Name is Harlequin 213

Naidenko, A. 195
narcissism 211
National Front 251
national humiliation 209
national pride 249–50
Nava, M. 192
needs: irrational 196–201; rational 193–5
neformaly (informal youth groups) 201, 213, 233, 259
neo-fascism 202–3, 249
Nevar, S. 3, 8, 202, 203
Nevskii, A. 115
new-born babies 275–8, 279–80
'new Russians' 236, 239–41
newspapers *see* press
Night Wolves 246, 261, 262, 263; girls and 246–7, 247, 262; Sexton Club 240, 244
nomenklatura 44
Novii Vzgliad 172
nylon stockings 190–1

object of defence 218–19
obstetric problems 11, 158
officials, state 170–1
Ogonek 209
Oi music 252
older women: murder of for housing 182; prospects and responses in labour market 23–8; service sector 45–6; *see also* generation
'On the Prevention of the Neglect of and Crime Among Juveniles . . .' 205
organizational abilities 50–1
organizational culture 58, 68, 73
organizational structure 58, 71–2
organized crime 222, 224–6, 226, 227, 233, 237–9
Orlik, E. 201
Orlov, S. 200
Osheverova, A. 203, 205, 206, 214

paedophilia 103
Panthers 246, 262
parents: students' relationships with 148
part-time work 86, 88
partnership model of family 64–5, 66
'pathology' approach 217
patriarchy 58, 65–6, 87–8, 129
P'ekha, E. 172
perestroika period 196–7
'permanent war' hypothesis 233
personality, psychology of 95
personification 68
personnel issues 67–8
Pertsova, L. 13
pestushki ('baby-talk') 277, 281
Philadelphia 141
physical attributes 30–1, 267–8
Piatigorsk: University of Foreign Languages 132–3
Pilkington, H. 3, 189, 193, 201, 257; girls 196, 243; *lichnost'* 41; women's power 43
pill, contraceptive 161
Pilot Club 240
Pisklakova, M. 179
Pitlura 241
playful approach to work 68
Plesko, G. 194
Ploshchad' Revoliutsii 248
Plotnikov, A. 201, 202, 206–7
Podkolodnii, F. 107, 108, 118
Pokrovskii, V. 109
Poliakov, V. 210
police: corruption 238; and gangs 205, 222, 223; and violence against women 173, 175, 182–3

political instability 220–1; education and 82, 89
politics, chauvinist 236, 243–55, 257–8
pollution 155
Poole, M. 77, 78–9
Popov, A. 153
Popov, G. 270, 271, 272, 274, 275
Popova, N. 111
popular music (*estrada*) 107, 197–8, 213
pornography 113–14, 208
portentous signs 265, 269, 277–8
Posadskaya, A. 30, 45, 47
posidelki (evening gatherings) 193
Potapova, E. 201
Potekhina, I. 11
poverty 220; feminization of 21–2
power 43; femininity, sexuality and 9–12
pragmatism 77
pregnancy: folklore 264–81; health beliefs 158
presents, symbolic 268, 281
press: read by trainee teachers 140–1; women's publications 171–2; youth publications 113, 118; *see also under names of individual publications*
'prestigious girls' ('toughs') 227, 228, 230–1
prison sentences: gangs and 217, 222, 224–6; homosexuality and 103; skinheads 254, 263
prisons, rape in 186
private training courses 24–5
privatization 44
productivity 49–50
professional orientations 77–8
progressive management style 68, 69–70
promotion (for women) 72–3; against their wishes 60–2
'pro-prostitution propaganda' 32, 37
Prospekt café 248, 262
prostitution: 175–6, 199, 227; impact of market 114–15, 206; juveniles 208–9; prostitutes in gangs 228, 232; 'undercover' 33, 34, 37; younger women in labour market 32–3, 33–4
protection rackets 237, 238, 240
provocative behaviour 173
psychological reports 174
psychological support 27
psychological tactics 68
Ptiuch Club 261
punks 252–3

qualifications 59–60
qualitative research methods 79, 153–5
'queue' 266–7

Rabotnitsa 98, 171
racial hatred 250–1, 253, 254, 255, 257–8
racial violence 251–2
rape 11, 165, 168; age and 174; gang 13, 117, 175; law and 173–4, 175; male inadequacy and 117; within marriage 177; of men 186; *see also* sexual violence
Rasputin, V. 197
rational needs 193–5
rationality 197
reading 140–1
redundancies 22; *see also* unemployment
registration (of organizations) 110
Reimer, B. 189
Repin, L. 205
reproductive health 10–11, 159–63
resistance, patterns of 43–4, 50, 51–5, 55
retraining 24–5, 26, 37
Rezanov, G. 207
'right-hand men' ('lieutenants') 223, 226, 228, 230
Right Radical Party 202
risk 35
Riurikov, I. 101
rock music 197–8, 213
rokery see bikers
role models 14–17
Roman, L. 191
Romper Stomper 257
Rozanov, V. 268–9
rural women 8
Rzhanitsyna, L. 22, 23, 26

Sablina, L. 13
Sade 215
Sadko Ltd 46, 56
safety-net, education as 82
Samara 154, 158, 166, 178, 209
Samuseva, A. 173
Sanachev, I. 197
Saratov 178
Sargin, A. 173
Sarkitov, N. 197
Savel'ev, V. 176–7
Savichev, V. 173
school-leavers' expectations 7–8, 75–91 boys' attitudes 87–8; education and professional orientations 76–80; motives for continuing education 81–6
schools: exclusion from 205; *see also* education
segregation 70–2
Seidler, V. 17
selection, discrimination in 22–3

self-assertiveness 51–5
self-induced abortion 163
self-medication 157, 166
self-realization, creative 123–4, 125
self-reflection 68
Semashchko, L. 173
Semenchenko, F. 195
Semenov, L. 2, 4
Sementsov, M.V. 270–1, 271
Sem'ia i Shkola 141
'sensitive' type 131
Serdiukov, M. 207
service sector 39–56
sex, information on 140–3
sex education 96–7
sex industry: market's impact on gender
    relations 113–16, 118; young women
    in labour market 32–5; youth culture
    207–10
sex instinct 101
sex roles 9–10, 164–5; 'initiating' type
    122, 125–6, 128–30; sex-role
    socialization 96–102, 132; young
    people's attitudes to 132–51
Sexton Club 238, 241, 242, 247, 262;
    bikers 240, 244
sexual behaviour: age of beginning 164;
    girls in gangs 232; influence of AIDS
    142–3; 'initiating' type 130; Soviet
    writings 96–102; youth culture and
    consumption 199, 200–1, 206–7,
    207–10; youth self-regulation 193
sexual discrimination 22–3, 25–6, 30–1,
    36–7, 70–2, 183
sexual equality *see* equality
sexual harassment 7, 31–2, 33, 64
sexual identity *see* identity
sexual intercourse, banishment of 275
sexual trade in people 33–4, 175, 209
sexual violence 11–12, 169–86; gender
    images, violence and 170–2; law and
    173–6; support for victims 176–81
sexuality: female 118, 191–2; femininity,
    power and 9–12; teenage 116–18;
    young people's attitudes to 132–51
Shashkova, T. 208
Shavyrin, D. 198
Shchepanskaia, T. 196, 280
Shlapentokh, D. 114
shopping sprees 191
short time 21
shouting 69
Shreeves, R. 113, 114
Shubkin, V.N. 77
signs, portentous 265, 269, 277–8
single-parent families 221

sistema 196, 213
'Sisters' centre 179–80, 181; principles of
    work of 183–4
skills 35; mismatch 22; women managers
    and diverse 58–9
skinheads (*skinkhedy*) 244, 249–55,
    256–8, 263; masculinity and the street
    253–5; politics and style 249–51; style
    and political expression 251–3
'sleeper districts' 218, 221, 235
small businesses 24, 237, 256
smiles, babies 276–7
Snegireva, T. 96
social attitudes *see* attitudes
social change 41, 164–5; and health 155,
    158–9
social conditioning 147
social dislocation 4–6
social problems 2–4, 220–1
social tension 216
social work 72
socialization 52–3, 60–2
Sorokin, V.V. 99
'spheres of influence' 222
SPID-info 107–9, 115, 118, 119, 141, 143
sponsors 207–10
St Petersburg 109–10, 154, 166
St Petersburg Centre for Gender
    Problems 181, 184–6
St Petersburg Crisis Centre 179, 181
Stankevich, S. 17
state 42–4, 90
state officials 170–1
status, loss of 27–8
Stepanov, V. 272
'stepping over' 269, 270, 275
stereotypes *see* gender stereotypes
stiliagi 243, 261, 263; becoming bikers
    244, 248, 255–6; becoming skinheads
    249, 256–7
Stimson, G. 153
stockings, nylon 190–1
street children 203–4, 214
street crime 165
stress: and health 155, 158–9; women and
    labour market 26–8
Strish, K. 215
'strong' women 10, 122–3
style: bikers 244, 247; and consumption
    196, 198–9; girls in gangs 227–32
    passim; 'initiating' type 124–5;
    skinhead 249–53; *see also* dress
subcultures: aggressive 202–3; mothers
    13–14, 265–9; subcultural styles 196
subjectivity 190–3
Sudarushka 171

suffering 177–8, 186
suicide attempts 173
Sukhareva, L. 201
Sumgait 181
superiority complex 257
support: psychological for older women 27; for victims of violence 176–81
Surkov, V. 170
Suvorova, T. 103
swearing 63, 245, 262
symbolic presents 268, 281
Sysenko, V. 102

taboos 264, 273–5, 278–80
Tarkhova, T. 99
Tartsan, N. 76
teachers, trainee 132–51
technical educational institutions 76
teenage sexuality 116–18
telephone help-lines 178–9, 180
telephone sex 115–16
Tema 109
Terkhov, V. 8
territorial gangs 200, 204–5, 218–22, 234 *see also* gangs
territory, defence of (skinheads) 249–50
Tikhonova, O. 15, 209
Timoshchenko, L. 96, 97, 99
Tiumen' 178
Tiurina, I. 16
Toktalieva, G. 104–5
'toughs' ('prestigious girls') 227, 228, 231
trade in people, sexual 33–4, 175, 209
trainee teachers 132–51
training: older women 24–5, 26, 37; younger women 29
traits 134–8, 147
Trud (labour) class 147
TsDKh bikers 244, 246, 262
Turkey 209
tusovki (central gatherings) 13, 236–43, 260; drugs 241–2; end of 242–3; money, mafia and masculinity 237–9; Westernization and club scene 239–41
2X2 Club 240
Ty 110

Ul'ianovsk 204; gang activity 13, 222–32
'undercover prostitution' 33, 34, 37
'underground' clubs 240–1
unemployment 21–2, 48, 49; gender, employment and 46–8; stress 26–8
Union of Russian Women 24–5
United Nations Convention on the Elimination of Discrimination against Women 171, 175–6

value, education as 81
value orientations 10, 121–31
Vasil'ev, V.L. 117
venereal disease 176, 232
Veselkin, V. 107
victims: rape 173–4; support for victims of violence 176–81
village culture 193–4
violence 11–12, 169–86; bikers 245; concept 169–70; inter-ethnic and military conflict 181; prostitution and 115; sexual *see* sexual violence; skinhead 251, 251–2, 263; support for victims 176–81
'Violence Towards Women' conference 180
virginity 185
Visser, A. 153
Viukova, N. 98
Voice of America 195
Volovich, A.S. 112–13, 203
Volskaia, L. 107
Voronina, O. 127–8
Vospitanie Shkol'nikov 141

'wannabees' 191
water supply 158
Watson, P. 43, 164
weakness, feelings of 272
wealthy families 182
weather 155, 158
Westernization of youth culture 194–5, 236, 239–41, 241–2, 245
'White Bows' ('*Belie bantiki*') 219, 226
'white slave trade' 33–4, 175, 209
Wild Vixens/Foxes 246, 262
Willems, H. 251–2
Window to Paris 39–40, 55
'wives' 227, 228, 229–31
'Wolves' 223
women: dependency on men 134, 148–9; importance of producing children 148; male attitudes to women's education and work 86–8; 'Men Killers' 172; role in morality 104, 114–15; unemployment 21, 26–8, 47; violence towards 11–12, 115, 169–86, 245; *see also* girls, older women, young women
women managers 7, 57–74; attitudes to promotion 60–2; family-career dilemma 64–7; family life 62–4; feminine management style 67–70; path to the top 58–60; segregation and equal opportunities 70–2
'Women of Russia' 43, 179

Women's Crisis Centre 179, 181
women's enterprises (light industry) 70–1, 71–2
Women's Global Fund 180, 181
women's journals 171–2
work 164; employment strategies in service sector 39–56; 'initiating' type 123–4, 125, 128, 129, 129–30; school-leavers' expectations 88; trainee teachers' attitudes 135–6, 139–40; *see also* career, labour market
World Bank 47
World War II 130
Worobec, C. 193

Yakov, V. 7, 11, 12
young people: attitudes to sex roles and sexuality 132–51; sex and sexual identity 95–120; social problems 2–3; symbolic role 4
young women: foreign firms and 46, 53–4; health beliefs 10–11, 152–68; opportunities and obstacles in labour market 28–35; value orientations 10, 121–31
youth culture 12–14, 189–215; classification of cultural groups 236, 259; consumption of girls 200–1; female treachery and sex 207–10; gender and consumption 196–201; gender and subjectivity 190–3; market and male marginalization 201–7, 212; Moscow youth scene 236–63; music 197–8, 213; style and dress 198–9; *tusovki* 13, 236–43, 260; Westernization 194–5, 236, 239–41, 241–2, 245; youth and consumption 193–5; *see also* bikers, gangs, skinheads
'Youth and the Future' project 79–80, 91
youth leisure facilities 204
youth publications 113, 118
youth service 192
Yugoslavia, former 181, 186

Zabelina, T. 175
Zaitsev, I. 237
Zaitsev, S. 260–1
Zelenin, D. 268, 275
Zhirinovsky, V. 249, 250, 251
Zimina, V. 205
Zotova, A. 115–16